The Whites And The Blues

THE ROMANCES OF

ALEXANDRE DUMAS

Handy Library Edition

The Napoleon Romances

THE WHITES AND THE
BLUES

VOLUME TWO

Madame de Staël.

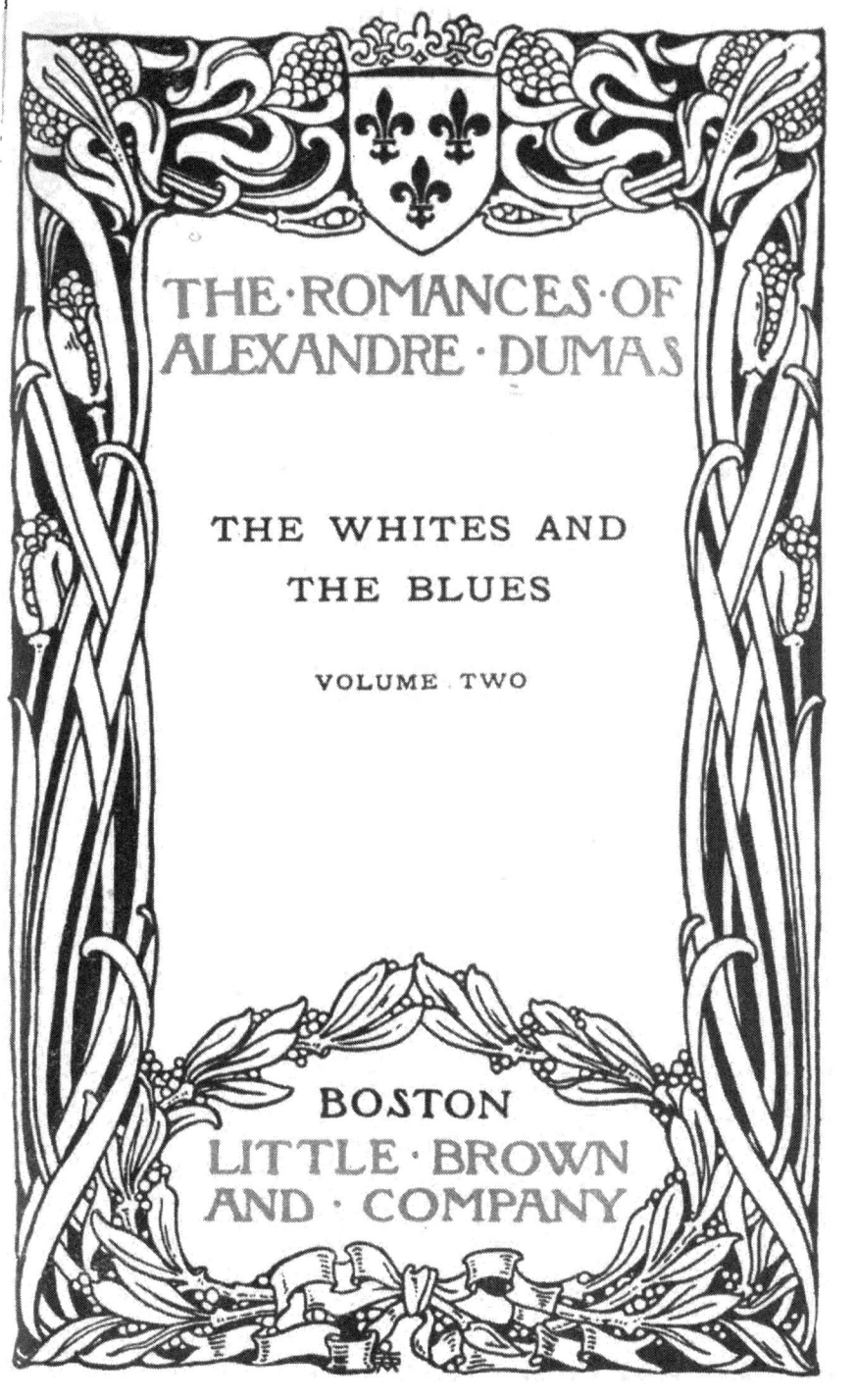

THE·ROMANCES·OF
ALEXANDRE·DUMAS

THE WHITES AND
THE BLUES

VOLUME TWO

BOSTON
LITTLE·BROWN
AND·COMPANY

Copyright, 1894,
BY LITTLE, BROWN, AND COMPANY.

Printers
S. J. PARKHILL & CO., BOSTON, U.S.A.

CONTENTS.

———◆———

THE EIGHTH CRUSADE.

THE WHITES AND THE BLUES.

ILLUSTRATIONS IN VOL. II.

THE WHITES AND THE BLUES.

THE THIRTEENTH VENDÉMIAIRE
(CONTINUED).

CHAPTER XXIV.

THE SWORD OF THE VICOMTE DE BEAUHARNAIS.

AFTER events like those we have just described, when cannon have thundered in the public squares, and blood has run in the streets of a capital, society is always thrown into a turmoil from which it takes a long time to recover.

Although the 14th Vendémiaire had sufficed to take away the corpses and remove the most noticeable traces of the combat, people continued for a long time to discuss the details of that terrible day which had resulted in restoring to the Convention threatened with destruction, — that is to say, to the Revolution and its authors, — the power which they needed for the establishment of those new institutions, the fear of which had produced the event which we have related.

The Convention understood so well, on the morning of the 14th, that its power was fully restored, that it gave itself very little uneasiness as to what had become of the sectionaries, who had disappeared without leaving any other trace of their passage than the blood which one day had sufficed to efface, if not from the memories of the citizens, at least from the pavement of the streets.

They contented themselves with dismissing the staff of the national guard, disbanding the grenadiers and chasseurs, who were almost all young men, placing the national guard under the orders of Barras, or rather of his colleague, Bonaparte, to whom he had abandoned all the active part of the work, ordering the disarming of the section Le Peletier and the section du Théâtre Français, and, finally, forming three commissions to try the leading sectionaries, who had almost all disappeared.

For some time anecdotes of the day were related, — this day which was destined to leave such a lasting and bloody souvenir in the minds of the Parisians. The magnificent words which had fallen from the lips of the wounded, or rather from the lips of the wounds, on that day of superb patriotism, were repeated and extolled. They told how the wounded, who had been carried to the Convention, to the Salle des Victoires, which had been transformed into a hospital, had been cared for by the gentle hands of the wives and daughters of the members of the Convention, transformed into sisters of charity.

They extolled Barras, who had shown such unerring judgment in selecting his second at the first glance, and they also extolled that second, who, unknown on the previous night, had suddenly burst upon them like a god from the midst of thunder and lightning.

Descending from this brilliant pedestal, Bonaparte remained general of the interior; and to be within reach of the staff, who had their headquarters on the Boulevard des Capucines, in what was formerly the Ministry of Foreign Affairs, he took two rooms in the Hôtel de la Concorde, Rue Neuve-des-Capucines.

In the room which he used for his cabinet, one morning a young man was announced under the name of Eugène Beauharnais.

Although already besieged with petitioners, Bonaparte had not yet got to the point of drawing a sharp line as to whom he would or would not receive.

Besides, the name of Eugène Beauharnais awakened only sympathetic memories.

He therefore gave orders that the young man should be admitted.

For those of our readers who have already seen him in Strasburg three years before, it is needless to say that he was a handsome and distinguished young man of some sixteen or seventeen years.

He had large eyes, thick black hair, full red lips, white teeth, and aristocratic hands and feet,— a mark of distinction which the young general immediately noticed, — and amid the embarrassment inseparable from a first interview, he had that attractive modesty which is so becoming to youth, above all when its possessor appears as a suppliant.

From the time he entered the room, Bonaparte followed him attentively with his eyes, — which did not tend to lessen Eugène's timidity.

But suddenly, as if he had shaken it off as unworthy of him, he raised his head, and standing upright, said :

"After all, I do not see why I need hesitate to prefer a request which is at once loyal and pious."

"I am listening," said Bonaparte.

"I am the son of the Vicomte de Beauharnais."

"Of the Citizen-General," corrected Bonaparte, gently.

"Of the Citizen-General, if you choose, or if thou choosest," rejoined the young man, "in case you absolutely insist upon the form of speech adopted by the government of the Republic — "

"I insist upon nothing," replied Bonaparte, "save what is clear and precise."

"Very well," continued the young man, "I come to ask at your hands, Citizen-General, the sword of my father, Alexandre de Beauharnais, who was a general like yourself. I am sixteen years old, my military education is almost completed. It is for me now to serve my country. I hope some day to wear at my side the sword which my father wore. That is why I come to ask you for it."

Bonaparte, who liked clear and concise replies, was much pleased with this firm and intelligent language.

"If I should ask you for more complete information concerning yourself and your family, Citizen," he said to the young man, "would you attribute the request to curiosity, or to the interest with which you inspire me?"

"I should rather believe," replied Eugène, "that the report of our misfortunes has reached your ears, and that it is to this that I owe the kindness with which you have welcomed me."

"Was not your mother a prisoner also?" asked Bonaparte.

. "Yes, and she was saved by a miracle. We owe her life to Citizeness Tallien and Citizen Barras."

Bonaparte reflected for a moment.

"How does your father's sword happen to be in my hands?" he asked finally.

"I do not say that it is in your hands, exactly, but I do say that you can cause it to be restored to me. The Convention ordered the disarming of the section Le Peletier. We are living in our former hôtel in the Rue Neuve-des-Mathurins, which General Barras caused to be restored to us. Some men came to my mother and asked for all the weapons in the house. My mother gave

orders that they should be given a double-barrelled hunting rifle of mine, a single-barrelled rifle which I bought
at Strasburg, and with which I fought against the
Prussians, and, finally, my father's sword. I regretted
neither the double-barrelled gun nor the other, although
I took pride in the memories they recalled. But I regretted, and I confess that I still regret, that sword which
fought so gloriously in America and France."

"If you were to see the weapons which formerly belonged to you," said Bonaparte, "you would doubtless
recognize them ?"

"Without any doubt," replied Eugène.

Bonaparte rang.

A subaltern entered.

"Accompany Citizen Beauharnais," said Bonaparte, "to
the rooms where they have put the arms of the sections.
You will allow him to take those which he shall point
out as belonging to him."

And he held out to the young man the hand which
was to lift him so high. Ignorant of the future, Eugène
darted towards it and pressed it gratefully.

"Ah, Citizen," he said, "my mother and sister shall
know how good you have been to me, and, believe me,
they will feel the same gratitude towards you that I do."

Just then the door opened, and Barras appeared,
unannounced.

"Ah," he said, "I am on ground with which I am
acquainted twice over."

"I have already told General Bonaparte what I owe
you," said Eugène, "and I am happy to repeat before you
that the widow and children of Beauharnais, if it had not
been for your protection, would probably have died of
hunger."

"Died of hunger!" repeated Bonaparte, laughing

"It is only those officers whom Citizen Aubry has put upon the retired list who are exposed to that kind of death."

"It is true, I was wrong," said Eugène ; "for while our mother was in prison I was with a carpenter, where I earned my daily bread, and my sister was with a seamstress, who supported her through charity."

"Well," said Barras, "the bad days are over, and the good ones have come back. Pray, what brings you here, my young friend ?"

Eugène told Barras the object of his visit.

"And why did you not apply to me," inquired Barras, "instead of disturbing my colleague ?"

"Because I wanted to know the Citizen-General Bonaparte," replied Eugène. "It seemed to me that it would be a good omen if my father's sword should be returned to me by him."

And bowing to the two generals, he went out with the officer, much less embarrassed than he had been at his entrance.

CHAPTER XXV.

THE MAP OF MARENGO.

THE two generals were left alone.　Both alike, but with different thoughts, followed the young man with their eyes, until the door had closed behind him.

"That boy has a heart of gold," said Barras.　"Just imagine that when he was thirteen and a half years old, — I did not know him then, — he went alone to Strasburg, in the hope of finding there some papers which would justify his father before the revolutionary tribunal.

"But the revolutionary tribunal was in a hurry. While waiting for the papers which the son was collecting, it cut off the head of the father.　It was time, any way, for Eugène to return, for had it not been for Saint-Just, whom he met there, I do not know what would have happened to him.　He attacked in the midst of a performance at the theatre one of the leaders of Strasburg, a president of a club named Tétrell, who was twice as big as he.

"If the people, who had seen him during the day fighting the Prussians, had not taken his part boldly, the poor boy would have been well singed."

"I suppose," said Bonaparte, always precise, "that you did not put yourself out simply to come and talk to me about this young man, since you did not know that I had received a call from him."

"No," replied Barras, "I came to make you a present."

" Me ?"

" Yes, you," said Barras.

And going to the door of the ante-chamber, he opened it and made a sign. Two men entered. They were carrying on their shoulders, as two carpenters carry a beam, an immense piece of canvas rolled and tied.

" Good God, what is that?" asked Bonaparte.

" You have often spoken to me of your desire to make a campaign in Italy, General."

" You mean," interrupted Bonaparte, " of the necessity which will arise, some day or other, for France to decide there the Austrian question."

" Well, for some time Carnot, who is of your opinion, has been occupying himself with the manufacture of the most complete map of Italy which exists in the world. I asked for it at the Ministry of War, and although they were inclined to refuse me, they finally gave it to me, and I give it to you."

Bonaparte seized Barras' hand.

" That is a true gift," he said, " particularly if this map is given to me as the one who is to make use of it. Open it," he continued, addressing the men who had brought it.

They knelt down and untied the cords; but when they tried to unroll it, they found that the room was not half large enough to hold it.

" The deuce !" said Bonaparte ; " you will force me to build a house just to hold this map."

" Oh," rejoined Barras, " when the time comes for you to use it, perhaps you will be living in a house large enough to nail it up between two windows. In the mean time, look at this part which is unrolled. Not a hill, not a brook is wanting."

The porters opened the map as far as possible. The

portion which they uncovered extended across the Gulf of Genoa, from Ajaccio to Savona.

"By the way," said Bonaparte, "is not that where Schérer, Masséna, and Kellermann ought to be, at Cervoni ?"

"Yes," replied Barras, "and we received news from them this very night. How could I have forgotten to tell you ! Augereau has won a great victory at Loano. Masséna and Joubert, whom Kellermann kept in the army in spite of the order of dismissal by the Committee of Public Safety, showed magnificent courage."

" It is not there, it is not there," murmured Bonaparte. " What do blows aimed at the limbs amount to ? Nothing. The heart is what we must strike at. At Milan, Mantua, Verona. Ah, if ever — "

" What ? " asked Barras.

"Nothing," said Bonaparte.

Then, turning suddenly towards Barras, he asked :

" Are you sure to be appointed one of the five directors ?"

" Yesterday," replied Barras, lowering his voice, " the members of the Convention met to agree upon the members of the Directory. They discussed it for some time ; the names which came out successfully from this first test are these : mine, then Rewbell's, Sieyès third, then La Réveillère-Lepaux, and Letourneur ; but one of the five will certainly not accept."

" Who is that ambitious one ? " asked Bonaparte.

" Sieyès."

" Is there any talk of the one who will replace him ?"

" In all probability it will be Carnot."

" You will lose nothing by that. But why not have introduced among all these names of civilians some name which represents the army, like Kléber, Pichegru, Hoche, or Moreau ?"

"They were afraid of giving the military too much influence."

Bonaparte began to laugh.

"Nonsense," he said; "when Cæsar took Rome, he was neither tribune nor consul; he had just returned from Gaul, where he had won eighty battles and conquered three hundred nations. That is what dictators do. But none of those men whom we have just named is built to play the *rôle* of Cæsar. If the five men whom you have named are chosen, things will go on well enough. You have popularity, talent for the initiative, and activity; you will naturally be the leading man of the Directory. Rewbell and Letourneur are men who will do the work, while you will represent the people. La Réveillère-Lepaux is wise and honest, and will furnish morality for you all. As for Carnot, I do not quite know what part of the work you will assign him."

"He will continue to make plans and lay out victories on paper," said Barras.

"Let him make as many plans as he likes. If I ever have any command, you need not take the trouble to send me any of them."

"Why not?"

"Because battles are not won with a map, a compass, and red, blue, or green headed pins. It needs instinct, an unerring glance, genius. I should like to know if Hannibal had plans of the battles of the Trebia, of Lake Trasymene, and of Cannes sent to him from Carthage. I snap my fingers at your plans! Do you know what you ought to do? You ought to give me the details which you have received concerning the battle of Loano; and since this map is unrolled at that place, it would interest me to follow the movements of our troops and the Austrians."

Barras drew from his pocket a note written with the brevity of a telegraphic despatch, and handed it to Bonaparte.

"Patience," he said; "you have the map, and perhaps the command will come."

Bonaparte eagerly read the despatch.

"Good!" he said. "Loano is the key to Genoa, and Genoa is the magazine of Italy."

Then, continuing to read the despatch, —

"Masséna, Kellermann, Joubert, what men; what might one not do with them! He who could bring them together, and make the most of their varying qualities, would be the veritable Olympian Jove, with thunderbolt in hand."

Then he murmured the names of Hoche, Kléber, and Moreau, and with a compass in his hand he lay down upon the great map of which only one corner was uncovered.

There he began to study the marches and counter-marches which had led up to the famous battle of Loano.

When Barras took his leave, Bonaparte scarcely noticed his departure, so absorbed was he in his strategic combinations.

"It cannot have been Schérer," he said, "who devised and executed this plan. Neither can it have been Carnot; there was too much of the unexpected about the attack. It was doubtless Masséna."

He had been for about half an hour lying upon this map, which was never to leave him, when the door opened, and a voice announced, —

"Citizeness Beauharnais."

In his preoccupation, Bonaparte understood the announcement "Citizen Beauharnais," and thought that the young man whom he had already seen had returned to thank him for the favor which he had just granted him.

"Let him come in," he said ; "let him come in."   .

As he spoke, there appeared at the door, not the young man whom he had already seen, but a charming woman, of twenty-seven to twenty-eight years of age. He half rose in his astonishment ; and it was thus, with one knee upon the ground, that Bonaparte saw for the first time Marie-Rose-Joséphine Tascher de la Pagerie, the widow Beauharnais.

CHAPTER XXVI.

MARIE-ROSE-JOSÉPHINE TASCHER DE LA PAGERIE, VICOM-
TESSE DE BEAUHARNAIS.

BONAPARTE remained motionless, smitten with admiration.

Madame de Beauharnais at the time of which we are writing was, as we have said, about twenty-eight years old, of indisputable beauty, and with a charming grace of manner, exhaling from her whole person that subtle fascination which resembles the perfume that Venus gave to her chosen ones to command their love.

Her hair and eyes were black, her nose was straight, she had a smiling mouth, the oval outline of her face was irreproachable, her neck gracefully set upon her shoulders, her figure flexible and undulating, her arm of perfect shape, and her hand beautiful beyond comparison.

Nothing could have been more attractive than her Creole accent, of which there remained only sufficient trace to betray her tropical birth.

As was indicated by her maiden name, Madame de Beauharnais belonged to a noble family. Born at Martinique, her education had been, like that of all Creoles, left under her own control; but rare qualities of mind and heart had made Mademoiselle Tascher de la Pagerie one of the most cultivated women of any age. Her kind heart had taught her early in life that although they had wool on their heads instead of hair, negroes were more to be pitied than other men, since the power and cupidity of the whites had torn them from their own country, to transfer them to a climate which caused them constant suffering, and sometimes killed them.

The first sight which attracted her attention was that of these wretched beings, all their family ties sundered, but brothers in toil, offering, to a sun almost directly overhead, a body constantly bent beneath the overseer's whip, and delving in a soil which their sweat and their blood did not fertilize for themselves.

She asked herself, in her youthful intelligence, why these men were beyond the pale of the law, why they had to drag out wretched lives, naked, without shelter, unable to own property, without honor, without liberty ; and she herself found the answer, — that it was for the sake of enriching avaricious masters that they were, from infancy and for life, condemned to hopeless and unending torture. And young Joséphine's pity had made of the estate of her parents an earthly paradise for the slaves.

There was still a distinction between whites and blacks ; but, almost to the extent of being free, the blacks shared in all the advantages and some of the pleasures of life ; and while nowhere in the island was a negro sure of marrying the negress he loved, marriages for love rewarded the labor and the affection of the slaves of their young mistress Joséphine more surely than was the case among other slave-owners.

She was about thirteen years old when there came to Martinique a young officer of noble birth and great merit, whom she met at her Aunt Renaudin's house.

It was Vicomte Alexandre de Beauharnais.

The one had in his person everything calculated to please. The other, in her heart everything calculated to inspire love.

They loved each other, therefore, with all the ardor of

two young people who have the delight of realizing their mutual dreams of souls akin to each other.

"I have chosen you," said Alexandre, pressing her hand tenderly.

"And I have found you," said Joséphine, holding up her forehead for him to kiss.

Her Aunt Renaudin thought that it would be disobeying the decrees of Providence to oppose the love of the two young people. The relatives of both were in France. Their consent had to be obtained to this marriage, to which Aunt Renaudin saw no obstacle. Obstacles were raised, however, by Messieurs de Beauharnais, the father and the uncle of the young man. In an access of fraternal friendship, they had once promised to marry their children to each other. He whom the young girl already regarded as her husband was the destined spouse of his cousin.

Alexandre's father yielded first. When he saw that the young people were in despair at his refusal, he relented little by little, and finally agreed to go himself and tell his brother of the change which had come over their plans. But the latter, who was of coarser fibre, claimed the fulfilment of the agreement, and told his brother that although he might consent to break his word, which was a thing unworthy of a gentleman, the uncle himself should not do so.

The father of the viscount went away in despair at having quarrelled with his brother; but preferring, all things considered, his brother's hate to his son's unhappiness, he not only renewed his promise to consent, but actually did consent.

It was then that the young Joséphine, who was later to give the world an example of such great self-sacrifice and absolute devotion, sounded the prelude, as it were, to the great divorce scene, by insisting that her lover should sacrifice his passion for her to the peace and tranquillity of his family.

She declared to the viscount that she wished to have an interview with his uncle, and took him with her to Monsieur de Beauharnais' house. She caused him to enter a smaller room adjacent to the salon where Monsieur de Beauharnais, marvelling at her visit, had said that he would receive her. Monsieur de Beauharnais rose, for he was a gentleman, and was receiving a lady.

"Monsieur," she said to him, " you do not and cannot like me ; but what do you know of me that you should hate me ? Whence have you derived the hate that you declare for me, and what justifies it ? Certainly not my attachment for the Vicomte de Beauharnais, for that is pure, legitimate, and returned by him. When we first confessed our love for each other we were ignorant that social *convenances*, and interests of which I know nothing, could ever make that first confession of our love a crime. However, Monsieur, since all our misfortunes, and mine above all, come from this marriage, which was planned by my aunt and agreed to by Monsieur de Beauharnais ; if Alexandre and I, more considerate of your wishes than careful of our own happiness, have the terrible courage to sacrifice that happiness to you ; if he and I renounce this marriage, which makes impossible the one that you had planned, — will you still think your nephew unworthy of your friendship, and will you still deem me deserving of your scorn ? "

The Marquis de Beauharnais, amazed at what he had heard, looked at Mademoiselle Tascher de la Pagerie for some time without speaking ; but not being able to believe in the sincerity of the sentiments she had expressed, he said, covering with a varnish of politeness the insulting nature of his reply, —

" Mademoiselle, I have heard the beauty, the wit, and the noble sentiments of Mademoiselle de la Pagerie spoken of in the highest terms of praise ; but this union which I feared, in which my nephew is so well justified, or at least excusable, I find all the more blameworthy because it is hard to cŏntend with, and because a rival, far from overcoming its influence, can only increase it, and because it was very difficult to foresee that it alone had the power to stay its own progress.   This, Mademoiselle, is the spectacle which you present to-day, — a spectacle so singular, permit me to say, that in order not to suspect you of the most adroit egotism or the most profound and well-acted dissimulation, I must have recourse to a third supposition, which you would perhaps resent just because it is a natural one."

" What is that supposition, Monsieur ?" asked Mademoiselle de la Pagerie.

" That you have ceased to love my nephew, or to be loved by him."

The viscount, who was listening, full of astonishment and grief, opened the door and sprang into the room.

" You are mistaken, Monsieur," he said to his uncle. " She still loves me, and I love her more than ever.   But, as she is an angel, she is sacrificing herself and me for the sake of our families.   But you have just proved, by not understanding her and by calumniating her, that you are not worthy of the sacrifice which she was willing to make.   Come, Joséphine, come ; all that I can do — and this is my last concession — is to leave it to my father : what he decides, we will do."

And they returned to their home, where Mademoiselle de la Pagerie related to Monsieur de Beauharnais what had just passed, asking his final decision, and promising, on behalf of herself and his son, to abide by it.

But the count, with tears in his eyes, took the hands of the young people.

"Never," said he, "were you more worthy of each other than since you have renounced your hopes of mutual happiness. You ask my final decision : it is, that you shall be married; it is my earnest hope that you will be happy."

A week later Mademoiselle de la Pagerie became the Vicomtesse de Beauharnais.

Nothing had happened to disturb the happiness of the young people when the Revolution began. The Vicomte de Beauharnais took his place among those who favored it ; but he made a mistake in thinking that any one could direct the avalanche, which rushed on, carrying all before it. He was swept off to the scaffold.

CHAPTER XXVII.

WHERE AN ANGEL STEPS, A MIRACLE IS PERFORMED.

ON the evening of the day before that on which the Vicomte de Beauharnais was to die upon the scaffold, he wrote his wife the following letter; it was his final adieu : —

NIGHT OF THE 6TH AND 7TH THERMIDOR, AT THE CONCIERGERIE.

Yet a few moments to give to love, to tears and regrets, and then every thought shall be devoted to the glory of my destiny and to the great dreams of immortality. When you receive this letter, O my Joséphine, your husband, in the language of this world, will long have ceased to be; but he will already, in the bosom of his God, have tasted of the true existence. You see, then, that you must not weep for him ; the wicked men, the senseless ones who survive him, should have all your tears, for they do evil, and cannot repair it.

But do not let us blacken with their guilty image these last moments. I would brighten them, on the contrary, by reflecting that, beloved by an adorable wife, the short day of our wedded life has passed without the slightest cloud. Yes, our union has lasted but a day, and that thought draws a sigh from me. But how serene and pure was that day which passed so rapidly; and how grateful ought I to be to the Providence which has you in its keeping ! To-day that same Providence is taking me away before my time; and that is another of its favors. Can a good man live without grief and almost remorse when he sees the whole universe in the clutches of the wicked ? I should therefore be glad to be taken away from them, were it not for the feeling that I am leaving to their tender mercies lives which are so dear and so precious to me. If, however, the thoughts of the dying are trustworthy presentiments, I feel one in my heart, which assures me that these butcheries will cease before long, and that the executioners will follow their victims to the scaffold. . . .

I resume these incoherent, almost illegible, lines, after having been interrupted by my keepers. I have just undergone a cruel formality, which I would have died rather than endure, under other circumstances. But why cavil at necessity? Reason teaches us to make the best of it.

After they cut my hair, it occurred to me to buy back a part of it, in order to leave to my dear wife and to my children unequivocal proofs and tokens of my dying remembrance. . . . I feel my heart breaking at this thought, and my paper is wet with tears.

Adieu, all that I love! Love me, speak of me, and never forget that the glory of dying a victim to tyrants and a martyr to liberty makes the scaffold illustrious.

As we have already mentioned, the Vicomtesse de Beauharnais was arrested in her turn, and she wrote to her children just before she was to die, even as her husband had written to her.

She ended with these words a long letter which we have before us : —

"For my part, my children, as I am about to die, like your father, a victim to the mad excesses which he always opposed, and which finally devoured him, I leave this life with no feeling of hatred for his executioners and my own, whom I despise.

"Honor my memory, even as you share my sentiments ; I leave you for an inheritance the glory of your father and the name of your mother, — which some poor wretches have blessed, — our love, our regrets, and our blessing."

Madame de Beauharnais was finishing this letter when she heard in the courtyard of the prison shouts of "Death to Robespierre! *Vive la liberté !*" It was the morning of the 10th Thermidor.

Three days later, Madame la Vicomtesse de Beauharnais, thanks to the friendship of Madame Tallien, was free ; and a month later, thanks to the influence of Barras, such of her property as had not been sold was restored to her. A part of it was the hôtel in the Rue Neuve-des-Mathurins, No. 11.

When her son — who had not told her of the step that he proposed to take — returned home with his father's sword in his hand, and when she heard how the sword had been restored to him, in the first outburst of enthusiasm she left her house, and having only the Boulevard to cross, hastened to thank the young general, who was so much astonished at her appearance.

Bonaparte immediately held out his hand to the beautiful widow, more beautiful than ever in the mourning robes which she had worn since her husband's death, and made a sign to her to step over the map, and take a seat in a part of the room to which it did not extend.

Joséphine remarked that she had come on foot, and that she did not dare to put her dainty little shoe upon the map, for fear of soiling it.

Bonaparte insisted. Aided by his hand, she leaped over the Gulf of Genoa, and the toe of her shoe touched the little town of Voltri, where it made a mark.

An arm-chair was there, and Joséphine seated herself in it ; and near her, Bonaparte, who had remained standing, partly from respect and partly from admiration, put his knee on a chair, and leaned upon the back of it.

He was at first embarrassed. He was not much accustomed to society, and had rarely talked with women ; but he knew that there are three things to which their hearts are always alive, — fatherland, youth, and love.

He therefore spoke to Madame de Beauharnais of Martinique, of her relatives, and of her husband.

An hour slipped by, which, for all his skill in mathematics, seemed to him no more than a few minutes.

They spoke little of the present position of affairs; but Bonaparte noticed that Madame de Beauharnais seemed to have more or less close relations with all those who were in power, or likely to attain power, her husband having been a prominent exponent of the reactionary opinions which were then in high favor.

For her part, Madame de Beauharnais was too clear-headed a woman not to notice at once, through all his innate eccentricity, the powerful intellect of the conqueror of the 13th Vendémiaire.

This complete and rapid success had made Bonaparte the hero of the day; his name had often been mentioned to Madame de Beauharnais; curiosity and enthusiasm, as we have said, had induced her to pay him this visit. She found Barras' *protégé* to be intellectually far beyond what Barras had claimed for him, so that when her servant came to tell her that Madame Tallien awaited her at her house to go "she knew where, as they had planned," she exclaimed, —

"But we were not to meet until half past-five!"

"It is six o'clock, Madame," said the servant, bowing.

"*Mon Dieu!*" she said, in surprise, "what shall I say to her?"

"Tell her, Madame," said Bonaparte, "that I was so charmed by your conversation that I prevailed upon you by my entreaties to give me another quarter of an hour."

"That is bad advice," said Joséphine; "for in that case I should have to say what is not true, in order to excuse myself."

"Let me see," said Bonaparte, like a man dying with the wish to prolong the visit for a few moments more. "Was Madame Tallien contemplating another 9th Ther-

"I am a Corsican, Madame.'

midor? I thought that the days of Robespierre had gone by forever."

"If I were not ashamed to make the confession, I would tell you what we are going to do."

"Tell me, Madame. I shall be delighted to share a secret with you, and especially one which you are ashamed to confess."

"Are you superstitious?" asked Madame de Beauharnais.

"I am a Corsican, Madame."

"Then you will not laugh at me.

"We were at Madame Gohier's yesterday, and she told us that in passing through Lyons ten years or more ago she had her fortune told by a young woman named Lenormand. Among other predictions which had been fulfilled, the fortune-teller told her that she would love a man whom she would not marry, but that she would marry another one whom she did not love; and that after marriage she would grow extremely fond of this man whom she had married. That has been precisely her history.

"Now, she has heard that this sibyl, named Lenormand, is at present in Paris, living at Rue de Tournon, No. 7.

"Madame Tallien and I felt curious to go and see her; and Madame Tallien agreed to come to my house, where we were to disguise ourselves as *grisettes*. The appointment was, as I have said, for half-past five; it is now a quarter-past six.

"I must go and make my excuses to Madame Tallien, change my dress, and, if she still wishes it, go with her to Mademoiselle Lenormand's.

"I will confess that we flatter ourselves, thanks to the completeness of our disguise, that we shall succeed in misleading the prophetess completely."

"You have no use for a companion, a locksmith, or blacksmith, or gunsmith, I suppose?" said Bonaparte.

"No, Citizen," said Madame de Beauharnais, "I regret to say we have not. I have already committed one indiscretion in telling you what we are going to do. It would be a vastly greater indiscretion to permit you to make a third in our party."

"Your will be done, Madame, here on earth as in heaven," said Bonaparte.

And giving her his hand to lead her to the door, he this time avoided making her step upon the beautiful map, upon which her foot, light as it was, had left a trace.

CHAPTER XXVIII.

THE SIBYL.

As she had told the young general, Madame de Beauharnais found Madame Tallien waiting for her.

Madame Tallien (Thérèse Cabarus) was, as everybody knows, the daughter of a Spanish banker. She was married to M. Davis de Fontenay, a councillor of the parliament of Bordeaux, but was soon divorced from him. This was at the beginning of '94, when the Terror was at its height.

Thérèse Cabarus wished to join her father in Spain, in order to escape evils of which proscription was the least. Arrested at the gates of the city, she was brought before Tallien, who at first sight fell passionately in love with her. She made use of this passion to save a great number of victims.

At this time love was the most puissant opponent of death, its most cruel enemy.

Tallien was recalled. Thérèse Cabarus followed him to Paris, where she was arrested; from the depths of a prison she brought about the 9th Thermidor, and when Robespierre was overthrown she was free.

It will be remembered that her first care had been to secure the safety of Joséphine, her companion in prison.

From that time Joséphine Beauharnais and Thérèse Tallien had been inseparable. Only one woman in Paris disputed the palm of beauty with them; that woman was Madame Récamier.

This evening, as we know, they had resolved to go, dressed as *femmes-de-chambre* and under false names, to consult the fashionable sibyl Madame Lenormand.

In a twinkling the two great ladies were transformed into two charming *grisettes*.

Their lace caps fell over their eyes, the hood of a little silk mantle enveloped the head; clad in short dresses of Indian muslin, and bravely shod in shoes with paste buckles, and stockings embroidered in pink or green, which their skirts did not hide, they jumped into the *fiacre* which they had ordered to be driven in at the great gate of the house No. 11 Rue Neuve-des-Mathurins, and in a voice which trembled slightly, like that of all women when they are doing anything which is outside of their accustomed routine, Madame de Beauharnais said to the driver, —

"Rue de Tournon, No. 7."

The *fiacre* stopped at the place indicated, the driver got down from his seat, opened the door, received his fare, and knocked at the house-door, which opened at once.

The two ladies hesitated an instant, as if their hearts failed them at the critical moment. But Madame Tallien urged her friend on. Joséphine, light as a bird, alighted upon the pavement without touching the step; Madame Tallien followed her. They crossed the formidable threshold, and the door was shut upon them.

They found themselves under a *porte-cochère*, the arch of which extended into the court. At the farther end they saw, by the light of a sort of reflector, these words written on an outside shutter : —

"Mademoiselle Lenormand, bookseller."

They advanced towards the light, which rendered visible a short flight of four steps.

They went up the four steps, and found themselves in front of the porter's lodge.

"Citizeness Lenormand?" inquired Madame Tallien, who, although the younger of the two, seemed on this occasion to take the initiative.

"Ground floor, left-hand door," replied the porter.

Madame Tallien stepped first, holding up her already short dress, and thereby discovering a leg which, although it might vie in shape with the most beautiful Greek statues, had this evening condescended to the *grisette's* garter, tied below the knee.   Madame de Beauharnais followed, admiring her friend's free and easy manner, but unable to emulate it.   She was still on the steps when Madame Tallien, having reached the door, had already rung.   An old servant opened the door.

The new arrivals, whose faces were more of a recommendation than was their attire, were examined with the most scrupulous minuteness by the *valet-de-chambre*, who simply made them a sign to sit down in a corner of the first room.   The second, which was a salon, and through which the valet had to pass in order to reach his mistress, was occupied by two or three women, whose rank it would have been difficult to determine, all ranks at that time being practically merged in that of the *bourgeoisie*.   But, to their great astonishment, the door of the salon opened again after a few moments, and Mademoiselle Lenormand herself came and spoke to them.

"Mesdames," she said, "be good enough to enter the salon."

The two pretended *grisettes* looked at each other in astonishment.

Mademoiselle Lenormand was said to make her predictions in a state of somnambulism.   Was this true, and had she, by means of her second-sight, recognized, even without seeing them, two ladies of rank in the self-styled *grisettes* whom the valet had announced?

To be sure, at the same time, Mademoiselle Lenormand made a sign to one of the two ladies waiting in the salon to enter the fortune-telling cabinet.

Madame Tallien and Madame de Beauharnais then began to examine the room into which they had been shown.

Its principal ornaments were two portraits, one of Louis XVI. and the other of Marie-Antoinette. Notwithstanding the terrible days which had just passed, and the fact that the heads which the portraits represented had fallen upon the scaffold, the pictures had not left their place for a moment, and had not ceased to be regarded with all the respect with which Mademoiselle Lenormand regarded their originals.

After these paintings, the most remarkable thing in the room was a long table, covered with a cloth upon which sparkled necklaces, bracelets, rings, and pieces of silver ware elegantly wrought; most of the last being of the eighteeth century. All these objects had been given to the sibyl by persons to whom she had made agreeable predictions, which had doubtless been fulfilled.

Soon the door of the cabinet opened, and the last person who had occupied the salon before the arrival of the two ladies was called. The friends remained alone.

A quarter of an hour passed by, during which they conversed in low tones, and then the door opened again, and Mademoiselle Lenormand came out.

"Which of you desires to come in first, Mesdames?" she asked.

"Can we not go in together?" asked Madame de Beauharnais, quickly.

"Impossible, Madame," replied the sibyl. "I have sworn never to read the cards for one person in the presence of another."

"May we know why?" asked Madame Tallien, with her usual impulsiveness, we might almost say her usual indiscretion.

"Because in a portrait which I had the misfortune to draw too true to life, one of two persons whom I was receiving recognized her husband."

"Go in, go in, Thérèse," said Madame de Beauharnais, urging her friend.

"So I am always to be the one to sacrifice myself," replied the latter.

And then, looking smilingly at her friend, she said:

"Well, so be it; I will risk it."

And she entered.

Mademoiselle Lenormand was at that time a woman from twenty-four to twenty-nine years of age, short and stout in figure, vainly attempting to disguise the fact that one shoulder was higher than the other; she wore a turban adorned with a bird of paradise.

Her hair fell in long curls around her face. She wore two skirts, one above the other: one was short, scarcely falling below the knees, and pearl-gray in color; the other was longer, falling in a short train behind her, and was cherry-colored.

Beside her, on a cushion, was her favorite greyhound, named Aza.

The table upon which she made her experiments was nothing but a common round table covered with a green cloth, with drawers in front, in which the sibyl put her different materials. The cabinet was of the same length as the salon, but narrower. On each side of the door was an oak bookcase filled with books. Facing her seat was an arm-chair for the person who was consulting her.

Between her and the subject was a steel rod, which was called the divining-rod. At the end towards the client was a little coiled steel serpent; the opposite end was like the handle of a whip.

This was what Madame de Beauharnais saw in the brief moment during which the door remained open to give entrance to her friend.

Joséphine took up a book, drew near the lamp, and tried to read ; but her attention was soon diverted from her reading by the sound of the bell and the entrance of another person.

It was a young man dressed in the height of the fashion adopted by the *Incroyables*. Between his hair, which fell down to the level of his eyebrows, his "dog's-ears," falling over his shoulders, and his neckcloth, which reached to his cheek-bones, one could scarcely distinguish a straight nose, a firm and resolute mouth, and eyes as brilliant as black diamonds.

He bowed without speaking, twirled his knotty stick two or three times around his head, hummed three false notes, as if he were just finishing or beginning the air of a song, and sat down in a corner.

But although this "griffin's eye," as Dante would have said, was hardly to be seen, Madame de Beauharnais was beginning to feel ill at ease in this *tête-à-tête*, although the *Incroyable* was seated in one corner of the salon and she at the farther end, when Madame Tallien came out.

"Ah, my dear," she said, going straight to her friend, without seeing the *Incroyable*, who was seated in shadow, "ah, my dear, go in quickly. Mademoiselle Lenormand is a charming woman. Only guess what she predicted for me!"

"Why, my dear," replied Madame de Beauharnais, "that you will be loved, that you will be beautiful until you are fifty years old, that you will have love affairs all your life — "

And as Madame Tallien made a movement as if to say, " No, not that," Joséphine added : —

"And that you will have tall footmen, a beautiful house, and fine carriages with white or bay horses."

"I shall have all that, my dear, and, furthermore, if I am to believe our sibyl, I shall be a princess."

" I congratulate you sincerely, my beautiful princess," replied Joséphine, " but I do not see that there is anything further that I can ask for ; and as I shall probably never be a princess, and as my pride already suffers at being less beautiful than you, I will not give it this other subject for envy, which might make us quarrel."

" Are you in earnest, dear Joséphine ? "

" No ; but I will not expose myself to the inferiority which threatens me on all sides. I leave you your principality ; let us run away ! "

She made a movement as if to go, and to take Madame Tallien with her ; but just then a hand was placed lightly upon her arm, and a voice said, —

" Remain, Madame ; and perhaps, when you have heard me, you will find that you have no occasion to envy your friend."

Joséphine greatly desired to know what could be in store for her so great that she need not envy a princess ; she therefore yielded, and in her turn entered Mademoiselle Lenormand's cabinet.

CHAPTER XXIX.

FORTUNE-TELLING.

MADEMOISELLE LENORMAND made a sign to Joséphine to sit down in the chair which Madame Tallien had just vacated, and then she drew a fresh pack of cards from her drawer, — probably so that the destinies of one should not influence those of the other.

Then she looked fixedly at Madame de Beauharnais.

"You sought to deceive me," she said, "by coming to consult me in vulgar attire. I am a somnambulist, and I saw you leave a hôtel in the centre of Paris. I saw your hesitation about entering my house; I saw you finally in the ante-room, when your place was in the salon, and I went to look for you. Do not seek to deceive me; reply frankly to my questions, and since you come in search of truth, tell the truth."

Madame de Beauharnais bowed.

"If you care to question me, I am ready to answer."

"What animal do you like best?"

"The dog."

"What flower do you prefer?"

"The rose."

"What odor pleases you best?"

"That of the violet."

The sibyl placed before Madame de Beauharnais a pack of cards almost double the size of ordinary ones, which had not been invented more than a month, and which were called "le grand oracle."

" Let us see first where you are placed," said she.

And, turning over the pack, she separated the cards with the wand, and found the client; that is to say, a brunette in a white dress with broad embroidered flounces, and a cloak of red velvet with a long and flowing train. She was placed between the eight of hearts and the ten of clubs.

" Chance has placed you well, Madame, as you see ; the eight of hearts has three meanings in as many different rows.

"The first, which is the eight of hearts itself, represents the conjunction of stars beneath which you were born. The second, an eagle carrying away a toad from a pond over which he is hovering. The third, a female near a tomb.

" This is what I see, Madame, in this first card. You were born under the influence of Venus and the Moon. You have recently had a very satisfactory experience, which was almost in the nature of a triumph.

" Finally, this woman dressed in black approaching a tomb indicates that you are a widow.

" On the other hand, the ten of clubs promises success in an undertaking which has been begun, but of which you are scarcely cognizant.

" It would be impossible to find a more fortunate throw of the cards."

Then, taking up the cards, and leaving out the brunette, Mademoiselle Lenormand shuffled them, and asked Madame de Beauharnais to cut them with her left hand, and to draw fourteen cards, which she was to place, in any order she chose, beside the brunette, from right to left, as Orientals write.

Madame de Beauharnais obeyed, and cut and arranged the fourteen cards as requested.

Mademoiselle Lenormand followed them with her eyes more attentively than Madame de Beauharnais herself as the latter turned them.

"In truth, Madame," she said, "you are fortunate, and I am sure that you did well not to be frightened by the prediction which I made to your friend, brilliant though it was. Your first card is the five of diamonds; beside it is the beautiful constellation of the Southern Cross, which is invisible to us in Europe. The great subject of this card, which represents a Greek or Mohammedan traveller, indicates that you were born either in the East or in the colonies. The paroquet or the orange-tree, which form the third subject, lead me to favor the colonies. The flower, which is a veratrum, very common in Martinique, would almost justify me in saying that you were born in that island."

"You are not mistaken, Madame."

"Your third card, the nine of diamonds, which indicates distant journeys, makes me think that you left the island while you were still young. The convolvulus which is drawn on the lower part of this card, and which is the symbol of a woman seeking for some one to cling to, would indicate that you left Martinique in order to be married."

"That is also true, Madame," replied Joséphine.

"Your fourth card, which is the ten of spades, indicates the loss of your hopes; but the fruits and flowers of saxifrage which are on the same card make me think that your disappointment was but momentary, and that a happy conclusion — probably a marriage — succeeded these fears, which amounted even to loss of hope."

"If you had read in the book of my own life, Madame, you could not have seen more clearly."

"That encourages me," replied the sibyl, "for in your

cards I see such strange things that I should stop short if your denial were added to my doubts.

"Here is the eight of spades. Achilles is dragging Hector, chained to his car, around the walls of Troy; lower down, a woman is kneeling before a tomb. Your husband, like the Trojan hero, must have died a violent death, probably upon the scaffold. But here is a singular thing, on the same card : opposite the weeping woman, the bones of Pelops are crossed above the talisman of the moon. This means, 'Happy fatality.' To a great misfortune will succeed good fortune which is even greater."

Joséphine smiled.

"That belongs to the future ; I therefore cannot reply."

"You have two children?" asked the sibyl.

"Yes."

"A son and a daughter?"

"Yes."

"See, here is your son, who, on the same card, the ten of diamonds, takes, without consulting you, a resolution of the highest importance, not in itself, but in its results.

"At the bottom of the card, under this oak, which, you see, is one of the talking oaks of the forest of Dodona, Jason listens, lying beneath its shade. What does he hear? The voice of the future, which your son heard when he decided upon the step which he has just taken.

"The card which follows, the knave of diamonds, shows you Achilles, disguised as a woman, at the court of Lycomenes. The glitter of his sword will betray his sex. Is there something about a sword between your son and some other person?"

"Yes, Madame."

"Well, here at the bottom of the card is Juno in a cloud, crying, 'Courage, young man!' Help will not be wanting.

"I am not sure, but in this card, which is nothing less than the king of diamonds, I think I see your son addressing a powerful soldier, and obtaining of him what he asks.

"The four of diamonds represents you yourself, Madame, at the moment when your son is relating to you the fortunate result of his attempt. The flowers growing at the bottom of this card admonish you not to let yourself be overcome by difficulties, and tell you that you will reach the goal of your desires. And, finally, Madame, here is the eight of clubs, which positively indicates a marriage; placed as it is next to the eight of hearts, which is the eagle soaring towards the sky with a toad in his talons, the eight of hearts indicates that this marriage will lift you above the most eminent ranks of society.

"Then, if we still doubt, here is the six of hearts, which, unfortunately, goes so rarely with the eight, — here is the six of hearts, whereon is the alchemist watching the stone turn into gold; that is to say, the ordinary life changing into a life of nobility, honors, and lofty position. See among these flowers this same convolvulus, twining about a lily shorn of its blossoms; that means, Madame, that you will succeed, — you, who are simply seeking a support, will succeed — how shall I tell you? — to everything that is grandest and most powerful in France, in short, to the lily shorn of its blossoms, — and, as indicated by the ten of clubs, that you will succeed to all this by passing across battle-fields, where, as you see, Ulysses and Diomedes are carrying off the white horses of Rhesus, placed under the care of the talisman of Mars.

"There, Madame, you will have the respect and the affection of the whole world. You will be the wife of this Hercules stifling the lion of the Nemæan forest; that is to say, the useful and courageous man who exposes himself to every danger for the good of his country. The flowers with which you will be crowned will be the lilac, the arum, and the immortelle, for you will represent true merit and perfect goodness."

Finally, rising enthusiastically, seizing Madame de Beauharnais' hand, and falling at her feet, she said, —

"Madame, I know neither your name nor your rank, but I can read your future. Madame, remember me when you are — empress ! "

"Empress ? I ? You are mad, my dear woman ! "

"What, Madame, do you not see that your last card, the one to which the other fourteen lead, is the king of hearts, the great Charlemagne, who holds his sword in one hand and the globe in the other ? Do you not see on the same card the man of genius who, with a book in his hand and a sphere at his feet, meditates upon the destinies of the world ? And, finally, do you not see, on two desks placed opposite each other, the Book of Wisdom and the laws of Solon ? — which proves that your husband will be a legislator as well as a conqueror."

Improbable as the prediction was, the blood rushed in a torrent to Joséphine's head. Her eyes grew dim, her forehead was covered with perspiration, and a shiver ran through her whole body.

"Impossible ! Impossible ! Impossible ! " she murmured. And she sank back in her chair.

Then, suddenly remembering that the consultation had lasted nearly an hour, and that Madame Tallien was waiting for her, she rose, threw her purse to Mademoiselle Lenormand without looking to see how much it contained, darted into the salon, took Madame Tallien by the waist and drew her away, scarcely replying to the bow which the *Incroyable* made to the two ladies, rising as they passed before him.

" Well ?" asked Madame Tallien, stopping Joséphine on the flight of steps which led down into the courtyard.

" Well," replied Madame de Beauharnais, " that woman is crazy ! "

" What did she predict for you ? "

" It is your turn first."

" I warn you, my dear, that I have already become accustomed to my prediction," said Madame Tallien. " She said that I should be a princess."

" Well," rejoined Joséphine, " I am not yet accustomed to mine ; she said that I should be — empress ! "

And the two would-be *grisettes* got into their *fiacre*.

CHAPTER XXX.

THE PRETENDED INCROYABLE.

As we have said, the two ladies, excited with their predictions, had scarcely paid any attention to the young man who was awaiting his turn.

During the long *séance* which Madame de Beauharnais had had with the sibyl, Madame Tallien had more than once tried to ascertain to what class of *Incroyable* the young man belonged. But he, evidently little inclined to respond to her attempts at conversation, had drawn his hair over his eyes, his cravat over his chin, and his " dog's ears " over his cheeks, and with a sort of grunt had settled down in his chair, like a man who would not be sorry to shorten the time of waiting by a short nap.

Madame de Beauharnais' long *séance* had passed thus, Madame Tallien pretending to read, and the *Incroyable* pretending to sleep.

But as soon as the ladies had gone out, and he had followed them with his eyes as long as possible, he presented himself in his turn at the door of Mademoiselle Lenormand's cabinet.

The appearance of the new client was so grotesque that it brought a smile to her lips.

" Mademoiselle," he said, affecting the ridiculous mode of speech of the young dandies of the time, " will you have the goodness to tell me the fortunate or unfortunate vicissitudes which destiny has in reserve for the person of your humble servant? He will not conceal from you that

that person is so dear to him that whatever agreeable things you predict will be most gratefully received by him. He must add, however, that, owing to his great self-control, he will listen with equanimity to any catastrophes with which you may be pleased to threaten him."

Mademoiselle Lenormand looked uneasily at him for a moment. Did his indifference amount to madness, or had she to do with one of those young men who at this time, as they took pleasure in mocking even the holiest things, would have had no great scruples about insulting the sibyl of the Rue de Tournon, firmly anchored though she was in the esteem of the noble inhabitants of the Faubourg Saint-Germain ?

"Do you wish me to cast your horoscope ? " she asked.

" Yes, my horoscope, — one like that which was cast at the birth of Alexander, son of Philip, king of Macedon. Without expecting to attain the renown of the conqueror of Porus and the founder of Alexandria, I intend some day to make a stir in the world. Have the goodness, therefore, to prepare whatever is necessary, and predict the best of good fortune for me."

"Citizen," returned Mademoiselle Lenormand, "I have several different methods."

" Let us hear what they are," said the *Incroyable,* making his stomach protrude, slipping his thumbs into the arm-holes of his waistcoat, and letting his cane hang by its cord from his wrist.

"For example, I use at various times the whites of eggs, the analysis of coffee grounds, spotted or algebraic cards, and I sometimes read the future by means of a cock."

" The last would suit me very well," said the young man ; " but we should need a living cock and a glassful of wheat : have you them ? "

" I have them," replied Mademoiselle Lenormand. " I also use captromancy at times."

" I am looking for a Venetian mirror," said the young man ; " for, as nearly as I can remember, captromancy is performed with a Venetian mirror and a drop of water thrown thereon."

" You are right, Citizen ; you seem to be well acquainted with my art."

" Bah ! " said the young man. " Yes, yes, one takes a turn at the occult sciences occasionally."

" There is also chiromancy," said Mademoiselle Lenormand.

" Ah, that is what I want ! All the other practices have something more or less diabolical about them, while chiromancy has never been censured by the Catholic Church, being a science founded upon principles drawn from Holy Writ and from transcendental philosophy. As much cannot be said, remember, Citizeness, for hydromancy, which has to do with a ring thrown into the water ; for pyromancy, which consists in placing the victim in the midst of fire ; of geomancy, which is performed by means of cabalistic signs traced upon the ground ; of capnomancy, which consists in sowing poppy seeds on glowing coals ; of coscinomancy, in which the hatchet, the tongs, and the sieve are employed ; nor, finally, of anthropomancy, in which human victims are sacrificed."

Mademoiselle Lenormand looked uneasily at him. Was he speaking seriously ? Was he making fun of her ? Or did he conceal beneath assumed indifference a desire to remain unrecognized ?

" Then you prefer chiromancy ? " she said.

" Yes," replied the *Incroyable;* " for with chiromancy, were you the devil himself, or his wife Proserpine," and he bowed gallantly to Mademoiselle Lenormand, " I should not fear for the safety of my soul, since the patriarch Job has said (chapter xxxvii., verse 7), ' God hath drawn lines in the hands of all men, in order that each may know his destiny.' Solomon, the pre-eminently wise king, added : ' Length of life is marked in the right hand, and the lines of the left hand betoken riches and glory.' Finally, we read in the prophet Isaiah : ' Your hand denotes that you will live a long time.' Here is mine. What does it say ? "

As he spoke, the *Incroyable* drew off his glove and put out a hand that was delicate and well-shaped, although thin, and tanned by the sun. The proportions were perfect, the fingers long and smooth ; it was entirely without rings.

Mademoiselle Lenormand took it and looked at it carefully. Then her eyes turned from the young man's hand to his face.

" Monsieur," she said, " it must have cost your natural dignity much to clothe yourself thus, and you must have yielded, in doing so, either to a great curiosity or to the first expression of an unconquerable feeling. You wear a disguise, and not your ordinary attire. Your hand is that of a soldier, accustomed to wield the sword rather than twirl the cane of the *Incroyable* or the switch of the dandy. Neither is your natural language that which you now affect. Cease, then, to dissimulate : in my presence all disguise is useless. You know all that you have said, but you have learned these sciences only while studying others which you deem to be more important. You have a taste for occult research, it is true, but your future is not to be that of a Nicolas Flamel or a Cagliostro. You have laughingly asked for a horoscope like that which was cast at the birth of Alexander, son of

Philip.　It is too late to cast the horoscope of your birth ;
but I can tell you both what has happened to you since
your birth, and what will happen to you from now until
you die."

"Faith, you are right !" said the young man, in his natural voice, "and I confess that I am ill at ease in this disguise ; neither, as you have said, is this language that which
I am in the habit of speaking.　If you had been taken in
by my dress and my mode of speech I should have said
nothing, and I should have left you with a shrug of the
shoulders.　The discovery which you have made, in spite
of my efforts to deceive you, indicates to me that there is
something real in your art.　I well know that it is tempt-
ing God," he added gloomily, "to attempt to wrest from
Him the secret of the future ; but where is the man who
feels within himself a vast power of will, who does not
desire to aid, by a more or less complete knowledge of
the future, the events which the future has in store for
him ?　You have said that you will relate my past life.
I ask only a few words from you on that point, being
more eager to know the future.　I repeat, here is my
hand."

Madèmoiselle Lenormand's eyes rested for a moment
on the palm of his hand ; then, raising her head, she
said, —

"You were born on an island, of a family which,
though noble, has neither wealth nor renown.　You left
your country to be educated in France ; you entered the
service in a special branch, the artillery.　You gained
a great victory, which was worth much to your country,
but which was poorly recompensed.　For a moment
you thought of leaving France.　Fortunately, obstacles
stood in your way, and kept you here.　You have
just found your way into notoriety by means of a

brilliant stroke which has assured you the support of the future Directory. This very day, — mark well the date, — although it has been marked only by ordinary events, will become one of the most important landmarks of your life. Do you believe in my art now, and shall I go on?"

"Certainly," was the reply; "and that you may have every facility, I will begin my showing you my veritable features."

At these words he took off his hat, threw aside his wig, untied his cravat, and revealed that head of bronze which seemed to have been modelled from an antique medal. He frowned slightly, smoothed his hair upon his temples with his hand, his eye became fixed, haughty, almost stern, as did his voice ; and no longer with the lisp of the *Incroyable* or the gentleness of a man addressing a lady, but with the firmness of the word of command, he said, as he presented his hand for the third time to the sibyl, —

"Behold me!"

CHAPTER XXXI.

"MACBETH, THOU SHALT BE KING!"

MADEMOISELLE LENORMAND took, almost with a feeling of veneration, the hand which her client held out to her.

"Will you have the whole truth?" she asked, "or shall I tell you only the good, and conceal the evil, as I would to one of those effeminate creatures to whose nervous irritability you are sometimes liable?"

"Tell everything," said the young man, briefly.

"Be sure that you remember the *order* which you have given," she replied, emphasizing the word "order." "Your hand, the most perfect of any that I have ever seen, presents to me a mixture of all virtuous sentiments and all human weaknesses; it shows at once the most heroic and the most hesitating of characters. Most of the signs on your palm dazzle by their brilliancy, while others seem to point to the deepest and most painful darkness. What I am about to reveal to you is an enigma more difficult to read than that of the Theban Sphinx; for even as you will be greater than Œdipus, so will you be more unhappy. Shall I go on, or shall I stop?"

"Go on," he said.

"I *obey* you" (emphasizing the word "obey").

"We will begin with the most powerful of the seven planets; all seven are impressed upon your hand, and are placed according to their recognized order.

"Jupiter is at the extremity of the index finger. Let us begin with him. Perhaps some confusion will result from this method of procedure, but out of chaos we will draw forth light.

"Jupiter then in your hand is placed at the extremity of the index finger, which means that you will be the friend and the enemy of the great ones of this world and of the fortunate men of the age. On the third joint of this finger, notice this sign in the form of a fan ; it announces that you will forcibly levy tribute upon peoples and kings. See, on the second joint, this sort of grating, broken at its seventh branch : that means that you will occupy in succession six positions of dignity, and that you will stop only at the seventh."

"Do you know what those positions are ? " he asked.

"No. All that I can tell you about them is that the last is that of Emperor of the West, which is to-day in the house of Austria.

"Under the grating see that star; it announces that a good genius will not cease to watch over you until your eighth lustre, or, in other words, until you are forty years old. At that time you will apparently forget that Providence chose a companion for you, for that companion will be abandoned by you, as a result of a false calculation of human prosperity. The two signs which are placed immediately under that star, and which resemble, the one a horse-shoe and the other a chess-board, indicate that after long and continuous prosperity you will inevitably fall, and from the greatest height that man has ever reached. You will fall more through the influence of women than the strength of men. Four lustres will be the term of your triumph and power.

"This other sign at the feet of Jupiter, accompanied by these three stars, signifies that during the last three years of your power your enemies will be occupied in trying to undermine it, that three months will be sufficient to hurl you from it, and that the crash of your fall will resound from the East to the West. Shall I go on?"

"Go on," said the young man.

"These two stars on the extremity of the middle finger, which is the finger of Saturn, positively indicate that you will be crowned in the same metropolis which has witnessed the coronation of the kings of France, your predecessors. But the sign of Saturn, placed exactly below these two stars and governing them, as it were, is a sign of gloomiest import for you.

"On the second joint of this middle finger there are two signs which are peculiar, in that they seem to contradict each other. The triangle denotes a curious, suspicious man, not at all lavish with his means, except to his soldiers, and who during his life will receive three wounds : the first on the thigh, the second on the heel, and the third on the little finger. The second of these signs is a star which denotes the magnanimous sovereign, the lover of the beautiful, forming gigantic projects which are not only incapable of being realized, but which none but he would be capable of conceiving.

"This line, which resembles an S winding over the root of the second joint, forebodes, besides various other perils, several attempts at assassination, among which there is a premeditated explosion.

"The straight line, the letter C, and the letter X, which go down almost to the root of the finger of Saturn, betoken a second alliance, more illustrious than the first."

"But," said the young man, impatiently interrupting the sibyl, "this is the second or third time that you have spoken of this first alliance which is to protect the first eight lustres of my life. How shall I recognize the lady when I see her?"

"She is dark," replied the sibyl, "the widow of a fair-haired man who wore a sword and perished by the axe. She has two children, whom you will adopt for your own. In examining her face you will recognize her by two things : one is that she has a noticeable mark on one of her eyebrows ; and the other, that in familiar conversation she frequently raises her right wrist, being in the habit of holding a handkerchief in her hand, which she carries to her mouth whenever she smiles."

"Very well," he returned ; "now let us return to my horoscope."

"See, at the base of the finger of Saturn, these two signs, one of which resembles a gridiron without a handle, and the other the six of diamonds.

"They predict that your happiness will be destroyed by your second wife, who, unlike the first, will be fair, and born of a race of kings.

"The figure representing the image of the Sun at the end of the third joint of the ring finger, which is the finger of Apollo, proves that you will become an extraordinary personage, rising by your own merit, but especially favored by Jupiter and Mars.

"These four straight lines, placed like palisades below this image of the Sun, betoken that you will struggle in vain to overcome a power which, unaided, will stop you in your course.

"Beneath these four straight lines we find again that serpentine line, in the form of the letter S, which has already twice predicted misfortune for you on the finger of Saturn ; if the star which is below that line were above it instead, it would indicate that you would remain for seven lustres at the zenith of your power.

"The fourth finger of the left hand bears the sign of Mercury at the end of its third joint. This means that

few men will possess your knowledge, sagacity, finesse,
exactness of reasoning, and keenness of mind. You will
bend several nations to your vast projects; you will
undertake expeditions which will be marvelled at; you
will cross deep rivers, climb steep mountains, and traverse
immense deserts. But this sign of Mercury also denotes
that you will have an abrupt and capricious temper; that
this temper will raise up powerful enemies against you;
that, in the spirit of a true cosmopolite, tormented by lust
of conquest, you will not be contented anywhere, and that
sometimes you will even feel that Europe is too confined
a sphere for you.

"As for this sort of ladder which is drawn between
the first and third joints of the finger of Mercury, it
signifies that in the days of your power you will carry
out immense works, for the embellishment of your capital, as well as other cities of your kingdom.

"And now we pass to the thumb, which is the finger
of Venus.

"As you see, here is her all-powerful sign on the
second joint. It announces that you will adopt children
which are not your own, and that your first union will be
childless, although you have had and will again have
natural children. But as compensation, here are the
three stars which are dominated by it; this is a sign that,
in spite of the efforts of the enemy, surrounded by great
men who supplement your genius, you will be crowned
between your sixth and seventh lustre, and that the Pope
himself, to gain your favor for the Church of Rome, will
come from Rome to place on your head and that of your
wife the crown of Louis XIV. and of Saint Louis.

"Beneath the three stars do you see the sign of Venus
and that of Jupiter? Beside them, and on the same line,
do you see those numbers which are so lucky when in

conjunction, — 9, 19, 99 ? They are the proof that the East and the West will clasp hands, and that the Cæsars of the House of Hapsburg will consent to ally their name with yours.

"Below these numbers we find the same Sun which we have already seen at the tip of the finger of Apollo, and which indicates that, contrary to the celestial luminary, which goes from east to west, your course will be from west to east.

"Now let us go up from the first joint of the thumb, and stop at this O which diagonally crosses a bar. Well, that sign means disordered vision, political blindness. As for the three stars of the first joint, and the sign which surmounts them, they are only the confirmation of the prediction that women will have a great influence upon your life, and they indicate that, even as happiness will come to you through a woman, so through a woman will it take its flight.

"As for the four signs scattered over the palm of the hand in the form of an iron rake, one in the field of Mars, another adhering to the line of life, and the remaining two adjoining the base of the mountain of the Moon, they indicate prodigal expenditure of the blood of soldiers, but only on the battle-field.

"The top of this forked line, divided towards the mountain of Jupiter, number 8, denotes extended journeys in Europe, Asia, and Africa. Some of these journeys will be forced ones, which is denoted by the X at the top of the line of life, overlooking the mountain of Venus ; finally, as its branches cross beneath Mars, it is the sure sign of great renown, due to glorious feats of arms. In speaking to you, men will exhaust the whole vocabulary of humility and eulogy ; you will be the glorious man, the man of prodigies and miracles. You will be Alexander, you will

be Cæsar ; you will be even greater than they, you will
be Atlas bearing the world. After having seen the whole
universe lighted up with your glory, you will see it dark
as night on the day of your death ; and men, seeing that
the world is out of joint, will ask, not whether a man has
just died, but whether the sun has set."

The young man had listened to this prophecy with an
air more expressive of gloom than of joy ; he had seemed
to follow the sibyl to all those heights where, fatigued,
she had stopped to take breath ; then, with her, he had
descended to the gulf in which she had predicted that his
fortune would be swallowed up.

After she ceased speaking, he remained silent for a
moment.

"You have foretold for me Cæsar's fortune," he said at
last.

"It is greater than Cæsar's fortune," she replied, "for
Cæsar did not attain his end, and you will attain yours ;
Cæsar put his foot only on the first step of the throne,
while you will take your seat upon it. But do not forget
the dark woman who has a mark above the right eyebrow, and who carries her handkerchief to her mouth
when she smiles."

"And when shall I meet her ?" asked the young man.

"You have met her to-day," replied the sibyl. "And
she marked with her foot the spot where the long line of
your victories will begin."

It was so manifestly impossible that the sibyl could
have prepared beforehand this series of undoubted truths,
since they were already of the past, and this succession of
incredible facts which were still buried in the future,
that perhaps for the first time the young officer believed
thoroughly in what she had told him. He put his hand
in his pocket and drew forth a purse containing some gold
pieces ; but the sibyl put her hand on his arm.

"If I have prophesied lies to you," she said, "this price is too great. If, on the contrary, I have told you the truth, we can settle our account only at the Tuileries. At the Tuileries, then, when you are Emperor of the French!"

"So be it, at the Tuileries!" replied the young man. "And if you have told me the truth, you will have lost nothing by waiting." [1]

[1] We can vouch for the truth of this scene the more confidently because the details concerning Mademoiselle Lenormand were given to us personally by her admirer and pupil, Madame Moreau, who lived at the Rue de Tournon, No. 5, in the same house with the celebrated sibyl, and, who, devoting herself to the same art, met with very great success in it.

CHAPTER XXXII.

THE MAN OF THE FUTURE.

ON the 26th of October, 1795, at half-past two in the afternoon, the president of the Convention pronounced these words : " The National Convention declares that its mission is fulfilled, and that its sessions are at an end." These words were followed by repeated cries of " Long live the Republic ! "

To-day, after the lapse of seventy-two years and the lapse of three generations, he who writes these lines cannot forbear to bow his head in presence of that memorable date.

The long and stormy career of the Convention finished with an act of clemency.

It decreed that the death penalty should be abolished throughout the territory of the French Republic.

It changed the name of the Place de la Révolution to the Place de la Concorde.

And, finally, it pronounced an amnesty upon all deeds relating to the Revolution.

It did not leave in the prisons a single prisoner who had not received a trial, nor a political prisoner.

It was very strong and very sure of itself, this assembly which was resigning its power.

O terrible Convention, thou stern embalmer, who didst lay the eighteenth century in its blood-stained winding-sheet, thou didst find at thy birth, on the 21st of September, 1792, Europe in arms against France, a dethroned king, a constitution annulled, an administration overthrown, a discredited, paper currency, and skeletons of regiments without soldiers.

Thou didst pause an instant, and didst see that, unlike the two assemblies which preceded thee, it was not for thee to proclaim liberty before a worn-out monarchy, but to defend liberty against all the thrones of Europe.

On the day of thy birth thou didst proclaim the Republic in the face of two opposing armies, one of which was only fifty, and the other not more than sixty-five leagues from Paris. Then, in order to burn thy last bridge, thou didst carry to a conclusion the king's trial.

When voices, rising from thine own bosom, cried out, "Humanity!" thou didst reply, "Energy!"

Thou didst make thyself absolute. From the Alps to the coast of Brittany, from the ocean to the Mediterranean, thou didst lay hold of everything, saying: "I will answer for everything."

Like Louis XIII.'s minister, for whom there were neither friends nor family, but merely enemies of France, and who struck down with the same hand a Chalais and a Marillac, a Montmorency and a Saint-Preuil, thou didst not spare thine own members. And finally, after three years of such convulsions as never people knew before, after days which have come down to posterity as the 21st of January, the 31st of October, the 5th of April, the 9th Thermidor, and the 13th Vendémiaire, bleeding and mutilated, thou didst lay down thy functions, handing over to the Directory, safe and flourishing, the France which thou didst receive from the Constituent Assembly compromised and torn asunder.

Let those who accuse thee dare to say what would have happened if thou hadst weakened in thy course, if Condé had entered Paris, if Louis XVIII. had ascended the throne, if, instead of the twenty years of the Directory, the Consulate, and the Empire, there had been twenty years of restoration, twenty years of Spain instead of France, twenty years of shame instead of twenty years of glory.

Now, was the Directory worthy of the legacy bequeathed it by its bleeding mother ? That is not the question.

The Directory will answer to posterity for its deeds, even as the Convention has answered for its own.

The Directory was appointed.

The five members were Barras, Rewbell, La Réveillère-Lepaux, Letourneur, and Carnot.

It was decided that they should take up their official residence at the Luxembourg.

They did not know what condition the Luxembourg was in. They went there to begin their sittings.

They found not a single article of furniture.

"The concierge," says M. Thiers, "lent them a shaky table, a sheet of letter paper, and a writing-desk, with which to write the first message, which announced to the two Councils that the Directory was established."

They sent to the treasury.

There was not a single sou there.

Barras was the chief ; Carnot directed the movements of the armies ; Rewbell had charge of foreign affairs ; Letourneur and La Réveillère-Lepaux of the interior administration. Buonaparte had the command of the army of Paris. A fortnight later, he signed his name *Bonaparte.*

On the 9th of the following March, about eleven o'clock in the morning, two carriages stopped before the door of the *mairie* of the second district of Paris.

From the first descended a young man about twenty-six years old, wearing the uniform of a general officer.

He was followed by his two witnesses.

A young women of twenty-eight or thirty descended from the other.

She also was followed by her two witnesses.

The six presented themselves before the citizen Charles-Théodore François, civil magistrate of the second district, who asked them the questions usually propounded to matrimonial aspirants, to which they made the customary replies. Then he caused the following document to be read to them, which they afterwards signed : —

"The 19th day of Ventôse, in the year IV. of the Republic.

"Contract of marriage of *Napoline* BONAPARTE, general-in-chief of the army of the interior, aged *twenty-eight* years, born at Ajaccio, in the department of Corsica, residing in Paris, Rue d'Antin, son of Charles Bonaparte, gentleman, and of Lætitia Ramolini ;

"And of Marie-Josèphe-Rose de Tascher, aged twenty-eight years, born in the island of Martinique, in the Windward, Islands, living in Paris, Rue Chantereine, daughter of Joseph-Gaspard de Tascher, captain of dragoons, and of Rose-Claire Desvergers de Sanois, his wife.

"I, Charles-Théodore François, civil magistrate of the second district of the canton of Paris, after having caused to be read in the presence of these parties and their witnesses :

"1st, the certificate of birth of Napolione Bonaparte, which states that he was born on the *5th of February*, 1768, of the lawful marriage of Charles Bonaparte and Lætitia Ramolini ;

"2d, the certificate of birth of Marie-Josèphe-Rose de Tascher, which states that she was born on the 23d of June, 1767, of the lawful marriage of Joseph-Gaspard de Tascher and of Rose-Claire Desvergers de Sanois ;

"The certificate of the death of Alexandre François-Marie

Beauharnais being taken into consideration, which states that he died on the 5th Thermidor, in the year II., married to Marie-Josèphe-Rose de Tascher;

"Also that the certificate of publication of said marriage was duly posted without opposition during the time prescribed by law ;

"And also after Napolione Bonaparte and Marie-Josèphe-Rose de Tascher had declared aloud that they took each other for husband and wife, — I did pronounce Napolione Bonaparte and Marie-Josèphe-Rose de Tascher to be husband and wife.

" And this in the presence of the adult witnesses hereinafter named ; to wit: Paul Barras, member of the Executive Directory, living at the Palace of the Luxembourg ; Captain Jean Lemarrois, aide-de-camp, living in Rue des Capucines ; Jean-Lambert Tallien, member of the Corps Législatif, living at Chaillot ; and Étienne-Jacques-Jérôme Calmelets, lawyer, living in Rue de la Place Vendôme, No. 207, all of whom have signed with the principals, as I also have done after this reading."

Indeed, one may see the six signatures of M.-J.-R. Tascher, of Napolione Bonaparte, of Tallien, of P. Barras, of J. Lemarrois, junior, of E. Calmelets, and of Leclerc, at the foot of the certificate which we have quoted.

The remarkable thing, however, about this certificate is that it contains two false statements. Bonaparte is there alleged to be two years and a half older than he really was, and Joséphine four years younger than she was. She was born on the 23d of June, 1763, and Bonaparte on the 15th of August, 1769.

On the day after his marriage, Bonaparte was appointed commander-in-chief of the army in Italy.

This was Barras' wedding gift.

On the 26th of March, Bonaparte arrived at Nice, with two thousand louis in the box of his carriage, and a million in drafts.

Jourdan and Moreau had been given a magnificent army of seventy thousand men. But the Directory dared trust Bonaparte with only thirty thousand soldiers, who were famished, in want of everything, reduced to the last extremity, without clothes, shoes, or pay, and most of the time without provisions, but who, nevertheless, bore all their privations, even hunger, with admirable fortitude.

His officers were : Masséna, a young Niçard, headstrong and obstinate, but full of happy inspirations ; Augereau, whom we have already met in Strasburg, where we saw him handling the foil against Eugène, and the musket against the Austrians ; La Harpe, a banished Swiss ; Serrurier, a soldier of the old school, painstaking and brave ; and, finally, Berthier, the chief of his staff, whose good qualities he had already divined, — qualities which improved every day.

With his thirty thousand soldiers he had to fight sixty thousand, — twenty thousand Piedmontese under General Collé, and forty thousand Austrians under General Beaulieu.

These generals looked with disdain upon the arrival of a man younger than they, who was said to owe his rank to Barras' patronage, — small, thin, and proud, with an Arab complexion, a piercing eye, and Roman features.

As for the soldiers, they started at the first words which he addressed to them ; it was the kind of talk they needed. He said, —

"Soldiers, you are poorly fed, and almost naked ; the government owes you much, but can do nothing for you now. Your patience and your courage are worthy of all honor ; but if you remain here, they will procure for you neither profit nor glory. I am about to lead you to the most fertile plains in the world. You will find there great cities and beautiful provinces ; you will find there honor, glory, and riches. Follow me !"

The same day he distributed four gold louis to the generals, who had not seen gold for four or five years, and removed his headquarters to Albenga.

He was eager to reach Voltri, which was the place on the map where Joséphine, the first time she came to call upon him, had left the mark of her foot.

On the 11th of April he reached Arenzano.

Would he meet the enemy ? Would this pledge of his future fortune be given him ?

As he was ascending the slope of Arenzano, at the head of the division of La Harpe, which formed the advance-guard, he uttered a cry of joy : he had just seen a column leaving Voltri.

It was Beaulieu and the Austrians.

They fought for five days ; at the end of that time Bonaparte was master of the valley of the Bormida ; the Austrians, defeated at Montenote and at Dego, retreated towards Acqui, and the Piedmontese, after losing the passes of Millesimo, fell back upon Ceva and Mondovi.

Master of all the roads, having in his train nine thousand prisoners who were to go to France to announce his first victories, from the heights of Monte Remoto, which he had to cross in order to reach Ceva, he pointed out to his soldiers those beautiful plains of Italy which he had promised them ; he showed them the rivers which empty into the Mediterranean and the Adriatic, and pointing to a gigantic mountain covered with snow, he exclaimed, —

" Hannibal crossed the Alps, but we have turned them."

Thus we see that Hannibal naturally presented himself to his mind as a fit subject of comparison.

Later, it was Cæsar.

Later still, it was Charlemagne.

We have witnessed the birth of his fortune. Let us leave the conqueror at the first station in his journey across the world. He is fairly started on the road to Milan, Cairo, Vienna, Berlin, Madrid; and, alas! to Moscow.

THE EIGHTEENTH FRUCTIDOR.

CHAPTER I.

A GLANCE AT THE PROVINCES.

On the evening of the 28th of May, 1797, at the moment when, his glorious campaign in Italy finished, Bonaparte was enthroned with Joséphine at Montebello, surrounded by ministers from foreign courts ; when the Corinthian horses, having descended from the Duomo, and the Lion of St. Mark, having fallen from his column, were on their way to Paris ; when Pichegru, relieved from service on account of vague suspicions, had just been made president of the Five Hundred, and Barbé-Marbois president of the Ancients, — a horseman who was travelling, as Virgil says under the friendly silence of the moon, " per amica silentia lunæ," and who was trotting upon a powerful horse along the road from Mâcon to Bourg, left that road a little above the village of Pollias, leaped, or rather made his horse leap, the ditch which separated it from the ploughed fields, and followed for about five hundred metres the banks of the river Veyle, where he was not likely to meet either village or traveller. There, doubtless, no longer fearing to be recognized or noticed, he allowed his cloak to slip from his shoulders to his saddle, the movement betraying a belt in which were stuck two pistols and a hunting-knife. Then he raised his hat, and wiped his perspiring forehead. It could then be seen that the traveller was a young man of twenty-eight or twenty-nine, handsome, distinguished, and well set-up ; and that he was all ready to repel force by force, if any one had the imprudence to attack him.

And, by the way, the precaution which had caused him to put a pair of pistols in his belt was not out of place. The Thermidorian reaction, suppressed at Paris on the 13th Vendémiaire, had taken refuge in the provinces, and had assumed gigantic proportions. Lyons had become its headquarters ; on one side, by way of Nîmes, it stretched out the hand to Marseilles, and, on the other, by way of Bourg in Bresse, as far as Besançon. For further information concerning this reaction, we might refer the reader to our romance, the "Companions of Jehu," or to Charles Nodier's "Souvenirs of the Revolution and of the Empire ;" but as the reader in all probability has neither of these works at hand, we will reproduce briefly here what is requisite for our purpose.

It was not to be wondered at that the Thermidorian reaction, suppressed in the first capital of France, had taken up its abode in the second, with branches at Marseilles and Besançon. It is well known what Lyons suffered after its revolt. The guillotine was too slow : Collot d'Herbois and Fouché supplemented it with grape-and-canister. There were very few families at this time belonging to the rich commercial class, or to the nobility, who had not lost one or more of their members. The time had come now to avenge the lost father or brother or son ; and they were avenged openly, publicly, in broad daylight. "You caused the death of my son, my brother, my father," they would say to the informer, and then they would immediately strike him down.

"Speculation in regard to murder," says Nodier, "was much indulged in by the upper classes. There were in the

salons secrets of death which would have frightened
the galleys.   Men played *charlemagne* with death for the
stakes, and they did not even take the trouble to lower
their voices when they spoke of planning to kill some
one.   The women, sweet alleviators of all the passions of
men, took an aggressive part in these dreadful discussions.
Since horrible hags no longer wore guillotines as ear-rings,
'adorable' furies, as Corneille would have said, wore
daggers for breast-pins.   If you made objection on senti-
mental grounds to these frightful excesses, they would
take you to the 'Brotteaux,' and make you tread, in spite
of yourself, upon the elastic, springy soil, saying: 'Our
relatives are there.'   What a picture is presented by these
exceptional times, whose indefinable, nameless character
cannot be expressed except by the facts themselves, so in-
adequate are words to reproduce the unheard-of confusion
of ideas so antipathetic in themselves, the union of the most
refined methods with implacable fury, the horrifying compact between the doctrines of humanity and deeds worthy
of cannibals !   How can we convey an adequate impression
of this impossible period, when prison-cells did not protect the prisoners, when the executioner who came in
search of his victim found, to his astonishment, that he had
been anticipated by the assassin, — this endless 2d of
September, renewed every day by respectable young men
who had just left a ball-room, and were expected in a
boudoir ?

   "It was, in truth, a localized monomania, — a craving
for rage and murder which had sprung to life under the
wings of revolutionary harpies ; an appetite for larceny
sharpened by confiscations ; a thirst for blood inflamed by
the sight of blood.   It was the frenzy of a generation
nourished, like Achilles, upon the marrow of wild beasts ;
a generation which had no other models or ideal than

Schiller's brigands and the freebooters of the Middle Ages. It was the sharp and irresistible necessity for beginning society again by crime, as it had ended. It was what is always brought about by the inevitable tendency to compensation, in noteworthy times: the Titans after chaos; Python after the deluge; a flock of vultures after a battle; the unerring law of retaliation for these unaccountable scourges, which demands death for death, corpse for corpse, which pays itself with usury, and which Holy Writ has counted among the treasures of Providence.

" The unexpected amalgamation of these bands, whose object was unknown at first, exhibited in a slight degree the inevitable confusion of ranks, conditions, and persons which is noticeable in all factions, all parties which grow out of a disorganized society; but there was less of it here than was ever seen before. That portion of the lower classes which took part in it did not lack that varnish of manner which is furnished by expensive vices: an aristocratic populace, which ran from one debauch to another, and from excess to excess, in the wake of the aristocracy of name and fortune, as if to prove that there is nothing more easy than to outdo a bad example. The remainder concealed beneath the most refined exterior a more odious depravity, because it had to break down the barriers of conventionality and education. Never before had so many assassins in silk stockings been seen; and it would have been a great mistake to imagine that luxurious habits were in inverse ratio to ferocity of character. Pitiless exhibitions of mad fury were no less common among men of the world than among men of the people, and death was found to be capable of no less cruel refinements when inflicted by the dagger of the dandy than when dealt by the knife of the butcher.

"The proscribed class had at first eagerly sought the shelter of the prisons, as a refuge. When this melancholy bulwark of the unfortunate was broken down, like everything else that men formerly held sacred, like the churches and the tombs, the administration tried to provide for the safety of the victims by sending them away from the province. To put them beyond the reach of private vengeance, they sent them twenty and thirty leagues away from their wives and children, among people to whom they were not known either by name or deed. The fatal move only resulted in changing the place of sepulture. These partners in the death industry delivered their prey in exchange from one department to another with the regularity of commercial transactions. Never had business-like habits been carried so far as in this horrible traffic. Never was one of those barbarous drafts, which were payable in men's heads, protested when it came due. As soon as the letter of advice arrived, they would coolly balance the debits and credits, and carry forward the balances, and the check drawn in blood would be paid at sight.

"It was a spectacle, the very idea of which was revolting to the soul, and which was often renewed. Imagine one of those long carts, with racks upon which calves are loaded to be taken to the shambles, and upon them huddled in confusion, the feet and hands firmly tied with cords, with heads hanging down, and swaying with each jolt, panting for breath, in despair and terror, men whose greatest crime was almost always an excited outburst which spent itself in threatening words. Do not imagine for a moment that there was prepared for them on their return the feast of a martyr or the expiatory honors of sacrifice, or that they were even allowed the empty satisfaction of offering for a moment an impossible resistance to an attack without peril, as in the arenas of Constantius and Gallus. The assassins surprised them as they lay; they were murdered in their bonds, and the club, reddened with blood, kept playing upon their bodies long after they were beyond feeling."

Nodier once saw and described to me a septuagenarian, noted for his gentleness of manner and for that scrupulous courtesy which is esteemed above all other qualities in provincial salons; one of those men of breeding who are becoming almost extinct, who used to make one visit to Paris to pay their court to the minister and to be present at the king's card-party and hunting-party, but who owed to this happy memory the privilege of dining from time to time with the *intendant*, and of giving their opinion on important occasions on questions of etiquette. Nodier saw him, while women looked on placidly, holding children in their arms who clapped their little hands, — Nodier saw him, and I quote his own words, "wearying his withered old arm by striking with a little gold-headed cane a corpse in which the assassins had neglected to extinguish the last spark of life, and which had just betrayed its agony by a final convulsion."

And now that we have tried to give some idea of the state of the country through which the traveller was passing, no surprise will be felt at the precautions which he used, nor the attention which he paid to every characteristic of a region which was, besides, apparently unknown to him. In fact, he had scarcely followed for half a league the banks of the Veyle before he stopped his horse, stood up in his stirrups, and, leaning over his saddle, tried to pierce the obscurity which had become deeper since a cloud had passed over the moon. He began to despair of being able to find his way without being driven to take a guide, either at Montech or at Saint-Denis, when a voice which seemed to come out of the river made him start, so unexpected was it. It said, in a most cordial tone, —

"Can I do anything for you, Citizen?"

"Faith! yes," replied the traveller; "and as I cannot go to you, not knowing where you are, perhaps you will be so good as to come to me, since you apparently do know where I am."

And while he pronounced these words he covered with his cloak both his pistols, and the hand which was playing with the handle of one of them.

CHAPTER II.

THE TRAVELLER.

THE traveller was not mistaken; the voice did indeed come from the river. A shadow slowly climbed the bank, and in a moment was at the horse's head, with one hand resting on his neck. The rider, who seemed to be annoyed by such familiarity, caused his horse to take a step backward.

"Oh, I beg your pardon, Citizen," said the new comer; "I did not know that it was forbidden to touch your horse."

"It is not forbidden, my friend," replied the traveller, "but you know that in the night, and in these times, it is advisable to converse at some distance."

"*Dame!* I cannot distinguish what is advisable from what is not. You seemed to be unable to find your way; I saw it, and I am a good fellow. I said to myself: 'Here is a Christian who does not seem to be sure of his road; I will direct him.' You called out to me to come; here I am! You do not need me; adieu!"

"Your pardon, friend," said the other, recalling him with a gesture; "the movement which caused my horse to step back was an involuntary one. I did really need you, and you can do me a service."

"What is it? Tell me. Oh, I bear no malice."

"Do you belong to this region?"

"I am from Saint-Rémy, near by. You can see the church from here."

" Then you know the neighborhood ?"

" I should think so. I am a fisherman by trade. There is not a run of water for ten leagues around where I have not thrown my lines."

" Then you must know the abbey of Seillon ?"

" Do I know the abbey of Seillon ? I should think so ! But I can't say as much about the monks."

" Why not, pray ?"

" Why, because they have been driven out since 1791, of course ! "

" Then to whom does the monastery belong ?"

" To no one."

" What, are there in France a farm, a convent, a forest of ten thousand acres, and three thousand acres of land besides, which belong to no one ?"

" They belong to the Republic, which is the same thing."

" Then the Republic does not cultivate the property which it confiscates ?"

" As if it had the time ! It has plenty of other things to do, has the Republic."

" What has it to do ?"

" It has to make a new skin."

" To be sure, it is putting on its third skin. Do you bother your head with such things ?"

" Oh, a little, in my spare time. Our neighbors of the Jura have sent the Republic General Pichegru all the same."

" Yes."

" They can't have liked that very well over yonder. But I am chattering, and wasting your time. After all, though, if you are going to Seillon, you need be in no hurry."

" Why not ?"

" Why, because there is no one there."

"No one?"

"Except the ghosts of the old monks; but as they only come at midnight, you need be in no hurry."

"Are you sure, my friend," persisted the traveller, "that there is *no one* at the monastery of Seillon?"

And he emphasized the words "No one."

"I passed there yesterday, when I carried some fish to the Château des Noires-Fontaines, to Madame de Montrevel; there was not even a cat there."

Then he added emphatically:—

"They were all priests of Baal, so there is not much harm done."

The traveller started more visibly than at first.

"*Priests of Baal?*" he repeated, looking fixedly at the fisherman.

"Yes, and unless you come from a certain King of Israel whose name I have forgotten."

"From King *Jehu*, you mean, do you not?"

"I am not quite sure; it is a king who was consecrated by a prophet named — named — What was the name of the prophet who consecrated King Jehu?"

"Elisha," replied the traveller, without hesitating.

"That is it; but he consecrated him upon one condition. What was it? Help me to remember."

"That he should punish the crimes of the house of *Abab* and *Jezebel*."

"Ah, *sacrebleu!* tell me about it at once."

And he held out his hand to the traveller.

The traveller and the fisherman, in clasping hands, made a final sign of recognition, which left neither of them in doubt that they belonged to the same association. However, they did not question each other as to their personality, nor as to the work which they had in hand, the one in going to the abbey of Seillon, and the other in setting his lines and his nets, but the young fisherman said, —

"I am very sorry that I am kept here by superior orders; if it were not for that, I would gladly serve as your guide; but I cannot return to the monastery until I am summoned by a signal. But there is no need to deceive you longer. You see those two black masses, of which one is higher up than the other? The higher one is the town of Bourg; the lower is the village of Saint-Denis. Pass between the two, at an equal distance from each, and continue on your way until you are stopped by the bed of the Reyssouse. You will cross it, for the water will scarcely come to your horse's knees; then you will see a great black curtain before you; that is the forest."

"Thanks," said the traveller; "once on the edge of the forest, I know what to do."

"Even if they do not reply from the forest to your signal?"

"Yes."

"Well, go, then, and *bon voyage!*"

The two young men shook hands once more, and the fisherman descended the bank with the same rapidity with which he had scaled it.

The traveller mechanically stretched out his neck to see what had become of him. He was invisible. Then the traveller gathered up his reins, and as the moon had reappeared, and he had an open field to cross, he put his horse to a gallop, and was soon between Bourg and Saint-Denis.

The clock struck in both places at once. The traveller counted eleven strokes.

After crossing the road from Lyons to Bourg, the traveller found himself, as the guide had said, on the bank of the little river. With two strides his horse reached the other side ; and when there, he saw before him a plain about two kilometres in width, bounded by the dark line which he had been told was the forest. He spurred his horse straight for it.

At the end of ten minutes he was on a country road which skirted the forest along its whole length. There he stopped a moment, and looked around him. He did not hesitate to give the signal which he had been told to give, but he wished to make sure that he was quite alone. The silence of the night is sometimes so intense that the most daring men respect it, if they are not forced to break it. For a moment, as we have said, our traveller looked and listened ; but he saw and heard nothing. He put his hand to his mouth, and whistled thrice with the handle of his whip, the first and last times being firm and resonant, and the middle one tremulous, like a boat-swain's whistle. The sound was lost in the depths of the forest, but no other sound, either similar or different, replied to it. While he listened, midnight struck at Bourg, and was repeated by all the clocks in the neighborhood. The traveller repeated the signal a second time, and again silence was his only reply.

Then he appeared to make up his mind, and following the country road until he came to one at right angles with it, he resolutely plunged into the latter ; at the end of ten minutes, coming to another one which crossed it again, he followed the cross-road, bearing to the left, and five minutes later he was out of the forest.

Before him, two hundred yards away, arose a dark mass which was doubtless the end of his journey. As he approached it, he remarked certain details to make sure that the old monastery was really before him.

Finally he stopped before a great door, surmounted by three statues, — those of the Virgin, Our Lord Jesus Christ, and Saint John the Baptist. The statue of the Virgin, placed immediately over the centre of the door, formed the most elevated point of the triangle. The two others came down to the cross piece forming the branch of the stone cross, in which was set a double door of massive oak, which, more fortunate than certain parts of the façade, and more particularly the windows of the first floor, seemed to have defied the ravages of time.

"Here it is," said the traveller. "Now let us see which of the three statues is that of Saint John."

CHAPTER III.

THE CARTHUSIAN MONASTERY OF SEILLON.

THE traveller found that the statue he sought was the one in the niche at the right of the great door. He made his horse approach the wall, and, standing up in his stirrups, he reached the pedestal of the statue. There was a space between the base and the side of the niche; he slipped his hand into it, felt a ring, drew it to him, and guessed at, rather than heard, the tinkling of a little bell. He did this three times. After the third time he listened. He thought he heard a hesitating step approaching the door.

"Who rang?" asked a voice.

"He who comes in the name of the prophet," replied the traveller.

"What prophet?"

"He who left his mantle to his disciple."

"What is his name?"

"Elisha."

"Who is the king whom the children of Israel must obey?"

"Jehu."

"What is the house that they must exterminate?"

"That of Ahab."

"Are you a prophet or a disciple?"

"I am a disciple; but I have come to be made a prophet."

"Then welcome to the house of the Lord."

Scarcely had the words been pronounced when the iron bars which held the door were noiselessly removed, the bolts shot noiselessly back in their places, and the door opened silently, as if by magic.

The rider and his horse disappeared under the arch. The door closed behind them. The man who had opened it so slowly and closed it so quickly, approached the new-comer as he dismounted.

The latter looked curiously at him. He was dressed in the long white robe of the Carthusian monks, and his head was entirely concealed by his hood. He took the horse's bridle, but evidently more as a favor than as a duty. In the mean time the traveller unfastened his valise from the saddle, and drew out the pistols from the holsters, putting them in his belt with the others.

The horseman looked around him, and seeing no light and hearing no sound, he asked, —

"Are the Companions absent?"

"They have gone on an expedition," replied the brother.

"Do you expect them to-night?"

"I hope for them to-night, but I hardly expect them before to-morrow night."

The traveller reflected for a moment. Their absence seemed to disturb him.

"I cannot lodge in the town," he said; "I should be noticed, if not recognized. Can I wait here for the Companions?"

"Yes, if you will give your word of honor not to try to go away."

"You have it."

In the mean time the robe of a second monk had appeared in the shadow, growing whiter as it approached the spot where they were standing. He was doubtless a Companion of lower grade, for the first one threw the horse's bridle to him, telling him, more in the form of an order than a request, to take the horse to the stable. Then, holding out his hand to the traveller, he said, —

"You understand why we have no lights. This monastery is supposed to be uninhabited, or inhabited by ghosts only; a light would betray us. Take my hand and follow me."

The traveller removed his glove and took the monk's hand. It was a soft hand, evidently unused to all those kinds of work which take from this member its pristine aristocratic appearance. In the circumstances in which the traveller found himself, everything was significant. He saw at once that he had to do with a man of breeding, and followed him with the utmost confidence. After several turns in corridors that were perfectly dark, they entered a rotunda which took its light from above. This was evidently the dining-room of the Companions. It was lighted by candles placed in candelabra on the walls. A fire was burning in a large fireplace, fed by dry wood, which made little or no smoke.

The monk handed a chair to the traveller, and said :

"If our brother is weary, let him rest ; if our brother is hungry, supper will be served him; if he wishes to sleep, he will be shown to his bed."

"I accept them all." said the traveller, stretching his shapely and powerful limbs. "The chair because I am weary, the supper because I am hungry, the bed because I am sleepy. But, with your permission, my very dear brother, we will take them in turn."

He threw his broad-brimmed hat upon the table, and passing his hand through his wavy hair, he showed a high forehead, beautiful eyes, and a serene expression.

The monk who had led the horse to the stable now entered, and replied to his companion's questions that he had given the animal fresh straw, and that his manger was full of hay. Then, in obedience to an order, he laid a napkin at the end of the table, and on it a bottle of wine, a glass, a cold chicken, a pie, a plate, a knife, and a fork.

"When you like, my brother," said the monk to the traveller, pointing to the laden table.

"At once," he replied.

And without leaving his chair, he drew it up to the table and sat down. He bravely attacked the chicken, of which he took first the leg, then the wing upon his plate. Then came the pie, of which he ate a slice, while he sipped the rest of his wine. In the mean time the monk stood quietly a few steps behind him. The monk was not inquisitive, and the traveller was hungry, so neither of them uttered a word. When the meal was finished, the traveller drew his watch from his pocket.

"Two o'clock," he said. "There are two hours more before daylight."

Then, addressing the monk, he added, —

"If our Companions do not come to-night, we may not expect them before to-morrow night, I suppose ? "

"Probably not," replied the monk. "Unless it is absolutely necessary, our brothers do not travel by day."

"Well," said the traveller, "I will wait one of the two hours. If our brothers are not here at three o'clock, you may show me to my room. In the mean time, if you have anything to do, do not disturb yourself about me. You belong to a silent order, and I never chatter except with women. You have none here, have you ? "

"No," replied the monk.

"Well, go about your business, if you have any, and leave me to my thoughts."

The monk bowed and went out, leaving the traveller alone; but before he went, he placed a second bottle of wine upon the table. The guest acknowledged the attention with a bow, and mechanically continued to sip his wine and nibble at the crust of his pie.

"If this is the ordinary fare of our Carthusians," he murmured, "I do not pity them. Pomard for every-day wine, a chicken (to be sure, we are in the country of chickens), and snipe pie. However, there is no dessert."

The thought had scarcely taken form when the monk who had previously attended to the wants of both horse and rider entered, bearing on a dish a slice of fine Sassenage cheese dotted with green, the invention of which, it is said, dates back to the fairy Melusine. Without being a gourmand, the traveller, as we have seen, seemed able to appreciate a good supper. He did not say, with Brillat-Savarin, "A meal without cheese is like a woman without an eye," but doubtless he thought so.

An hour passed, while he finished his wine and picked up the crumbs of cheese with the point of his knife. The monk had left him alone, and he was consequently at liberty to devote himself to this double occupation. He drew out his watch; it was three o'clock.

He looked for a bell, but found none. He was on the point of striking his glass with his knife; but it occurred to him that this would be taking a great liberty with the good monks who had so hospitably entreated him.

Consequently, wishing to keep the promise which he had made himself, of going to bed, he laid his weapons on the table, so that he should not be suspected of having broken his word, and bareheaded, and with only his hunting-knife at his side, he passed into the corridor by which he had entered. Half way down, he met the monk who had received him.

"Brother," said the latter, "two signals have announced that our Companions are approaching; in five minutes they will be here. I was just on my way to tell you."

"Well," said the traveller, "let us go to meet them."

The monk made no objection; he turned back and reentered the courtyard, followed by the stranger. The second monk opened the double door, as he had done for the traveller. The door once open, it was easy to hear the gallop of several horses which were rapidly approaching.

"Make room!" said the monk quickly to the traveller, drawing him aside against the wall.

And at the same time a whirlwind of men and horses swept under the arch with a noise like thunder.

The traveller thought for a moment that the Companions were pursued; he was mistaken.

CHAPTER IV.

THE TRAITOR.

THE door closed behind them. Daylight had not yet come, but the darkness was less profound. The traveller was surprised to see that the Companions had a prisoner with them. His hands were tied behind his back, and he was fastened on a horse which two of the Companions were leading. These three had entered first, and had galloped to the end of the court. Two by two, the others had followed, and had surrounded them. All had then dismounted.

For a moment the prisoner had remained on horseback, but they had taken him down also.

"Let me speak to Captain Morgan," said the traveller to the monk who had waited on him. "He must know at once that I am here."

The monk went and said a few words in the ear of the chief, who quickly approached the traveller.

"From whom do you come?" he inquired.

"Shall I reply by the ordinary formula," asked the stranger, "or shall I simply tell you from whom I really come?"

"Since you are here, you have probably satisfied all requirements. Tell me who sent you."

"General Roundhead."

"You have a letter from him?"

"Here it is."

And the traveller put his hand to his pocket; but Morgan stopped him.

"Later," he said. "First we must try and punish a traitor. Take the prisoner to the council hall," he added.

Just then they heard the galloping of a second troop of horsemen. Morgan listened.

"Those are our brothers," he said; "open the door."

The door was opened.

"Take care!" cried Morgan.

And a second company of four men entered almost as rapidly as the first had done.

"Have you the prisoner?" cried the commander.

"Yes," replied the Companions of Jehu, in chorus.

"And you," asked Morgan, "have you the report?"

"Yes," replied the four with one voice, who had just arrived.

"Then all goes well," said Morgan, "and justice will be done."

This is what had happened.

As we have said, several bands, known by the name of Companions of Jehu, or Avengers, sometimes by both, scoured the country from Marseilles to Besançon. One had its headquarters in the neighborhood of Avignon, another in the Jura, and the third, as we have seen, in the monastery of Seillon.

As all the young men who formed these bands belonged to families in the neighborhood, as soon as each undertaking, whether successful or not, was accomplished, they separated, and each one returned to his own home. A quarter of an hour later, our robber of diligences, with his hat perched on his ear, his eye-glass in his eye, and his stick in his hand, was walking through the town, asking news of what had happened, and marvelling at the incre-

dible insolence of these fellows, to whom nothing was
sacred, not even the cash of the Directory. Now, how
could young men, some of whom were rich and others of
noble birth, and all of whom were connected with the
ruling powers of the town, be suspected of being highway
robbers? Therefore they were not suspected; but even
if they had been, no one would have taken it upon himself to denounce them.

However, the government were much annoyed to see
their money turned from its destination, and sent to Bretagne instead of Paris, to find a resting-place in the coffers
of the Chouans instead of those of the Directory. They
therefore decided to play a trick upon their enemies.

In one of the diligences used to convey money, they
placed seven or eight gendarmes, dressed as citizens, who
had sent their carbines and pistols beforehand to the diligence, and who had received express orders to take one
of the outlaws alive. The thing had been done so
cleverly that the Companions of Jehu had heard nothing
about it. The vehicle, with the modest appearance of an
ordinary diligence, — that is to say, filled with honest bour-
geois, — ventured into the pass of Cavaillon, and was stopped
by eight masked men. A sharp discharge of firearms
from the interior of the carriage betrayed the *ruse* to the
Companions of Jehu, who, not desirous of entering into a
profitless struggle, set off at a gallop, and, thanks to the
excellence of their horses, soon disappeared. But one
horse had his leg broken by a ball, and fell on his rider.
The horseman, held down by the animal, could not escape,
and was taken prisoner by the gendarmes, who thus fulfilled their double commission of defending the government money and capturing one of those who sought to
lay hands upon it.

Like the old freebooters, like the Illuminati of the

eighteenth century, like the modern Freemasons, the members of this society, in order to be received as companions, underwent brutal tests, and were required to take blood-curdling oaths. One of these oaths was never to betray a companion, no matter what tortures were inflicted. If weakness overcame him, if the name of an accomplice escaped the prisoner's mouth, then the Companions, taking the place of that justice which granted mercy, or softened the penalty as a reward of his treachery, had ordained that the first of their number who should meet the traitor was justified in burying a dagger in his heart.

Now, the prisoner taken on the road from Marseilles to Avignon, whose *nom de guerre* was Hector, and whose true name was Fargas, after having resisted promises as well as threats for a long time, finally, weary of prison, tortured with loss of sleep, — that worst of all tortures, — and being known by his real name, had ended by confessing and naming his accomplices.

But as soon as the thing was known, the judges had received such a deluge of threats, both by letter and by word of mouth, that they resolved to carry on the trial at the other end of France, and had chosen for the purpose the little town of Nantua, at the extremity of the department of the Ain.

But at the same time that the prisoner was sent to Nantua, with every precaution taken for his safety, the Companions of Jehu of the monastery of Seillon received word of the betrayal, and of the removal of the traitor.

"It is for you," they were told, "who are the most devoted brothers of the order, it is for Morgan, your leader, the most daring and venturesome of us all, to save the Companions by destroying the report which accuses them, and to make a terrible example upon the person of the traitor. Let him be tried, condemned, and executed, and exposed to the gaze of all, with the avenging poniard in his breast."

This was the terrible mission which Morgan had just accomplished.

He had gone, with ten of his companions, to Nantua. Six of them, after having gagged the sentinel, had knocked at the prison door, and with a pistol at his throat had forced the doorkeeper to open it. Once in the prison, they had learned which was Fargas' cell, and had compelled the doorkeeper and the jailer to lead them to it, after which they had shut them both in the prisoner's cell, had bound the latter upon a horse which they had led with them, and had set off at a gallop.

The other four, in the mean time, had seized upon the clerk, and had forced him to admit them to the registry office, of which he had the key, and where he sometimes worked all night when there was a press of business. There they made him give them the entire court record, including the interrogatories, which contained the charges, signed by the accused. Then, to save the clerk, who begged them not to ruin him, and who had, perhaps, not made all possible resistance, they emptied a number of boxes and set fire to them, shut the door, returned the key to the clerk, who was then free to go home, and set off at a gallop themselves, carrying the papers with them, and leaving the office to burn quietly.

It is needless to say that all who took part in this expedition were masked.

This is why the second troop, when they entered the courtyard of the monastery, asked, "Have you the prisoner?" and why the first-comers, after replying, "Yes," had asked, "And have you the report?" And this is also why, upon receiving an affirmative reply, Morgan had said, "Then all goes well, and justice will be done."

CHAPTER V.

THE JUDGMENT.

THE prisoner was a young man of some twenty-two or twenty-three years, looking more like a woman than a man, so fair and slender was he. He was bare-headed and in his shirt-sleeves, with pantaloons and boots. The Companions had taken him from his cell just as he was, and hurried him away without giving him an instant for reflection.

His first thought had been that he was rescued. These men who had entered his cell were beyond question Companions of Jehu ; that is to say, they were men who held the same opinions and belonged to the same band as himself. But when he found that they bound his hands, when he saw through their masks the angry flashing of their eyes, he understood that he had fallen into hands yet more terrible than those of his judges, — the hands of those whom he had betrayed, — and that he had nothing to hope for from accomplices whom he had chosen to denounce.

On the way he had not asked a question, and no one had spoken to him. The first words that he had heard from the mouths of his judges had been the ones that they had just pronounced. He was very pale, but this pallor was the only sign of emotion which he showed.

At Morgan's order, the pretended monks crossed the cloister. The prisoner walked first between two of them, each holding a pistol in his hand.

The cloister crossed, they entered the garden. The procession of twelve monks, marching silently in the darkness, had something terrifying about it. It approached the door of the subterranean vault. One of the two who were walking with the prisoner moved a stone. Beneath it there was a ring, by means of which he raised a flagstone which covered the entrance to a staircase.

The prisoner hesitated a moment, so closely did the mouth of the vault resemble that of a tomb. The two monks who walked beside him went down first; then from a groove in the stone they took two torches which had been placed there to light the way for those who might have occasion to enter the darksome vaults. They struck a light, kindled the torches, and uttered the one word, —

" Descend."

The prisoner obeyed.

The monks disappeared to the last man into the vault. They walked on for three or four minutes, when they came to a grating; one of the two monks drew a key from his pocket and opened it.

It opened into the place of burial.

At the end of the vault was the door of an old subterranean chapel which the Companions of Jehu used for their council-chamber. A table covered with a black cloth stood in the centre, and twelve carved stalls, where the monks used to sit when the burial service was chanted, extended along the wall on either side of the chapel. On the table were an inkstand, several pens, and some paper; two iron brackets projected from the wall, like hands ready to receive the torches which were placed in them.

The twelve monks took their seats in the twelve stalls. They made the prisoner sit down on a stool at the end of the table; on the other side of the table stood the traveller, the only one who did not wear a monk's robe, the only one who was not masked.

Morgan began to speak.

"Monsieur Lucien de Fargas," he said, "was it of your own free will, and without being constrained or forced by any one, that you asked of our brothers in the South to admit you to our association, and that you became a member thereof, after the usual initiation, under the name of Hector?"

The young man bowed in token of assent.

"It was of my own free and unconstrained will, without being forced to it," he said.

"You took the customary oaths, and you therefore knew the terrible punishment which awaits any one who proves false to them?"

"I knew it," replied the prisoner.

"You knew that when any Companion, even under torture, reveals the names of his accomplices, he incurs the death-penalty, and that this penalty is to be executed, without reprieve or delay, the moment the proof of his crime is furnished?"

"I knew it."

"What could have induced you to break your oaths?"

"The impossibility of resisting the torture which is caused by loss of sleep. I resisted it for five nights; on the sixth I asked for death, which was sleep. They would not give it to me. I sought for means to take my own life; my jailers had taken their precautions so well that I could find nothing. On the seventh night I yielded. I promised to make disclosures on the morrow. I hoped that they would let me sleep; but they demanded that I should speak at once. It was then that, in despair, insane from want of sleep, held up by two men who prevented me from sleeping where I stood, I stammered the four names of M. de Valensolles, M. de Barjols, M. de Javat, and M. de Ribier."

One of the monks drew from his pocket the record which he had taken from the clerk, and held it before the prisoner's eyes.

"That is it," said the latter.

"And your signature," said the monk, "do you recognize it?"

"I recognize it," replied the young man.

"You have no excuse to make?" asked the monk.

"None," replied the prisoner. "When I put my name at the bottom of that page, I knew that I was signing my death-warrant; but I wanted to sleep."

"Have you any favor to ask before you die?"

"Only one."

"What is it?"

"I have a sister whom I love, and who adores me. Being orphans, we were educated together; we grew up side by side; we have never been parted. I should like to write to my sister."

"You are free to do so; but at the end of your letter you will write the postscript which we shall dictate."

"Thanks," said the young man.

He rose and bowed.

"Will you untie my hands," he said, "so that I may write?"

This wish was complied with. Morgan, who usually had addressed him, pushed towards him the paper, pen, and ink. The young man wrote a page, with a hand which did not tremble.

"I have finished, gentlemen," he said. "Will you dictate the postscript?"

Morgan approached, and laid one finger on the paper while the prisoner wrote.

"Are you ready?" he asked.

"Yes," replied the young man.

"I die because I have broken a sacred oath; consequently, I acknowledge that I deserve death. If you wish to give my body Christian burial, it will be placed to-night in the market-place at Bourg. The dagger which will be found buried in my breast will indicate that I do not die the victim of a cowardly assassination, but of a just vengeance."

Morgan then drew from beneath his robe a dagger, both blade and handle of which were forged from the same piece of metal. It was in the form of a cross, so that the condemned, in his last moments, could kiss it, in the absence of a crucifix.

"If you wish, Monsieur," he said, "we will grant you the favor of giving yourself the death-blow. Here is the dagger. Is your hand sure enough?"

The young man reflected a moment.

"No," he said, "I am afraid I should fail."

"Very well," said Morgan. "Put the address on your letter."

The young man folded the letter and wrote : —

Mademoiselle Diana de Fargas,
Nimes.

"Now Monsieur," said Morgan, "you have ten minutes in which to say your prayers."

The old chapel altar still stood, though mutilated. The condemned man went and knelt down before it. In the mean time, a piece of paper was torn into twelve parts, on one of which was drawn a dagger. The twelve pieces were put into the hat of the messenger who had arrived just in time to be present at this act of vengeance. Then, before the condemned had finished his prayer, each of the monks drew out a piece of paper from the hat. The one upon whom the functions of

executioner had fallen said not a word ; he merely took
the dagger from the table and tried the point of it with
his finger. The ten minutes having passed, the young
man rose.

"I am ready," he said.

Then, without hesitation or delay, mute and erect, the
monk who had drawn the fatal slip walked straight
towards him, and plunged the dagger into the left side
of his breast. There was a cry of agony, then the fall
of a body on the flags of the chapel, and all was over.
The condemned man was dead ; the blade of the dagger
had pierced his heart.

"Thus perish all companions of our holy association
who break their oaths," said Morgan.

And all the monks in chorus answered, —

"Amen."

CHAPTER VI

DIANA DE FARGAS.

ABOUT the time when the unfortunate Lucien de Fargas was drawing his last breath in the subterranean chapel of the monastery at Seillon, a postchaise stopped before the inn of the Dauphin, at Nantua.

This inn of the Dauphin had a certain reputation in Nantua and the neighborhood, a reputation which it owed to the well-known opinions of Master René Servet, its proprietor.

Without knowing why, Master René Servet was a royalist. Thanks to Nantua's distance from all great centres of population, thanks also to the mild temperament of its inhabitants, Master René Servet had passed through the Revolution without being in the least degree molested on account of his opinions, well known though they were.

It must be confessed, however, that the worthy man had done all in his power to invite persecution. Not only had he kept the title of "Dauphin" for his inn, but in the tail of the fantastic fish on his sign, a tail which insolently protruded from the water, he had caused to be drawn the profile of the poor little prince who had remained shut up for four years in the prison of the Temple, and who died soon after the reaction of Thermidor.

Therefore all those who, for twenty leagues around, within or without the Department of the Ain, — and their number was great, — shared the opinions of René

Servet, did not fail to patronize his inn, and would not for the world have consented to go elsewhere.

It was not astonishing, therefore, that a postchaise having to stop at Nantua should leave its passengers at the aristocratic hotel of the Dauphin, rather than at the rival democratic hostelry of the Boule d'Or.

At the sound of the chaise, although it was scarcely five o'clock in the morning, René Servet leaped out of bed, and putting on his drawers, a pair of white stockings, list slippers, and a great bath robe over his sholders, and holding in his hand his cotton cap, reached the doorstep just as a beautiful young woman of eighteen or twenty years descended from the carriage.

She w s dressed in black, and, in spite of her youth and great beauty, was travelling alone.

She replied by a nod to the obsequious salutation given her by Master René Servet, and, without paying any attention to his offers of service, asked him if there was in his inn a good room with a dressing-room.

Master René mentioned No. 7, on the first floor, as the best that he had.

The young lady impatiently went herself to the wooden frame on which were hanging the keys of the different rooms, with numbers indicating the rooms to which they respectively belonged.

"Monsieur," she said, "will you be good enough to accompany me to my room? I want to ask you some questions. You can send the chambermaid to me when you go down."

René Servet bowed almost to the floor, and hastened to obey. He went first, and the young lady followed. When they reached the room, the traveller closed the door behind her, and as she seated herself, addressed the inn-keeper, who remained standing.

"Master Servet," she said, with decision, "I know you both by name and reputation. Throughout the bloody years which have just passed, you have remained a partisan, if not a defender, of the good cause. Therefore I came directly to you."

"You do me honor, Madame," replied the innkeeper, bowing.

She continued : —

"I shall, therefore, omit all the circumlocution and beating about the bush which I might employ with a man whose opinions were unknown to me or suspected by me. I am a royalist : that gives me a claim upon your interest. You are a royalist : that gives you a right to my confidence. I know no one here, not even the president of the tribunal, for whom I have a letter from his brother-in-law at Avignon ; it is therefore perfectly natural that I should address myself to you."

"I am waiting, Madame," said René Servet, "for you to do me the honor to tell me what it is that I can do for you."

"Have you heard, Monsieur, that a young man named M. Lucien de Fargas was brought to the prison at Nantua two or three days ago ?"

"Alas! yes, Madame ; it seems that he is to have his trial here, or rather at Bourg. He is a member, so I am told, of the secret society called the 'Companions of Jehu.'"

"Do you know the purposes of that society ?" inquired the young girl.

"I believe that they are to seize the government money and to pass it on to our friends in La Vendée and Bretagne."

"Exactly, Monsieur, and the government would treat these men like ordinary thieves!"

"I believe, Madame," said René Servet, confidently, "that our judges are intelligent enough to know the difference between them and malefactors."

"But to come to the object of my journey. It was thought that the accused, who is my brother, ran some danger in the prison at Avignon, and so they brought him to the other end of France. I wish to see him. To whom ought I to apply to obtain this favor?"

"Why, Madame, to the very president for whom you have a letter."

"What sort of a man is he?"

"A prudent man, but a well-meaning, I hope. I will have you taken to his house as soon as you wish."

Mademoiselle de Fargas drew out her watch. It was scarcely half-past five in the morning.

"But I cannot present myself at such an hour," she murmured. "Shall I go to bed? I am not sleepy."

Then, after thinking a moment, she asked, —

"On which side of the town is the prison?"

"If Madame would like to take a turn that way," said Master Servet, "I would beg the honor of accompanying her."

"Very well, Monsieur, send me a glass of milk, coffee, tea, whatever you please, and finish your toilet. While I am waiting for leave to enter, I should like to see the walls within which my brother is confined."

The innkeeper made no remark; the desire was a natural one. He went down, and sent up a cup of milk and some coffee to her. After some ten minutes she came down, and found him dressed in his Sunday clothes, ready to guide her through the streets of the little town, which was founded by the Benedictine Saint Amand, and in whose church Charles the Bold sleeps more tranquilly, probably, than he ever did in life.

The town of Nantua is not large. At the end of five
minutes' walk they reached the prison, before which was
a great crowd full of excitement.

Everything arouses a foreboding in the minds of those
whose friends are in danger. Mademoiselle de Fargas
had something more than a friend, — an adored brother,
who was lying in prison charged with a capital offence.
It suddenly seemed to her that her brother must be
involved in the presence of this noisy crowd; and growing pale and seizing her guide's arm she cried, —

"O my God! what has happened?"

"We shall soon know, Mademoiselle," replied René
Servet, much less easily moved than his companion.

No one knew positively what had happened. When
they had come, at two o'clock in the morning, to relieve the
sentinel, they had found him gagged and tied hand and
foot in his sentry-box. All that he could tell was that,
being surprised by four men, he had offered a desperate
resistance, which had resulted in their leaving him in the
state in which he was found. He could tell nothing of
what had passed after he had been overpowered and
gagged. He believed, however, that the object of the
attack was the prison. The mayor, the commissioner of
police, and the firemen's sergeant had then been notified
of what had happened. These three dignitaries had held
a council, and had summoned the sentinel, who had repeated his story to them.

After half an hour of deliberation and of guesses, each
one of which was more absurd than the last, they resolved to end where they ought to have begun, by going
to the prison. But in spite of their resounding blows,
no one came to admit them; the strokes of the
knocker, however, awakened the people in the neighboring houses. They came to their windows, and ques-

tions and answers passed, which resulted in the locksmith being sent for.

In the mean time day had come, the dogs had begun to bark, and the occasional passers-by had grouped themselves inquisitively around the mayor and the police commissioner; and when the sergeant returned with a locksmith, about four o'clock in the morning, he found quite a gathering at the prison doors. The locksmith remarked that if the doors were bolted on the inside, all the picklocks in the world would do no good. But the mayor, a man of great good sense, ordered him to try first, and then they would see what they would do. Now, as the Companions of Jehu had been unable to close the door on the outside and bolt it on the inside also, they had simply pulled the door to after them; and, to the great satisfaction of the constantly increasing crowd, the door opened at once.

Everybody then tried to rush into the prison; but the mayor placed the sergeant on guard at the door, with orders to keep every one out. They had to obey the law. The crowd increased, but the order given by the mayor was respected.

There are not many cells in the prison of Nantua; they comprise three subterranean chambers, from one of which proceeded groans. These groans attracted the attention of the mayor, who interrogated through the door those who were making them, and soon found that the authors of the groans were none other than the doorkeeper and the jailer himself.

They had proceeded thus far with the municipal investigation when Diana de Fargas and the proprietor of the Hôtel du Dauphin arrived in the square before the prison.

CHAPTER VII.

WHAT WAS TALKED ABOUT IN THE LITTLE TOWN OF NANTUA FOR THE NEXT THREE MONTHS.

To Master René Servet's first question, "What is going on at the prison, for Heaven's sake, friend Bidoux?" the person addressed replied, —

"The most extraordinary things that ever were known, Monsieur Servet. When they came to relieve the sentinel this morning, they found him gagged and tied up like a sausage; and just now it seems they have found Père Rossignol and his turnkey shut up in a cell. What times we live in, good Lord! what times we live in!"

By the grotesque form of the reply, Diana saw that he was telling the truth. It was clear to any intelligent mind that if the doorkeeper and the turnkey were inside the cell, the prisoner must be outside.

Diana dropped Master René's arm, darted towards the prison, made her way through the crowd, and reached the door.

There she heard some one say, —

"The prisoner has escaped!"

At the same time there appeared within the jail Père Rossignol and the turnkey, who had been released from their cell in the first place by the locksmith, who had opened the door, and in the second place by the mayor and the police commissioner, who had unbound them.

"No one can pass," said the sergeant to Diana.

VOL. II. — 7

"That order, although it applies to every one else, does not apply to me," replied Diana. "I am the sister of the prisoner who has escaped."

This reasoning was not perhaps very conclusive in point of law, but it carried with it that logic of the heart which few men can resist.

"Oh, that is another thing," said the sergeant, lifting his sword. "Pass on, Mademoiselle."

And Diana passed, to the great amazement of the crowd, who saw the curtain rising upon a new scene of the drama, and muttered, —

"It is the prisoner's sister."

Now, everybody in Nantua knew who the prisoner was, and why he was detained.

Père Rossignol and the turnkey were at first in such a state of prostration and terror that neither the mayor nor the police commissioner could get a word out of them. Fortunately, the latter conceived the idea of giving them each a glass of wine, which imparted to Père Rossignol the strength to relate how six masked men had forcibly entered the prison, had made him and the turnkey Rigobert go down to the cell with them, and after they had made sure of the prisoner, who had arrived two days before, had shut them up in his place. Since then, they did not know what had happened.

This was all that Diana cared to know just then; convinced that her brother had been taken away by the Companions of Jehu, since Père Rossignol had described the invaders of his dominion as masked men, she hastened from the jail. But she was at once surrounded by the eager crowd, who, having heard that she was the prisoner's sister, wanted to hear the details of his escape.

In a few words Diana told them all she knew, and then with great difficulty rejoined Master René Servet;

she was about to give him the order for post-horses,
to start at once, when she heard a man announce in a
loud voice that the office had been set on fire, — a piece
of news which was privileged to share with the prisoner's
escape the attention of the crowd.

Indeed, they had learned almost all there was to know
in the prison square, when this unexpected episode bade
fair to open a new field for conjecture. It was practically certain that there was some connection between
the fire in the office and the abduction of Diana's brother.
The young girl certainly believed this. The order to put
horses to the carriage was arrested on her lips, for she
felt that the burning of the office would furnish her
with new details which might perhaps be useful to
her.

Time passed. It was eight o'clock in the morning.
This was the hour to present herself at the house of the
magistrate for whom she had the letter. Moreover, the
extraordinary events of which the little town of Nantua
had been the scene would explain this early visit, especially from a sister of the prisoner. Diana therefore
begged her landlord to take her to Monsieur Pérignon ; for
such was the name of the president of the tribunal.

Monsieur Pérignon had been one of the first to be
awakened by the news which had put all Nantua in a
tumult. But he had hurried to the spot in which he
was, as a judge, particularly interested, that is, the record
office. He had just come in when Mademoiselle Diana de
Fargas was announced.

When he reached the office, he had found the fire
extinct ; but it had already consumed a portion of the
papers which had been deposited there for safe keeping.
He had questioned the concierge, who told him that the
registry clerk had come to the office about half-past

eleven in the evening with two gentlemen ; that he, the concierge, had not thought it his duty to investigate, inasmuch as the clerk sometimes came there in the evening to procure papers which he engrossed at home.

But scarcely had the clerk gone away when he had seen a bright light through the blinds of the office. Not understanding what it could be, he had risen and had found a great fire lighted in such a way as to spread to the wooden cases along the wall, which contained the boxes of documents. Then he had not lost his head, but had separated the burning papers from those which had not yet been touched by the fire, and had succeeded in putting out the fire by bringing water in dippers from a tub in the cellar.

The worthy concierge had gone no farther than to think it an accident ; but as the flames had done some mischief, and as by his presence of mind he had probably prevented a much greater loss, he had told everybody about it when he awoke in the morning ; and as it was for his interest to exaggerate rather than suppress the details, at seven o'clock in the morning they were saying all over the town that if it had not been for the concierge, who had almost perished in the fire, and whose clothes had been completely burned off him, not only the registry office, but probably the whole court-house would have been devoured by the flames.

Monsieur Pérignon, after he had seen with his own eyes the state of the record office, thought, very sensibly, that the best way to get exact information was to apply to the clerk himself. Consequently, he went to his house and asked to see him. The reply was that during the night the clerk had been attacked with brain fever, and that he was raving of masked men, burning papers, and stolen records.

When he saw Monsieur Pérignon, the clerk's terror was at its height; but thinking that he would do better to tell all than to invent a fable which would have no other result than to cause him to be suspected of complicity with the incendiaries, he fell at Monsieur Pérignon's feet and confessed the truth. The coincidence between the events of the night left no doubt in the magistrate's mind that they were part of the same plot, and were intended to achieve the double purpose of carrying off both the guilty man and the proof of his guilt.

The presence of the prisoner's sister in his house, and her story of what had passed in the prison left him no room for doubt, even had he been in doubt.

These masked men had come to Nantua with the evident intention of taking away Lucien de Fargas and the report of the prosecution which had been begun against him. Now, for what purpose had the prisoner been abducted?

In the sincerity of her heart, Diana did not doubt that, moved by generosity, her brother's companions had united, and risked their own heads to save his.

But Monsieur Pérignon, whose mind was cold and logical, was not of this opinion. He knew the true reason for the removal of the prisoner to Nantua; he knew that, having informed against some of his accomplices, he had become the object of the vengeance of the Companions of Jehu. Thus his opinion was that, far from aiding him to escape from prison in order to restore him to liberty, they had taken him away only to punish him more cruelly than the law would have done. The important thing, there-fore, was to ascertain whether they had taken the road to Geneva, or had gone back towards the interior of the department. _

If they had taken the road to Geneva, and consequently

gone beyond the frontier, it would prove that they intended to save Lucien de Fargas, and their own lives as well. If, on the contrary, they had gone into the interior of the department, it would be because they felt themselves strong enough to defy justice twice over, — not only as highway-robbers, but as murderers.

At this suspicion, which came to her for the first time, Diana turned pale, and seizing Monsieur Pérignon's hand, cried, —

"Monsieur! Monsieur! do you think they would dare to commit such a crime?"

"The Companions of Jehu would dare do anything, Mademoiselle, and particularly that which one would suppose that they would not dare attempt."

"But," said Diana, trembling from terror, "how can we learn whether they have gone to the frontier or returned to the interior of France?"

"Oh, as to that, nothing is easier," replied the judge. "This is market-day; ever since midnight all the roads leading to Nantua have been covered with peasants who, with their carts and donkeys, have been bringing their produce to market. Ten men on horseback, taking a prisoner with them, could not have passed unperceived. We must find some people coming from Saint-Germain and Chérizy, and ask them if they saw such a party going in the direction of the Gex country; and then we must find others coming from Vollongnat and Peyriat, and learn whether they saw horsemen going towards Bourg."

Diana was so urgent with Monsieur Pérignon, she laid so much stress upon his brother-in-law's letter of introduction, and, moreover, her situation as sister of the man whose life was at stake aroused so much interest that Monsieur Pérignon consented to go with her to the market-place.

There they learned that the horsemen had been seen going towards Bourg.

Diana thanked Monsieur Pérignon, went to the Dauphin, ordered horses to be made ready at once, and started immediately for Bourg.

She alighted on the Place de la Préfecture, at the Hôtel des Grottes de Ceyzeriat, which had been recommended to her by Master René Servet.

CHAPTER VIII.

A NEW COMPANION IS RECEIVED INTO THE SOCIETY
OF JEHU, UNDER THE NAME OF ALCIBIADES.

JUST as Lucien de Fargas underwent the penalty to which he had condemned himself when, on entering the Society of Jehu, he had sworn upon his life never to betray his companions, day was breaking. It was therefore impossible that on that day, at least, his body could be publicly exposed, as was proposed. Its removal to the Place de la Préfecture at Bourg was therefore postponed until the following night.

After leaving the underground vault, Morgan turned to the messenger.

"Monsieur," he said, "you have seen what has just passed, you know with whom you are, and we have treated you as a brother. If it is your pleasure that we should prolong this session, fatigued though we are, and if you are in a great hurry to take leave of us, we will give you your liberty at once, unconditionally. If, however, you do not intend to leave us before night, and if the affair upon which you have come is of considerable importance, grant us a few hours' sleep. Take some repose yourself; for you do not seem to have slept, any more than we. At noon, if you will remain so long, the council will hear you; and, if my memory does not play me false, having parted after our last meeting as companions in arms, we shall part this time as friends."

"Gentlemen," replied the messenger, "I was with you in heart long before I set foot upon your domains. The oath which I shall take can add nothing, I trust, to the confidence which you have done me the honor to grant me. At noon, if you please, I will present my letters of introduction to you."

Morgan exchanged a clasp of the hand with the messenger. Then, retracing the road they had come, the pretended monks went back through the underground passage, which they closed up, concealing the ring with the same care. They crossed the garden, skirted the cloister, re-entered the monastery, and disappeared silently through different doors.

The younger of the two monks who had received the stranger remained alone with him, and showed him to his room, after which he bowed and went out. The guest of the Companions of Jehu noticed with pleasure that the monk did not lock the door behind him. He went to the window, which opened from within, had no bars, and was almost on a level with the garden. Therefore the Companions evidently trusted in his word, and took no other precautions. He drew the curtains of his window, threw himself all dressed on the bed, and slept. At noon he was wakened by the opening of his door: the young monk entered.

"It is noon, Brother," he said; "but if you are weary, and desire to sleep longer, the council will wait."

The messenger sprang from his bed, opened his curtains, drew from his valise a brush and a comb, brushed his hair, combed his moustache, glanced over the rest of his toilet, and made a sign to the monk that he was ready to follow him. He was conducted to the hall where he had supped. Four young men awaited him, all of whom were unmasked.

It was evident from their clothing, the care which they had bestowed upon their toilet, and the refined courtesy of the salute with which they received the stranger that they all four were aristocrats either by birth or fortune.

Had not the messenger remarked this for himself, he would not long have been left in doubt.

"Monsieur," said Morgan, "I have the honor of presenting to you the four chiefs of the society Monsieur de Valensolles, Monsieur de Jayat, Monsieur de Ribier, and myself, the Comte de Sainte-Hermine. Monsieur de Ribier, Monsieur de Jayat, Monsieur de Valensolles, I have the honor of presenting to you Monsieur Coster de Saint-Victor, a messenger from General Georges Cadoudal."

The five young men bowed, and exchanged the usual greetings.

"Gentlemen," said Coster de Saint-Victor, "it is not astonishing that Monsieur Morgan should know me, nor that he should not hesitate to tell me your names, since we fought on the 13th Vendémiaire in the same ranks. That is why we were companions before we were friends; as Monsieur le Comte de Sainte-Hermine has said, I come from General Cadoudal, with whom I serve in Brittany. Here is the letter which accredits me with you."

At these words Coster drew from his pocket a letter bearing a seal stamped with the fleur-de-lis, and handed it to the Comte de Sainte-Hermine. The latter broke the seal and read aloud: —

MY DEAR MORGAN, — You will remember that at the meeting in the Rue des Postes you were the first to offer, in case I should carry on the war alone and without help either from home or abroad, to be my cashier. All our defenders have died with arms in their hands, or have been shot. Stofflet and Charette have been shot; D'Autichamp has submitted to the Republic; I stand alone, unshaken in my faith, unassailable in my Morbihan.

An army of two or three thousand men is enough with which to keep the field; but I must furnish arms, food, and ammunition for them, as they ask for no pay. Since Quiberon, the English have sent us nothing.

If you will furnish the money, we will furnish the blood. God forbid, however, that I should be understood to say that when the occasion offers you would be sparing of your blood! No, your devotion is so much greater than ours that ours grows pale before it. If we who are fighting here are taken, we shall only be shot; but if you are taken, you will die upon the scaffold. You write me that you have a considerable sum at my disposal. If I could be sure of receiving every month thirty-five or forty thousand francs, that would be enough.

I send you our common friend, Coster de Saint-Victor ; his name alone will tell you that you may have perfect confidence in him. I have given him the little catechism which will help him to reach you. Give him the first forty thousand francs, if you have them, and keep the rest of the money for me; it will be safer in your hands than in mine. If you are too much persecuted yonder, and find that you cannot stay there, cross France and come and join me.

Far and near, I love and thank you.

GEORGES CADOUDAL,
General-in-chief of the army in Brittany.

P. S. — They tell me, my dear Morgan, that you have a young brother of nineteen or twenty. If you do not think me unworthy of teaching him his first lessons in warfare, send him to me ; he shall be my aide-de-camp.

Morgan stopped reading, and looked questioningly at his companions. Each one made an affirmative sign.

" Will you trust me with the reply, gentlemen ? " asked Morgan.

The question was received with a unanimous "yes." Morgan thereupon took the pen, and while Coster de Saint-Victor, Monsieur de Valensolles, Monsieur de Jayat, and Monsieur de Ribier were talking together in the embrasure of a window, he wrote. Five minutes later, he called Coster and his three companions, and read them the following letter, —

MY DEAR GENERAL, — We have received your kind and noble letter by your brave and noble messenger. We have about a hundred and fifty thousand francs in hand, and therefore we are prepared to do as you request. Our new associate, to whom I have on my own authority given the name of Alcibiades, will start this evening, taking with him the first forty thousand francs.

Every month you can procure the forty thousand francs you require at the same bank. In case of our death or dispersion, the money will be buried in as many different places as we have times forty thousand francs. Subjoined you will find a list of the names of those who will know where the sums are, and will be, deposited.

Brother Alcibiades came just in time to be present at an execution; he has seen how we punish traitors.

I thank you, my dear General, for your very kind offer regarding my young brother ; but my intention is to keep him out of danger until he may be called to take my place. My eldest brother was shot, bequeathing to me the duty of avenging his death. I shall probably die, as you have said, upon the scaffold; and I shall die bequeathing a similar duty to my brother. In his turn he will enter the road which we have trod; and he will contribute to the triumph of the good cause as we have done, or will die like us. No less powerful a motive would induce me, while asking your friendship for him, to deprive him of your immediate protection.

Send us again, as soon as you can, our beloved brother Alcibiades; we shall be doubly glad to send you the message by such a messenger.

MORGAN.

The letter was unanimously approved, and was then folded, sealed, and given to Coster de Saint-Victor.

At midnight the door of the monastery opened to permit two horsemen to pass out. One, the bearer of the letter to Cadoudal, together with the desired sum, took the road to Mâcon. The other, carrying the corpse of Lucien de Fargas, was on his way to place it on the Place de la Préfecture, at Bourg.

In the breast of the corpse was the knife with which he had been killed; and hanging to the handle of the knife by a thread, was the letter which the condemned man had written just before his death.

CHAPTER IX.

THE COMTE DE FARGAS.

IT is necessary that our readers should now learn who the unfortunate young man was, whose corpse has just been placed upon the Place de la Préfecture, and also who the young woman was who alighted at the Hôtel des Grottes de Ceyzeriat, in the same square.

They were the last remaining scions of an old family of Provence. Their father, formerly a colonel, and chevalier of Saint-Louis, was born in the same town as Barras, with whom he had been intimate in his youth; namely, Fos-Emphoux. An uncle who had died at Avignon, making him his heir, had left him a house in that city; in 1787 he went with his children, Lucien and Diana, to live in that house. Lucien at this time was twelve, and Diana eight. It was then the period of the early revolutionary ardor, hopeful or fearful, according as one was a patriot or a royalist.

To those who are acquainted with Avignon, there were then in that city, as there are now, and always have been, two cities in one, — the Roman city and the French.

There was the Roman city, with its magnificent papal palace, its hundred churches, each more splendid than the last, and its innumerable bells, always ready to sound the tocsin of incendiarism, or the ghastly signal for murder.

The French city, with its Rhone, its silk manufactories, and its cross-roads going from north to south, from west to east, from Lyons to Marseilles, from Nîmes to Turin, — the French city was the ill-fated city, the city that longed for a king, was anxious to secure its liberties, and trembled at the thought that it was a land of slaves, a land over which the clergy were omnipotent.

The clergy, not such as it has been from all time in the Gallican Church, and such as we see it to-day, pious, tolerant, strict in the fulfilment of duty, prompt in charity, living in the world only to give comfort and instruction, without mingling either in its joys or passions, — such was not the clergy to be found in Avignon; but the clergy such as intrigue, ambition, and cupidity had made it, — consisting, that is to say, of court abbés, rivals of the Roman abbés, idle, elegant, bold, kings of fashion, autocrats of the salon, and inveterate gossips. Will you have a specimen of them? Take the Abbé Maury, proud as a duke, insolent as a lackey, son of a shoemaker, and more aristocratic than the son of a lord.

We have spoken of Avignon as a Roman city; let us speak of it as a city of bitter passions as well. The heart of the child, everywhere else free from bad passions, was born there full of hereditary hate, bequeathed from father to son for eight hundred years; and, after a life of hatred, each man bequeathed in his turn the diabolical inheritance to his children. In such a city, every one was forced to choose one side or the other, and act a part in proportion to the importance of his position.

The Comte de Fargas had been a royalist before coming to Avignon. When he settled there, in order to find his level, he was obliged to become a fanatic. From that time he was looked upon as one of the royalist chiefs, and one of the standard-bearers of religion.

The time of which we are speaking was, as we have said, the year '87, the dawn of our independence. And so, at the first cry for liberty which was uttered in France, the French city rose, full of joy and hope. The moment had at last come for it to dispute aloud the grant made, by a young queen under age, of a city, a province, and half a million souls, in order to atone for her crimes. By what right had those souls been sold forever to a foreign master?

All France was about to meet on the Champ de Mars in the fraternal embrace of the Federation. All Paris had labored to prepare that immense piece of ground, where, sixty-seven years after the time of this fraternal kiss, it was to invite all Europe to the Universal Exposition,— the triumph of peace and industry over war. Avignon alone was excluded from this great love-feast; Avignon alone had no part in the universal communion. Was not Avignon, then, a part of France?

Avignon named deputies, who went to the papal legate and gave him twenty-four hours in which to leave the city. During the night the Roman party, by way of revenge, with the Comte de Fargas at its head, amused itself by hanging a manikin wearing the tricolored cockade.

It is possible to direct the course of the Rhone, to make a canal in the Durance, or to dam up fierce torrents which, on the melting of the winter's snow, precipitate themselves in liquid avalanches from the peaks of Mont Ventoux; but this terrible, living wave, this human torrent which rushed down the steep incline of the streets of Avignon, when once it was loosed, once launched upon its way, Heaven itself would not have attempted to stay.

At sight of the manikin with the national colors dangling at the end of a cord, the French city rose from its foundations with shrieks of rage. The Comte de Fargas, who knew the Avignonese well with whom he had to deal, had retired, on the night of this clever expedition which he had led, to the house of one of his friends in the valley of Vaucluse. Four of his retainers who were justly suspected of having been members of the party which had strung up the manikin, were torn from their houses and hanged in its place. For this execution they took ropes by force from a worthy man named Lescuyer, who was afterwards falsely accused by the royalists of having volunteered to furnish them. This took place on the 11th of June, 1790.

The French city as a unit wrote to the National Assembly that it gave itself to France, and with itself its Rhone, its commerce, the Midi, and half of Provence. The National Assembly happened to be having one of its days of reaction. It did not want to quarrel with Rome, and it was temporizing with the king; it therefore postponed the matter.

From that time, the patriotic movement in Avignon was a revolt, and the pope had the right to punish and repress. Pope Pius VI. ordained that everything which had been done in the Comtat Venaissin should be annulled, that the privileges of the nobles and clergy should be renewed, and that the inquisition should be restored in all its rigor. The Comte de Fargas returned triumphantly to Avignon, and not only no longer sought to conceal that it was he who had strung up the manikin with the tricolored cockade, but even boasted of it. No one dared say anything. The pontifical decrees were posted.

One man, and only one, in open day, in the sight of all, went straight to a wall to which the decree was

affixed, and tore it down. His name was Lescuyer.
He was the same one who had already been accused of
having furnished ropes to hang the royalists. It will be
remembered that he had been wrongfully accused. He
was not a young man, and he had not been carried away
by the passions of the age. No, he was almost an old
man, who was not even a native of the country. He
was a Frenchman from Picardy, impulsive and thoughtful at the same time. He was a notary who had been
long in business at Avignon. This act of his was a
crime at which Roman Avignon trembled, — a crime so
heinous that the statue of the Virgin shed tears in consequence of it.

As you see, Avignon was still a part of Italy; it
must have miracles at any cost, and since Heaven did
not provide them, it found some one who could invent
them. This particular miracle was exhibited in the
church of the Cordeliers. The crowd flocked to see it.

A report was started at the same time which put the
climax to the excitement. A large chest, tightly closed,
had been carried through the city. This chest had
excited the curiosity of the people of Avignon. What
could it contain? Two hours later, the report had it
that not one, but eighteen chests had been taken to the
Rhone. As for the contents of these chests, a porter
had revealed the secret: they were the hoards of the
Mont-de-piété, which the French party were carrying
with them on their departure from Avignon. The
hoards of the Mont-de-piété; that is to say, the goods
stolen from the poor! The more wretched a city, the
richer is its Mont-de-piété. Few of these establishments
could boast of as much wealth as that of Avignon. This
was not a matter of political opinion, it was a theft, an
infamous theft. Whites and Blues, or, in other words,

royalists and patriots, rushed to the church of the Cordeliers, not to see the miracle, but to shout that the municipality should answer to them for the crime.

Monsieur de Fargas was naturally at the head of those who cried the loudest.

CHAPTER X.

THE TROUILLASSE TOWER.

Now, Lescuyer, the man of the ropes, the patriot who
had torn down the decrees of the Holy Father, the
quondam Picard notary, was secretary to the municipality. His name was thrown to the crowd as having
not only committed the crimes already mentioned, but
as having signed the order to the keeper of the Mont-
de-piété to allow the property to be taken away.

Four men were sent to take Lescuyer and bring him
to the church.

They found him in the street, quietly going towards
the municipal buildings.

The four men threw themselves upon him, and dragged
him with ferocious cries into the church.

In the church, Lescuyer realized, from the flaming
eyes fixed upon him, the outstretched hands which men-
aced him, and the cries which demanded his death, that
he was in one of the circles of hell forgotten by Dante.
His only idea was that this hate was caused by the ropes
which had been taken forcibly from his shop, and by
the destruction of the pontifical decrees.

He got up in the pulpit, thinking to make a rostrum
of it; and with the voice of a man who not only has done
nothing of which he is ashamed, but who would do the
same thing over again, he began, —

"Citizens, I believed the revolution to be necessary,
and I have acted accordingly."

The Whites knew that if Lescuyer, whose death they desired, should explain, he would be saved. This was not what they wanted. Obeying a sign from the Comte de Fargas, they threw themselves upon him, tore him from the pulpit, and pushed him into the midst of the howling pack, which dragged him towards the altar, uttering that terrible cry which is like the hissing of the serpent and the growling of the tiger,— that murderous " Zou! zou! zou! " peculiar to the populace of Avignon.

Lescuyer knew that baleful cry! He tried to take refuge at the foot of the altar. He fell there.

A carriage-trimmer, armed with a club, dealt him such a blow on the head that the weapon was broken in two.

Then they pounced upon the poor body, and with that mixture of ferocity and gayety peculiar to the people of the South, the men sang as they stamped upon his body; while the women, that he might atone for the blasphemies he had uttered, cut off his lips, or rather made a fringe of them, with their scissors. From the midst of the group came forth a cry, or rather a death-rattle. It said,—

" In the name of Heaven! in the name of the Virgin! in the name of humanity, kill me at once! "

It was heard and understood. With one accord the crowd drew back. They left the wretched, disfigured, bleeding man to live in agony. It lasted five hours, during which, amid bursts of laughter, insults, and mockeries, the poor body quivered on the steps of the altar. That is how they kill at Avignon.

Wait, and you will see presently that they had still another method.

Just then, while Lescuyer was undergoing this mortal

agony, it occurred to one of the French party to go to the Mont-de-piété (something which might well have been done at first) in order to see if the story of the theft was true. He found everything in order there; not the smallest trifle had been removed.

From that time forth, the mob regarded the murder of Lescuyer, not as in consequence of theft, but because he was a patriot.

There was at that time in Avignon a man who ruled the destinies of that party which in times of revolution is neither white nor blue, but blood-colored. All those terrible leaders of the South have acquired such a fatal celebrity that it is enough to name them for any one, even the least intelligent, to recognize them. This was the famous Jourdan. Braggart and liar, he made the common people believe that it was he who had cut off the head of the governor of the Bastille; and so they dubbed him Jourdan Coupe-tête. This was not his name, it was Mathieu Jouve. He was not a Provençal, but from Puy-en-Velay. He had once been a muleteer on the steep heights which surrounded his native town; afterwards he became a soldier, but did not go to war (war might perhaps have humanized him), then an innkeeper at Paris. At Avignon he dealt in madder.

He got together three hundred men, took possession of the gates of the city, left half his troops there, and with the rest marched upon the church of the Cordeliers, preceded by two pieces of artillery. He set the battery up in front of the church, and fired at random. The assassins dispersed like a flock of frightened birds, some escaping through the windows, and others by way of the sacristy, leaving several dead upon the church steps. Jourdan and his men stepped over the corpses, and entered the sacred precincts.

There was nothing there but the statue of the Virgin and the wretched Lescuyer. He was still breathing, and when they asked him who had assassinated him, he gave the name, not of those who had dealt the blows, but of the one who had given the order to strike.

This was the Comte de Fargas.

Jourdan and his men were very careful not to despatch the dying man, for his agony was a most potent means of exciting the people. They took this remnant of a living man, this body which was three-fourths corpse, and carried it along, bleeding and panting, with the death-rattle in its throat. They cried,—

" Fargas! We must have Fargas! "

Every one fled at the sight, shutting doors and windows. At the end of an hour Jourdan and his men were masters of the city.

Lescuyer died, and no one knew when he drew his last breath; but it mattered little, for they needed his agony no longer.

Jourdan took advantage of the terror that he had inspired; and in order to assure the victory to his party, he arrested, or caused to be arrested, eighty persons as assassins, or alleged assassins, of Lescuyer, and in consequence accomplices of Fargas.

As for the latter, he had not yet been arrested; but they were sure that he would be, since all the gates of the city were scrupulously guarded, and the Comte de Fargas was known to every one.

Of the eighty persons arrested, more than thirty had not set foot within the church at all; but when one finds a good chance to get rid of one's enemies, one should take advantage of it; such chances are rare. These eighty persons were thrust into the Trouillasse tower.

This was the tower in which the Inquisition used to

put its victims to the torture. To this very day can be seen, along the walls, the greasy soot which rose with the flame of the pyre on which human flesh was being consumed. To this very day can be seen all the implements of torture, carefully preserved, — the copper kettle, the oven, the wooden horses, the chains, the oubliettes; yes, even down to the old bones, nothing is wanting.

It was in this tower, built by Clement IV., that they confined the eighty prisoners. When they were once safely there, their captors were much embarrassed.

By whom should they be tried? There were no courts legally constituted, save those of the pope.

Should they kill these wretches as they had killed Lescuyer? As we have said, there were at least a third of them, possibly a half, who not only had taken no part in the assassination, but who had not even set foot in the church. To make an end of them was the only safe way; the slaughter would pass under the head of reprisals.

But. a number of executioners was needed to kill eighty persons. A sort of tribunal, improvised by Jourdan, sat in one of the halls of the palace. They had a clerk named Raphel; a president, half Italian, half French, an orator in the popular dialect, named Barbe Savournin de la Roua; then there were three or four poor devils, a baker, a charcoal-burner (their names have been lost, because they were of low estate). These were the ones who exclaimed, —

"We must kill them all! If any of them escape, they will witness against us."

Executioners were wanting. There were scarcely twenty men at hand in the courtyard, all belonging to the lowest class in Avignon, — a wig-maker, a ladies' shoemaker, a cobbler, a mason, a carpenter, all with weapons caught up at hap-hazard. One had a sword, another a bayonet; this one a bar of iron, that one a piece of wood that had been hardened in the fire. They were all shivering in a fine October rain; it was difficult to make assassins of such creatures. Nonsense! Is anything difficult for the devil? There come times in matters of this sort when it seems as if Providence had abandoned its *rôle;* then it is Satan's turn.

Satan in person entered this cold and muddy court. He had taken the appearance, form, and face of an apothecary of the neighborhood, named Mende. He set up a table, lighted by two lanterns; upon it he placed glasses, pitchers, jugs, and bottles. What was the infernal beverage that was contained in these mysterious receptacles? No one knows; but its effect is well known. All those who drank the diabolical liquor felt a sudden fever raging through their veins, — the thirst for murder and blood. After that, they needed only to be shown the door, and they hurled themselves into the cells.

The massacre lasted all night. All night long, cries, moans, and dying shrieks were heard in the darkness. They killed them all, men and women. It took a long time, for the executioners, as we have said, were drunk and poorly armed; however, the task was got through in time. As fast as the victims were killed, they were thrown, dead and wounded together, dead bodies and dying bodies, into the Trouillasse courtyard; they fell from a height of sixty feet. The men were thrown first, and then the women. At nine o'clock in the morning, after the massacre had lasted twelve hours, a voice from the depths of the sepulchre cried out, —

"For God's sake, come and finish me, for I cannot die!"

One man, the armorer Bouffier, leaned over the hole; the others did not dare.

"Who called?" they asked him.

"It was Lami," replied Bouffier, drawing back.

"Well," asked the assassins, "what did you see down there?"

"A queer marmalade," he replied; "all pell-mell together, men and women, priests and pretty girls. It is enough to make one split one's sides with laughing."

At that moment shouts of triumph and cries of grief were heard, and the name of Fargas was repeated by a hundred mouths. It was indeed the count, whom they were bringing to Jourdan Coupe-tête. He had just been found, hidden in a cask, in the Hôtel du Palais-Royal. He was half naked, and so covered with blood that they did not know but that he would fall dead when they loosened their hold.

CHAPTER XI.

BROTHER AND SISTER.

THE executioners, who might have been thought to be weary, were only drunk. Just as the sight of wine seems to give strength to the drunkard, so does the odor of blood seem to give strength to the assassin.

All these cut-throats, who were lying in the court-yard half asleep, opened their eyes and jumped to their feet at the name of Fargas.

He, far from being dead, had received only some slight wounds. But when he found himself in the midst of these fiends, he believed his death to be inevitable; and having but one idea,— that of making it as swift and painless as possible,— he threw himself upon the man who was nearest to him, with a naked knife in his hand, and bit him so savagely in the cheek that he thought of nothing but putting an end to the horrible pain. He instinctively thrust out his hand, and his knife, coming in contact with the count's breast, was buried in it up to the hilt. The count fell dead, without a cry.

Then they did with his corpse what they had been cheated of doing with his living body. They flung themselves upon it, struggling to secure a piece of his flesh.

When men get to such a point, there is little difference between them and the South Sea Islanders, who live on human flesh.

They lighted a pile of wood, and threw Fargas' body upon it; and as if no new god or goddess could be glorified without human sacrifice, the Liberty of the pontifical city had on the same day its patriot martyr in Lescuyer, and its royalist martyr in Fargas.

While these things were going on at Avignon, the two children, ignorant of what was happening, were living in a little house which was called the Three Cypresses, because of three trees which stood in front of it. Their father had gone in the morning to Avignon, as he often did; and it was on his way back to them that he had been stopped at one of the gates.

The first night passed without giving them much uneasiness. As he had a house in the city as well as one in the country, the Comte de Fargas often remained at Avignon for a day or two, — for business it might be, or for pleasure.

Lucien liked to live in the country, of which he was very fond. He and his sister were alone there, except for the cook and one other servant. He was passionately fond of Diana, who was three years younger than he. She returned his fraternal love with the passion of Southern natures, which can neither love nor hate by halves.

The young people were brought up together, and had never been parted. Although they were of different sex, they had had the same masters, and pursued the same studies; the result was, that when Diana was ten years old she somewhat resembled a boy, while Lucien at thirteen had some girlish ways.

As their country place was scarcely three quarters of a league away from Avignon, on the morning of the second day the tradespeople brought the news of the murders that had been committed. The two children were very anxious on account of their father. Lucien gave orders for his horse to be saddled; but Diana would not let him go alone. She had a horse like her brother's, and was quite as good a horseman as he, if not better; so she saddled her horse herself, and they set out at a gallop for the city.

Scarcely had they arrived, and begun to make inquiries, when they were told that their father had just been arrested and hurried off to the papal castle, where a tribunal was sitting in judgment upon the royalists. They no sooner heard this than Diana set off at full speed and galloped up the steep slope which led to the old fortress. Lucien followed her at a short distance. They reached the courtyard almost at the same time, and saw the smoking remains of the wood which had just consumed their father's body. Several of the assassins recognized them, and cried, —

"Death to the wolf's cubs!"

At the same time they endeavored to seize the horses' bridles, in order to make the orphans dismount. One of the men, who put his hand to the bit of Diana's horse, received a stinging blow across the face from her riding-whip. This was only an act of legitimate defence, but it exasperated the assassins, who redoubled their cries and threats. But just then Jourdan Coupe-tête came forward. Whether from satiety or from a tardy sense of justice, a ray of humanity shone in upon his heart.

"Yesterday," he said, "in the heat of the struggle and the desire for vengeance, we may possibly have mistaken the innocent for the guilty; but to-day such an error cannot be permitted. The Comte de Fargas was guilty of insulting France and murdering human beings. He hung the national colors on an infamous gallows, and he caused Lescuyer to be killed. The

Comte de Fargas deserved death, and you meted it out
to him; it is well.   France and humanity are avenged.
But his children have never taken part in an act of bar-
barity or injustice, and they are innocent.   Let them
go in peace, and let them not be able to say of us, as we
can say of the royalists, that the patriots are assassins."

Diana did not wish to flee, for, to her mind, to go
without wreaki· ʒ vengeance was equivalent to fleeiŋ:
but she and her brother by themselves could do nothiŋ .
Lucien took the bridle of her horse and led her away.

When they reached their home once more, the two
orphans threw themselves into each other's arms and
burst into tears; they had no one left in the world to
love except each other.

Their mutual love was touching and beautiful to see.

They grew up together until Diana was eighteen, and
Lucien twenty-one.

The reaction of Thermidor occurred at this time.
Their name was a pledge of their political opinions;
they went to no one, but others came to them.   Lucien
listened coldly to the propositions which were made to
him, and asked time for reflection.   Diana seized upon
them eagerly, and made signs that she would undertake
to convince her brother.   Indeed, she was no sooner left
alone with him than she brought up the great question,
noblesse oblige.

Lucien had been educated as a royalist, and on religious
principles.   He had his father to avenge, and his sister
had great influence over him; he therefore gave his word.
From that time, towards the end of 1796, he had been
a member of that branch of the Companions of Jehu
which was called " Du Midi."

We know the rest.

It would be difficult to describe the violence of Diana's

feelings from the moment her brother was arrested until she learned that he had been taken to the department of the Ain. She immediately took all the money at her disposal, and started in a post-chaise for Nantua.

We know that she arrived too late, that she learned at Nantua of the abduction of the prisoner and the burning of the register's office, and that, thanks to the judge's acumen, she was able to understand the object of the two exploits.

On the same day, about noon, she reached the Hôtel des Grottes de Ceyzeriat, and immediately upon her arrival she presented herself at the prefecture, where she related what had occurred at Nantua, which was still unknown at Bourg.

This was not the first time that news of the prowess of the Companions of Jehu had reached the prefect's ear. Bourg was a royalist town. Most of its inhabitants sympathized with the young "outlaws." Often, when the prefect had given orders that one of them should be watched or arrested, he had felt something like a net drawn around him; and although he could not see it clearly, he had at least conjectured the source of the hidden resistance which paralyzed his authority. But this time the accusation was clear and precise: armed men had taken their accomplice from prison by force; they had by force and arms compelled the registry clerk to give them a paper which compromised the names of four of their accomplices in the South. These men, finally, had been seen on their way to Bourg, after the perpetration of their double crime at Nantua.

He summoned before him and Diana the commander of gendarmerie, the president of the court, and the police commissioner; he made Diana repeat her long accusation against these formidable unknown persons; he declared that he proposed within three days to have some definite information; and he asked Diana to pass those three days at Bourg. Diana had divined how great an interest the prefect was likely to take, personally, in the apprehension of those whom she was hunting down. She returned at nightfall to the hôtel, worn out with fatigue, and dying with hunger, for she had eaten hardly anything since she left Avignon.

She ate, and went to bed, where she slept the deep sleep with which youth conquers grief.

The next morning she was awakened by a great uproar beneath her windows. She rose and looked through her blinds, but all she could see was a great crowd moving about in every direction; but something in the nature of a presentiment of evil told her that a new trial awaited her.

She put on a dressing-gown, and without knotting up her hair, which had become disordered in her sleep, she opened the window and leaned out over the balcony.

But she had no sooner cast one look into the street than she uttered a loud cry, rushed back into the room, darted down the stairs, and threw herself, mad with grief, dishevelled, and ghastly pale, upon the body which formed the centre of the crowd, crying, —

"My brother, my brother!"

CHAPTER XII.

IN WHICH THE READER WILL MEET SOME OLD ACQUAINTANCES.

WE must now ask our readers to follow us to Milan, where, as we have said, Bonaparte, who no longer called himself Buonaparte, had his headquarters.

On the same day and at the very hour when Diana de Fargas recovered her brother in such tragic and pitiful fashion, three men came out of the barracks of the Army of Italy, while three others issued from neighboring barracks occupied by the Army of the Rhine. After his first victories, General Bonaparte had demanded a reinforcement, and two thousand men had been detached from Moreau's army and sent, under the command of Bernadotte, to the Army of Italy.

The six men made their way towards the eastern gate, walking in two groups, at a little distance from each other. This gate, the nearest one to the barracks, was the one behind which took place the numerous duels caused by rivalry in the matter of personal valor and by difference of opinion between the soldiers from the North and those who had always fought in the South.

An army is always formed upon the model of its general. His peculiarities spread to the officers, and from them extend to the soldiers. The division of the Army of the Rhine commanded by Moreau, which had come south to join the Army of Italy, was formed upon Moreau's model.

The royalist faction looked longingly to Moreau and Pichegru. The latter had been all ready to yield; but weary of the indecision of the Prince de Condé, and not willing to introduce the enemy into France without having determined beforehand the conditions which should circumscribe the rights of the prince whom he was bringing in, as well as those of the people who were to receive him, nothing had occurred between him and the Prince de Condé except a correspondence which had had no result; and he had resolved to bring about his revolution, not by the aid of his military influence, but of the high position which had just been bestowed upon him by his fellow-citizens in making him president of the Five Hundred.

Moreau's republicanism could not be shaken. Careless, moderate, unemotional, with no taste for politics beyond his capacity, he held himself in reserve, sufficiently flattered by the praise which his friends and the royalists bestowed upon his masterly retreat from the Danube, which they compared to that of Xenophon.

His army, therefore, was, like him, cold and phlegmatic, and submissive to his discipline.

The Army of Italy, on the contrary, was composed of our Southern revolutionists, — brave hearts who were as impulsive in their opinions as in their courage.

Having been in evidence for more than a year and a half, at the very centre of the glory the French arms were reaping, the eyes of all Europe were fixed on it. It could take pride, not in masterly retreats, but in victories. Instead of being forgotten by the government, as were the armies of the Rhine and the Sambre-et-Meuse, generals, officers, and soldiers were overwhelmed with honors, gorged with money, and sated with pleasure. Serving first under General

Bonaparte, — that is to say, under the star which had been giving forth for a year and a half a brilliant light which had dazzled the world, — then under Generals Masséna, Joubert, and Augereau, who set the example of the most ardent republicanism, they were informed, by the command of Bonaparte, who caused to be distributed among them all those journals which were animated by his spirit, of the events which were taking place in Paris, — that is to say, of a reaction which threatened to be equal to that of Vendémiaire. For these men, who did not discuss their opinions, but who received them ready made, the Directory — the heir and successor of the Convention — was still the revolutionary government to whose service they had devoted themselves in 1792. They asked only one thing, now that they had conquered the Austrians, and thought they had nothing more to do in Italy, and that was to cross the Alps again, in order to put to the sword the aristocrats at Paris.

A fair sample of each of these armies was presented by the two groups which were on their way to the eastern gate.

One, which betrayed by its uniform that it belonged to that tireless infantry which had started from the foot of the Bastille to make the tour of the world, was composed of Sergeant-major Faraud, who had married the Goddess of Reason, and his two inseparable companions, — Groseiller and Vincent, — who had both reached the high rank of sergeant.

The other group, which belonged to the cavalry, was composed of the Chasseur Falou — who, it will be remembered, had been appointed quartermaster-general by Pichegru — and two of his companions, the one a quartermaster, and the other a brigadier.

Falou, who belonged to the Army of the Rhine, had not advanced a step since his promotion by Pichegru.

Faraud, of the Army of Italy, had remained, it is true, in the same rank which he had received within the lines at Weissembourg, — the rank at which so many poor fellows stop whose lack of education does not permit them to pass the examination for a commission; but he had twice been mentioned in the order of the day of his regiment, and Bonaparte had ordered him brought before him, and had said to him, —

" Faraud, you are a fine fellow! "

The result was that Faraud was as well satisfied with the two orders of the day and with Bonaparte's words as he would have been with his promotion to the rank of *sous-lieutenant.*

Now, Quartermaster-general Falou and Sergeant-major Faraud had had a few words on the previous night, which had seemed to them sufficient to require a promenade to the eastern gate, — which means that the two friends (to use the terms employed under such circumstances) were about to refresh themselves with a sword-thrust or two.

And, in fact, as soon as they were outside the gate, the seconds on both sides began to look for a suitable spot, where each party would have an equal advantage of ground and sun. When a satisfactory spot was found, they so informed the two principals, who followed their seconds, apparently content with the choice made by them, and put themselves at once in a condition to utilize it by throwing on the ground their foraging caps, coats, and waistcoats. Then each turned back the right sleeve of his shirt as far as the elbow.

Engraved upon his arm, Faraud had a flaming heart, with the words, " All for the Goddess of Reason."

Falou, less concentrated in his affections, had this Epicurean device: " *Vive le vin! vive l'amour!* "

The fight was to take place with the infantry swords known as *briquets*. Each received his weapon from the hands of his second, and darted towards his adversary.

" What the devil can a man do with such a kitchen-knife as this? " growled the Chasseur Falou, who was accustomed to his long cavalry sabre, and who handled the *briquet* as if it had been a pen. " This is only fit to cut cabbages and scrape carrots. "

" It will serve also, " said Faraud, with the movement of the neck which was habitual to him, and which we have noticed before, — " it will serve also for one who is not afraid to come to close quarters to shave his enemy's mustache. "

And making a feint to strike at his thigh, the sergeant-major made a thrust at his adversary's head, which was successfully parried.

" Oh, " said Falou, " very good, Sergeant! The mustaches are according to orders. It is forbidden in the regiment to cut them off, and, above all, to let any one else cut them off. And those who permit such a thing are usually punished for it. Punished for it, " he repeated, watching his chance, — " punished for it by the *coup de manchette.* "

And with such rapidity that Faraud had not time to parry, his opponent made the thrust which goes by the name of the part of the body at which it is aimed.

The blood spurted from Faraud's arm on the instant. But furious at being wounded, he cried, —

" It is nothing, it is nothing! Let us go on! "

And he stood on guard.

But the seconds sprang between the combatants, and declared that honor was satisfied.

Upon this declaration, Faraud threw down his weapon and held out his arm. One of the seconds drew a handkerchief from his pocket, and with a dexterity which proved that he was no novice in such affairs, he bound up the wound. He was in the midst of the operation when, not twenty yards away from them, a group of seven or eight horsemen appeared from behind a clump of trees.

"The deuce! The commander-in-chief!" exclaimed Falou.

The soldiers sought for some way of escaping the notice of their chief; but he had already seen them, and was urging his horse towards them with whip and spur. They remained motionless, with the right hand at salute and the left at the side. The blood was streaming from Faraud's arm.

" So you are fighting a duel here."

CHAPTER XIII.

CITIZENS AND MESSIEURS.

BONAPARTE stopped four paces from them, making a sign to his staff to remain where they were. Motionless upon his horse, which was as motionless as he, slightly stooping because of the heat and of the malady from which he was suffering, his piercing eyes half covered by the upper lid, and darting gleams of light through the eyelashes, he looked like a bronze statue.

" So you are fighting a duel here," he said, in his incisive voice. " It is well known that I do not approve of duels. The blood of Frenchmen belongs to France, and it should be shed for France alone."

Then, looking from one to the other of the adversaries, and letting his glance rest upon the sergeant-major, he said, —

" How does it happen, Faraud, that a fine fellow like you — "

Bonaparte at this time made it a matter of principle to retain in his memory the faces of those men who distinguished themselves, so that upon occasion he could call them by name. This was a distinction which never failed to have its effect.

Faraud started with delight when he heard his name spoken by the general, and raised himself upon tiptoe.

Bonaparte saw the movement; and smiling inwardly, he went on, —

" How does it happen that a fine fellow like you, who have twice been mentioned in the order of the day of your regiment, — once at Lodi, and again at Rivoli, — should disobey my orders thus? As for your opponent, whom I do not know — "

The commander-in-chief purposely emphasized these words.

Falou frowned, for the words pierced him like a needle in his side.

" I beg your pardon, General," he interrupted. " The reason you do not know me is because you are too young; because you were not with the Army of the Rhine at the engagement at Dawendorff, at the battle of Frœschwillers, and at the recapture of the lines at Weissembourg. If you had been there — "

" I was at Toulon," interrupted Bonaparte, dryly. " And if you drove the Prussians from France at Weissembourg, I did as much by the English at Toulon, which was quite as important."

" That is true," said Falou. " We even put your name in the order of the day. I was wrong to say that you were too young. I acknowledge it, and beg your pardon. But I was right in saying that you were not there, for you yourself admit that you were at Toulon."

" Go on," said Bonaparte. " Hast thou anything more to say? "

" Yes, General," replied Falou.

" Well, say on," rejoined Bonaparte. " But as we are republicans, be good enough to call me ' citizen-general,' and to say ' thou ' when thou addressest me."

" Bravo, Citizen-General! " cried Faraud.

Citizens Vincent and Groseiller — Faraud's seconds — nodded approvingly.

Falou's seconds remained motionless, without giving any sign either of approval or disapproval.

" Well, Citizen-General," continued Falou, with that familiarity of speech which the principle of equality had introduced into the ranks of the army, " if thou hadst been at Dawendorff, faith! thou wouldst have seen me, during a charge of cavalry, save the life of General Abatucci, who is as good as any man."

" Ah," said Bonaparte, " I thank thee. I believe that Abatucci is a sort of cousin of mine."

Falou picked up his cavalry sabre, and showing it to Bonaparte, who was much astonished to see a general's sabre in the possession of a mere quartermaster-general, said, —

" It was on that occasion that General Pichegru, who is as good as any man," and he emphasized this characterization of General Pichegru, " seeing the state to which my poor sabre was reduced, made me a present of his, which is not altogether according to orders, as you see."

" What, again! " said Bonaparte, with a frown.

" Pardon me, Citizen-General! *As thou seest.* I am always blundering; but what wouldst thou? Citizen-General Moreau has not accustomed us to the ' thou.' "

" What," said Bonaparte, " the republican Fabius is so lax as that with the republican vocabulary? But go on, for I see that thou hast something else to tell me."

" I have this to tell thee, General: that if thou hadst been at Frœschwillers on the day when General Hoche, who is also as good as any other man, put a price of six hundred francs on the Prussian cannon, thou wouldst have seen me capture one of those cannon, and have seen me made quartermaster for doing it."

"And didst thou receive the six hundred francs?"

Falou shook his head.

"We gave them up to the widows of the brave fellows who died on the day of Dawendorff, and I took nothing but my pay, which was in one of the Prince de Condé's chests."

"Brave, disinterested fellow! Go on," said the general. "I like to see such men as thou art, who have no journalists to sound their praises nor any to cry them down, pronouncing their own panegyrics."

"And then," continued Falou, "if thou hadst been at the carrying of the lines at Weissembourg, thou wouldst have known that when I was attacked by three Prussians, I killed two. True, I did not come to the parry in time to escape the blow of the third; hence the scar which you see, — which thou seest, I mean, — to which I replied with a thrust with the point which sent my man to join his two companions. For that I was made quartermaster-general."

"And is all this true?" asked Bonaparte.

"Oh, as for that, Citizen-General," said Faraud, drawing near, and bringing his bandaged hand to his right eyebrow, "if the quartermaster needs a witness, I can testify that he has told nothing but the truth, and that he has said too little rather than too much. It was well known in the Army of the Rhine."

"Very well!" said Bonaparte, looking benevolently at the two men who had just been exchanging blows, and one of whom was now sounding the other's praises. "I am delighted to make thy acquaintance, Citizen Falou. I trust that thou wilt do as well in the Army of Italy as thou didst in the Army of the Rhine. But how does it happen that two such fine fellows as you are should be enemies?"

"We, Citizen-General?" said Falou. "We are not enemies."

"Why the deuce were you fighting, then, if you are not enemies?"

"Oh," said Faraud, with his usual movement of the neck, "we fought for the sake of fighting."

"But suppose I tell you that I wish to know why you fought?"

Faraud looked at Falou, as if to ask his permission.

"Since the Citizen-General wants to know," said the latter, "I do not see why we should conceal it from him."

"Well, we fought — we fought — because he called me 'monsieur.'"

"And what dost thou want to be called?"

"Citizen, *mordieu!*" replied Faraud. "We paid dearly enough for that title to want to keep it. I am not an aristocrat like these messieurs of the Army of the Rhine."

"Thou hearest, Citizen-General," said Falou, tapping his foot impatiently, and putting his hand to the hilt of his sabre; "he calls us aristocrats."

"He was wrong, and thou also wert wrong to call him 'monsieur,'" replied the commander-in-chief. "We are all children of the same family, sons of the same mother, citizens of the same fatherland. We are fighting for the Republic; and the moment when kings recognize it is not the moment for good men like you to deny it. To what division dost thou belong?" he continued, addressing Quartermaster Falou.

"To the Bernadotte division," replied Falou.

"Bernadotte?" repeated Bonaparte, — "Bernadotte, a volunteer who was only a sergeant-major in '89, a gallant soldier who was promoted on the battle-field by

Kléber to the rank of brigadier-general, who was made
a general of division after the victories of Fleurus and
Juliers, and who took Maestricht and Altdorf! Bernadotte encouraging aristocrats in his army! I thought
he was a Jacobin. And you, Faraud, to what corps
dost thou belong?"

"To that of Citizen-General Augereau. No one can
accuse him of being an aristocrat. He is like you, — I
should say, like thee, — Citizen-General. He likes to
have us 'thee and thou' him. And so when we heard
these men from Sambre-et-Meuse calling us 'monsieur,'
we said to each other, 'For each "monsieur" a cut of
the sabre. Is it agreed?' 'Agreed.' And since then
we have stood up here perhaps a dozen times, our division against the Bernadotte. To-day it is my turn to
pay the piper. To-morrow it will be a 'monsieur.'"

"To-morrow it will be no one," said Bonaparte,
imperatively. "I will have no duelling in the army.
I have said it, and I repeat it."

"But —" muttered Faraud.

"Very well, I will talk over the affair with Bernadotte. In the mean time, you will please preserve
intact the republican traditions; and whether you belong
to Sambre-et-Meuse or Italy, you will 'thee and thou'
each other, and address each other as 'citizen.' You
will each of you pass twenty-four hours in the guard-
house now, as an example. And now shake hands, and
go away arm in arm, like good comrades."

The two soldiers approached each other and exchanged
a frank and manly grasp of the hand. Then Faraud
threw his vest over his left shoulder and passed his
hand through Falou's arm. The seconds did the same;
and all six entered the city by the eastern gate, and
went quietly towards the barracks.

General Bonaparte looked after them with a smile, murmuring, —

"Brave hearts! With men like you, Cæsar crossed the Rubicon; but it is not time yet to do as Cæsar did.

"Murat!" he cried.

A young man of twenty-four, with black hair and mustache and a quick, intelligent eye, dashed forward upon his horse, and was instantly beside the general.

"Murat," said the latter, "you will start at once for Vicenza, where Augereau now is. You will bring him to me at the Palace Serbelloni. You will say to him that the ground-floor of the palace is unoccupied, and that he can go there."

"The deuce!" murmured those who had seen but not heard. "It looks as if General Bonaparte was in an ill-humor."

CHAPTER XIV.

THE CAUSE OF CITIZEN-GENERAL BONAPARTE'S ILL-HUMOR.

BONAPARTE returned to the Palace Serbelloni.

He was, indeed, in an ill-humor.

While he was hardly at the beginning of his career, had hardly reached the dawn of his vast renown, calumny was already on his track, to take from him the merit of incredible victories, which could be compared only to those of Alexander, Hannibal, or Cæsar. Men said that it was Carnot who laid out his plans of battle, and that his pretended military genius only followed step by step the written instructions of the Directory. They said, too, as to the matter of administration, that he understood nothing about it, and that Berthier, his chief of staff, attended to everything.

He saw the struggle which was taking place at Paris against the partisans of royalty, then represented by the club of Clichy, as they had been represented two years before by the section Le Peletier.

Bonaparte's private correspondence with his two brothers urged him to take a stand between the royalists (that is to say, the counter-revolution) and the Directory, who still stood for a republic, — greatly diverted, no doubt, from its original starting-point and its original aim, but the only standard, nevertheless, around which republicans could rally.

In the majority of the two councils there was evident ill-will against him. Party leaders incessantly wounded his self-esteem by their speeches and their writings. They belittled his glory, and cried down the merits of the admirable army with which he had conquered five others.

He had attempted to enter into civil affairs; he had been ambitious to become one of the five directors in place of one who had resigned.

If he had succeeded in that attempt, he was convinced that he would soon be the sole director. But they had alleged his age — twenty-eight years — as an obstacle, since to be a director, he would have to be at least thirty. He had, therefore, withdrawn, not daring to ask for an exception in his favor, and thus violate that constitution for the maintenance of which he had fought on the 13th Vendémiaire.

The directors, moreover, were very far from desiring to have him for a colleague. The members of this body did not disguise the jealousy with which Bonaparte's genius inspired them, and had no hesitation in proclaiming that they were offended at his haughty manner and assumption of independence.

It saddened him to think that they represented him as a furious demagogue, and called him the " Man of the 13th Vendémiaire;" whereas on the 13th Vendémiaire he had been only the " Man of the Revolution," — in other words, of the public interest.

His instinctive inclination was, if not towards the Revolution, at all events against the royalists. He was therefore glad to notice the republican spirit of the army, and to encourage it. His first success at Toulon had been against the royalists; his victory in Vendémiaire had also been against royalists. And

what were the five armies which he had beaten?
Armies which sustained the cause of the Bourbons, —
or, in other words, royalist armies.

But at this period of all others, when he was waver-
ing between the safe *rôle* of a Monk and the hazardous
rôle of a Cæsar, that which made him fling high the
banner of the Republic, and prevented him from listening to any propositions which might be made to him,
was a strong presentiment of his coming grandeur.
Even more than that; it was the proud feeling, which
he shared with Cæsar, that he would rather be the first
man in a country town than the second man in Rome.

Indeed, no matter what exalted rank a king could
confer upon him, even though that of Constable of
France should be offered to him, the king would still
be above him, casting a shadow upon his brow.   Mounting with the aid of a king, he would never be anything
more than an upstart; mounting by his own unaided
strength, he would be no upstart, but would stand upon
his own feet.

Under the Republic, on the contrary, he was already
head and shoulders above other men, and he could but
continue to grow taller and taller.   Perhaps his gaze,
piercing though it was, had not yet extended to the vast
horizon which the empire revealed to him; but there
was in a republic an audacity of action and a breadth
of enterprise which suited the audacity of his genius
and the breadth of his ambition.

As sometimes happens with men who are destined to
greatness, and who perform impossible deeds, not because
they are predestined to do them, but because some one
has prophesied that they would do them, and they
thenceforth regard themselves as favorites of Providence, the most insignificant facts, if presented in a

certain light, sometimes led to momentous resolves with Bonaparte. The duel at which he had just been present, and the quarrel of the soldiers regarding the words "monsieur" and "citizen," had brought before him the whole question which was at the time agitating France. Faraud, in naming his general Augereau, and speaking of him as an inflexible partisan of democracy, which Bonaparte had known for a long time, had pointed out to the latter the agent he was seeking to second him in his secret plans.

More than once Bonaparte had thought of the danger of a Parisian revolution which would either overthrow the Directory or oppress it as the Convention had been oppressed, and which would lead to a counter-revolution, — or, in other words, a victory of the royalists, — and to the accession of some prince of the house of Bourbon. In that case, Bonaparte was fully determined to cross the Alps with twenty-five thousand men, and march upon Paris by way of Lyons. Carnot, with his sharp nose, had, no doubt, scented this design; for he wrote to him: —

"People ascribe to you a thousand projects, each one more absurd than the last. They cannot believe that a man who has done such great things can be contented to remain a simple citizen."

The Directory also wrote to him: —

"We have seen, Citizen-General, with the greatest satisfaction, the proofs of attachment which you are constantly giving to the cause of liberty and the Constitution of the year III. You can count upon the most complete reciprocity on our part. We accept with pleasure all the offers that you have made, to come at the first appeal to the succor of the Republic. They are only another proof of your sincere love for your country. You may rest assured that we shall make use of them only in the interest of its tranquillity, its happiness, and its glory."

This letter was in the handwriting of La Réveillère-Lepaux, and was signed, "Barras, Rewbell, and La Réveillère." The other two, Carnot and Barthélemy, either knew nothing about it, or refused to sign it.

But, as chance would have it, Bonaparte was better informed concerning the situation of the directors than were the directors themselves. A certain Comte Delaunay d'Entraigues — a royalist agent well known in the French Revolution — happened to be in Venice when that city was besieged by the French. He was regarded as being the moving spirit as well as the agent of the machinations which were on foot against France, and particularly against the Army of Italy. He was a man of sure judgment. He knew the peril of the Republic of Venice, and tried to escape; but the French troops occupied all the main land, and he was taken, with all his papers. When he was brought to Bonaparte as an *émigré*, Bonaparte treated him with the indulgence which · he always showed towards them. He caused all his papers to be returned to him, with the exception of three; and upon receiving his parole, he gave him the entire city of Milan for his prison.

One fine morning it was learned that Comte Delaunay d'Entraigues, abusing the confidence which the general had placed in him, had left Milan, and escaped into Switzerland.

But one of the three papers which had been left in Bonaparte's hands was, under the circumstances, of the greatest importance. It was an exact recital of what had passed between Fauche-Borel and Pichegru, following the first interview between them, which has been described in a previous chapter, and which had taken place at Dawendorff when Fauche-Borel had presented himself to Pichegru, under the name and garb of Citizen Fenouillot, travelling dealer in Champagne wines.

The famous Comte de Montgaillard, of whom we have already, I think, said a few words, was intrusted with the further attempts of the Prince de Condé upon Pichegru; and this paper, which had been retained by Bonaparte, written by Monsieur d'Entraigues from the dictation of the Comte de Montgaillard himself, contained the successive offers which had been made by the Prince de Condé to the general in command of the Army of the Rhine.

The Prince de Condé, who had all the authority of Louis XVIII., with the exception of the power of bestowing the blue ribbon, had offered Pichegru, if he would give up the town of Huningue and return to France at the head of the Austrians and *émigrés*, to make him Marshal of France and Governor of Alsace. He offered to give him, —

First. The red ribbon.

Second. The château of Chambord, with its park, and its twelve pieces of artillery taken from the Austrians.

Third. A million in ready money.

Fourth. Two hundred thousand livres of income, of which a hundred thousand, in case he should marry, should revert to his wife upon his death, and fifty thousand to each of his children, until his family should become extinct.

Fifth. A hôtel in Paris.

Sixth. Lastly, the town of Arbois, the native place of General Pichegru, should be re-christened Pichegru, and should be exempt from all taxes for twenty-five years.

Pichegru had flatly refused to give up Huningue.

" I will never enter into a conspiracy," he said. " I

do not wish to form the third volume of La Fayette and Dumouriez. My resources are as sure as they are great; they have roots, not only in my army, but in Paris, in the departments, and in the generals who are my colleagues, and who think as I do. I ask nothing for myself. When I have succeeded, I shall take my reward. But I am not ambitious; you may make your minds easy on that score at once. But to induce my soldiers to shout, '*Vive le roi!*' they must each have a full glass in the right hand, and six livres in the left.

"I will cross the Rhine, and enter France with the white flag; I will march upon Paris; and for the benefit of his Majesty Louis XVIII., I will overturn the government, whatever it may be, when I get there.

"But my soldiers must receive their pay every day, at least until we have made our fifth day's march upon French soil.

"They will give me credit for the rest."

The negotiation had fallen through on account of the obstinacy of Condé, who insisted that Pichegru should proclaim the king on the other side of the Rhine, and give up to him the town of Huningue.

Although possessing this precious document, Bonaparte had refused to use it. It would have cost him much to betray a general of Pichegru's renown, whose military talent he admired, and who had been his master in the school at Brienne.

But he was reckoning none the less on what Pichegru could do as a member of the Council of the Ancients, when, on that very morning, just as he was about to make a military reconnoissance in the neighborhood of Milan, he received a letter from his brother Joseph, telling him that Pichegru had not only been elected a

member of the Council of Five Hundred, but had almost
unanimously been elected its president.

He was, therefore, doubly armed, — with his former
popularity among his soldiers, and with his new civil
power.

Hence Bonaparte's rapid decision to send a messenger
to Augereau, to tell him that he wished to see him.

The duel which he had witnessed, and the causes
which had led to it, also threw their weight into the
scale with his wishes.   But the two adversaries little
suspected that they had just contributed in great measure towards making Augereau a marshal of France,
Murat a king, and Bonaparte an emperor.

And, indeed, none of this would have happened if
the 18th Fructidor had not, like the 13th Vendémiaire,
destroyed the projects of the royalists.

CHAPTER XV.

AUGEREAU.

On the next day, while Bonaparte was dictating his correspondence to Bourrienne, Marmont, one of his favorite aides-de-camp, who was discreetly looking out of the window, announced that he saw at the end of the street the waving plume of Murat and the somewhat diminutive form of Augereau.

Murat was then a handsome young man of some twenty-three or four years. He was the son of an innkeeper of Labastide, near Cahors; and as his father was also master of the post, Murat as a child became familiar with horses, and learned to be an excellent rider. Then, through some caprice of his father's, who probably wanted to have one priest in the family, he had been sent to a seminary, where, if we can judge from the letters which are lying before us, his studies did not extend so far as to give him a proper knowledge of orthography.

Luckily or unluckily for him, the Revolution opened the doors of the seminaries; young Joachim took flight, and enlisted in the constitutional guard of Louis XVI., where he distinguished himself by his extreme opinions, his duels, and his courage.

Dismissed, like Bonaparte, by the same Aubry who, in the Five Hundred, continued to wage such severe war against patriots, he met Bonaparte, became intimate with him, hastened to put himself under his orders on the 13th Vendémiaire, and followed him to Italy as aide-de-camp.

Augereau, whom we have already met at Strasburg, where he gave fencing lessons to our young friend Eugène de Beauharnais, was seventeen years older than Murat, and had already, when we renew our acquaintance with him, reached his fortieth year. After having stagnated for fifteen years in the lower grades, he had changed from the Army of the Rhine to the Army of the Pyrenees, commanded by Dugommier.

It was in that army that he won successively the grades of lieutenant-colonel, colonel, and brigadier-general, — in which last capacity he defeated the Spaniards on the banks of the Fluvia in such brilliant fashion that he was at once made general of division.

We have spoken of the peace with Spain, and have expressed our opinion of that peace, which made a neutral sovereign, if not our ally, of one of the nearest relatives of Louis XVI., whose head the Convention had just cut off.

After peace was signed, Augereau went into the Army of Italy under Schérer, and contributed largely to the victory of Loano.

At last Bonaparte appeared, and his immortal campaign of '96 began.

Like all the older generals, Augereau was sorry, almost scornful, to see a young man of twenty-five take command of the most important army of France. But when he had marched under the young general's orders; when he had contributed his part towards taking the pass of Millesimo; when, as the result of a manœuvre suggested by his young colleague, he had beaten the Austrians at Dego, and taken the redoubts of Montellesimo without knowing for what object they had been taken, — then he understood the power of the genius which had conceived the clever manœuvre, which, by separating the Sardinians from the imperial troops, assured the success of the campaign.

Thereupon he went straight to Bonaparte, confessed frankly his former prepossessions, apologized manfully, and, like the ambitious man he was, though recognizing how much his lack of education was against him, he asked Bonaparte to allow him to share in the rewards which the latter distributed to his lieutenants.

This was made all the easier for the young commander-in-chief to do by the fact that Augereau, one of the bravest soldiers of the Army of Italy, as well as one of the most active generals, on the day after that on which he had pressed Bonaparte's hand, carried the intrenched camp of Ceva, and penetrated into Alba and Casale. Finally, meeting the enemy at the head of the bridge of Lodi, bristling with cannon, and defended by a terrible fire, he rushed upon the bridge at the head of his grenadiers, took thousands of prisoners, defeated all the troops he met, released Masséna from a difficult position, and took Castiglione, which was one day to be made a duchy for him. At last came the famous day of Arcola, which was to crown for him most gloriously a campaign which he had made famous by so many daring exploits. There, as at Lodi, a bridge was to be crossed. Three times he led his soldiers to the middle of the bridge, and three times were they repulsed by the storm of grape and canister. Finally, seeing that his ensign was among the dead, he seized the flag, and with head down, not looking to see whether or no he was followed, he crossed the bridge, and found himself in the midst of the enemy's artillery and bayonets. But this time his soldiers, who adored him, followed him; the guns were captured, and turned against the enemy.

The victory, one of the most glorious of the campaign, was so justly recognized as the result of his valor that the government presented him with the flag which he had used to arouse the ardor of his soldiers.

Like Bonaparte, he also had reflected that he owed everything to the Republic, and that the Republic alone could give him the future of gratified ambition for which he hoped. Under a king, as he well knew, he would not have got beyond the rank of sergeant. The son of a mason and a fruit-seller, a common soldier and fencing-master at the beginning of his career, he had become a general of division, and at the first opportunity he might, thanks to his own courage, become commander-in-chief, like Bonaparte, although he had not his genius; like Hoche, although he had not his integrity; or like Moreau, although he had not his learning.

He had just given a proof of his greed, which had done him some harm among those pure republicans who sent their gold epaulets to the Republic, to have them melted up, wearing wool ones instead, until money should be more plenty.

He had granted his soldiers three hours of pillage in the town of Lago, which had risen against him. He did not take part in the pillage himself, it is true; but he bought at a ridiculously low price from the soldiers the articles of value which they brought away. He had with him an army wagon which contained, it was said, property worth a million; and " Augereau's wagon " was known throughout the army.

Having been notified by Marmont, Bonaparte was expecting him.

Murat entered first, and introduced Augereau.

Bonaparte thanked Murat with a gesture, and made a sign to him and to Marmont to leave them alone.

Bourrienne also rose to go; but Bonaparte, putting out his hand, made him sit down again; he had no secrets from his secretary.

Augereau entered. Bonaparte held out his hand to him, and motioned to him to sit down.

Augereau sat down, put his sword between his legs, placed his hat on its hilt, and his arms on the hat, and asked,—

"Well, General, what is it?"

"It is this," replied Bonaparte, "that I want to congratulate you upon the fine spirit of your army corps. I came upon a duel yesterday, where one of your soldiers was fighting because a soldier of Moreau's army had called him 'monsieur.'"

"Ah," said Augereau, "the fact is that I have some rascals who will not listen to reason on that subject. This is not the first duel that they have fought for the same reason. Therefore, when I left Vicenza this morning, I published an order of the day to the effect that any man of my division who should make use, verbally or in writing, of the word 'monsieur,' would be degraded from his rank, or, if he was a common soldier, would be declared incapable of serving in the armies of the Republic."

"Then, since you have taken this precaution, you do not think, do you," said Bonaparte, looking steadily at Augereau, "that there will be anything to prevent your leaving your division for a month or two?"

"Ah!" said Augereau. "Pray, why should I leave my division?"

"Because you have asked my permission to go to Paris on your own personal business."

"And a little on yours too, eh?" said Augereau.

"I thought," said Bonaparte, dryly, "that you knew no distinction in our affairs."

"No, no," rejoined Augereau, quickly; "and it ought to please you to think that I am modest enough to be content always with the second place."

"Have you not the second place in the Army of Italy?" asked Bonaparte.

"To be sure; but I did a little something myself towards that, and circumstances may not always be so favorable."

"You see," resumed Bonaparte, "that when you cease to be useful in Italy, — or, in other words, when opportunities are few, — I find an occasion for you to be useful in France."

"*Ah çà!* Tell me, you are sending me to the assistance of the Republic, are you not?"

"Yes. Unfortunately, the Republic is in poor hands just now; but, poor as they are, it still lives."

"And the Directory?" asked Augereau.

"Is divided," replied Bonaparte. "Carnot and Barthélemy incline towards royalty, and they have with them, it must be confessed, the majority of the councils. But Barras and Rewbell and La Réveillère-Lepaux stand firm for the Republic and the Constitution of the year III., and they have us behind them."

"I thought," said Augereau, "that they had thrown themselves into Hoche's arms."

"Yes, but it will not do to leave them there. There must be no longer arms in the army than ours; and ours must reach beyond the Alps, and, if necessary, bring about another 13th Vendémiaire at Paris."

"Well, why do you not go yourself?" asked Augereau.

"Because if I should go, it would be to overthrow the

Directory, not to sustain it; and I have not yet done enough to undertake the part of Cæsar."

"And you send me to play the part of your lieutenant? Very well, I am content. What is there to be done?"

"Make an end of the enemies of France, who were only half wiped out on the 13th Vendémiaire. As long as Barras goes straight towards a republican goal, second him with all your strength and all your courage; if he hesitates, resist him; if he betrays, collar him as you would the meanest citizen. If you fail, in a week I shall be at Paris with twenty-five thousand men."

"Very well," replied Augereau, "I will try not to fail. When shall I start?"

"As soon as the letter is written which you are to take to Barras."

Then, turning to Bourrienne, he said,—

"Write."

Bourrienne had pen and paper in readiness; Bonaparte dictated as follows:—

CITIZEN-DIRECTOR, — I send you Augereau, my right arm. For everybody else he is in Paris on leave, having some business of his own to attend to; for you he is there as the director who keeps pace with us. He brings you his sword, and is instructed to say to you that, in case of need, you may draw upon the chest here in Italy for one, two, or even three millions.

Particularly in civil war, money is the vital nerve.

I hope in the course of a week to hear that the councils are purified, and that the club of the Rue de Clichy no longer exists. Health and fraternity, BONAPARTE.

P.S. — What is all this that we hear about robberies of diligences, and Chouans who infest the highways of the South, under the name of Companions of Jehu? Put your hand on four or five of the rascals, and make an example of them.

B.

Bonaparte, according to his habit, read over the letter, and then signed it with a new pen, which did not make his writing any more legible; then Bourrienne sealed it and gave it to the messenger.

" Tell them to give Augereau twenty-five thousand francs from my cash-box, Bourrienne," said Bonaparte.

And to Augereau he added, —

" When you are out of money, Citizen-General, send to me for more."

CHAPTER XVI.

THE CITIZEN-DIRECTORS.

IT was time for the Citizen-General Bonaparte to have an eye upon the citizen-directors. There had been an open rupture, as we have said, among the five elect at the Luxembourg.

Carnot and Barthélemy had completely separated from Barras, Rewbell, and La Réveillère-Lepaux.

The result was that the ministry, such as it was, could not remain, some of the ministers being creatures of Barras, La Réveillère-Lepaux, and Rewbell, while others followed Barthélemy and Carnot.

There were seven ministers: Cochon, Minister of Police; Bénézech, Minister of the Interior; Truguet, Minister of Marine; Charles Delacroix, Minister of Foreign Affairs; Ramel, Minister of Finance; Merlin, Minister of Justice; and Pétiet, Minister of War.

Cochon, Pétiet, and Bénézech were tainted with royalism. Truguet was haughty and violent, and determined to have his own way. Delacroix was not equal to his post. In the opinion of the majority of the directors, —Barras, Rewbell, and La Réveillère, — Ramel and Merlin alone should be retained.

The opposition, on the other hand, demanded the removal of four ministers, — Merlin, Ramel, Truguet, and Delacroix.

Barras yielded Truguet and Delacroix; but he cut off three others, who were members of the Five Hundred, and whose loss would cause great trouble to the two chambers.

These were, as we have said, Cochon, Pétiet, and Bénézech.

We hope that Madame de Staël's salon has not been forgotten. It was there, it will be remembered, that the future author of "Corinne" formed a body of opinion almost as influential as that of the Luxembourg or the Rue de Clichy.

Now, Madame de Staël, who had made one minister under the monarchy, was haunted with the desire to make another under the Directory.

The life of her candidate had been an eventful one, interesting because of its many changes of fortune. He was forty-three years old, of one of the greatest families of France, born lame, like Mephistopheles, whom he in some respects resembled both in face and mind, — a resemblance which became still greater when he found his Faust. Destined to the Church because of his infirmity, although the eldest of the family, he had been made Bishop of Autun at the age of twenty-five. Then came the Revolution. Our bishop adopted all its principles, was elected a member of the Constituent Assembly, suggested there the abolition of ecclesiastical tithes, celebrated mass on the Champ de Mars on the day of the Federation, blessed the flags, admitted the new constitution of the clergy, and consecrated the bishops who took the oath, which led to his excommunication by Pope Pius VI.

Sent to London by Louis XVI. to assist our ambassador, Monsieur de Chauvelin, he received, in 1794, from the cabinet of St. James, an order to withdraw; and at the same time he received from Paris the news that he had been accused by Robespierre.

This double proscription was fortunate for him: he was ruined; he went to America, and made another fortune in commerce. He had returned to France only three months before this time.

His name was Charles-Maurice de Talleyrand-Périgord.

Madame de Staël, a woman of great intellect, had been attracted by this man's charming wit; she knew how much depth there was beneath the assumed frivolity of her new friend. She had introduced him to Benjamin Constant, who was then her *cicisbeo*, and Constant had put him in communication with Barras.

Barras was delighted with the prelate. After being presented by Madame de Staël to Benjamin Constant, and by Benjamin Constant to Barras, he induced Barras to present him to La Réveillère and Rewbell. He won them as he won everybody else, and it was agreed that he should be made Minister of Foreign Affairs in place of Bénézech.

The five directors held a meeting to elect by secret ballot the members of the new ministry who should replace those of the former one who were to go out. Carnot and Barthélemy did not know of the accord between their three colleagues, and thought they could successfully fight against them. But they saw their mistake when they found that the three were unanimous in their choice of those who were to go, of those who were to remain, and of those who were to come in.

Cochon, Pétiet, and Bénézech were dismissed, Merlin and Ramel retained; Monsieur de Talleyrand was appointed Minister of Foreign Affairs, Pléville-Lepeley, Minister of Marine, François de Neufchâteau went to the Department of the Interior, and Lenoir-Laroche to the Police Department.

They also selected Hoche as Minister of War, but

he was only twenty-eight, and the required age was thirty.

This was the selection which had disturbed Bonaparte in his headquarters at Milan.

The secret session terminated with a violent altercation between Barras and Carnot.

Carnot reproached Barras for his luxurious mode of life and his dissolute habits.

Barras accused Carnot of his defection in favor of the royalists.

From accusations they went on to the grossest insults.

" You are nothing but a vile rascal," said Barras to Carnot; " you have sold the Republic, and you want to cut the throats of those who defend it. Wretch, brigand," he continued, rising and shaking his fist, " there is not a citizen who would not be justified in spitting in your face."

" Very good! " said Carnot. " Between now and to-morrow I will reply to your insults."

The next day passed, and Barras received no call from Carnot's seconds.

The affair had no further consequences.

The appointment of this ministry, as to which the two councils had not been consulted, made a great sensation among the representatives. They instantly resolved to organize for the struggle.

One of the great advantages of counter-revolutions is that they furnish historians with documents which they could not otherwise obtain.

And in fact, when the Bourbons returned in 1814, each one tried to outdo the rest in proving that he had conspired against the Republic or the Empire, — that is to say, that he had betrayed his country.

The great object was to claim the reward of treason;

and thus it was that we witnessed the complete exposition and confirmation of all the conspiracies which precipitated Louis XVI. from the throne, — conspiracies of which people had had only a vague idea under the Republic and the Empire, because definite proofs were lacking.

But in 1814 the proofs were no longer lacking.

Each man presented with his right hand the proof of his treason, and held out his left hand for the reward.

It is therefore to that epoch of degradation of the moral sense and of self-accusation that we must have recourse in order to give official details of those struggles in which the guilty were sometimes looked upon as victims, and the administrators of justice as oppressors.

Moreover, it must have been noticed that in the work which we are now laying before the eyes of our readers, we appear as a romantic historian rather than as an historical romancist. We think that we have given sufficient proof of our imagination to be allowed, on this occasion, to prove our exactness, while preserving at the same time the element of poetical fancy which will make the perusal of the work easier and more attractive than that of history despoiled of all embellishment.

We have therefore had recourse to one of those counter-revolutionary revelations, in order to see just how far the Directory was threatened, and how urgent was the *coup d'état* which was determined upon.

We have seen that the three directors had turned to Hoche, passing Bonaparte by, and that this movement in the direction of the man who had pacified La Vendée had caused some anxiety to the commander-in-chief of the Army of Italy.

It was Barras who had applied to Hoche.

Hoche was preparing an expedition to Ireland; and he

had resolved to draw twenty-five thousand men from the Army of Sambre-et-Meuse, and take them to Brest.

In their march across France, these twenty-five thousand men could be stopped near Paris, and in one day's march be at the disposal of the Directory.

The approach of this army pushed the denizens of the Rue de Clichy to the last extremity. The principle of a national guard had been established by the Constitution. The Clichians, knowing that this national guard would be composed of the same elements as the sections, resolved to hasten its organization.

Pichegru was chosen president, and directed to draw up a plan.

He presented his report, drawn with the cleverness of which his genius and his hate combined rendered him capable.

Pichegru was equally bitter against the *émigrés* because they had not chosen to profit by his devotion to the royalist cause, and against the republicans, because they had punished him for his useless devotion. He had gone so far as to dream of a revolution got up by himself alone, and on his own account. At this time his reputation very justly equalled that of his three illustrious rivals, Bonaparte, Moreau, and Hoche.

If he had once overthrown the directors, Pichegru would have made himself dictator; and once dictator, he would have prepared the way for the return of the Bourbons, from whom he would, perhaps, have asked nothing, except a pension for his father and his brother, and a house with a vast library for himself and Rose.

The reader will remember who Rose was. She was the friend to whom he had sent, out of his savings in the Army of the Rhine, an umbrella, which little Charles took to her.

The same little Charles, who knew him well, has since said of him, —

"An empire would have been too small for his genius, and a farm would have been too great for his indolence."

It would take too long to describe Pichegru's scheme with reference to the national guard; but if it had once been organized, it would have been entirely in his hands, and, led by him, it might have caused another 13th Vendémiaire, which, in Bonaparte's absence, might have ended in the fall and destruction of the directors.

A book published by the Chevalier Delarue in 1821 takes us with him into the club in the Rue de Clichy.

The house where the club met belonged to Gilbert des Molières.

All the counter-revolutionary projects, which prove that the 18th Fructidor was not, on the part of the Directory, a simple abuse of power and a brutal caprice, emanated from this house.

The Clichians found themselves taken at a disadvantage by the passage of Hoche's troops and his alliance with Barras.

They immediately assembled at their usual meeting-place. They formed groups around Pichegru, and asked him what his means of resistance were.

Surprised, like Pompey, he had no real means at hand. His only resource was in the passions of the various factions.

They spoke of the projects of the Directory, and concluded, from the change in the ministry and the march of the troops, that the directors were preparing a *coup d'état* against the Corps Législatif.

They proposed the most violent resolutions. They wanted to suspend the Directory; they wanted to bring

charges against its members. They even went so far as
to propose to outlaw them.

But they lacked strength to attain this result. They
had only the twelve hundred grenadiers who formed the
guard of the Corps Législatif, — a part of the 21st
regiment of dragoons, commanded by Colonel Malo.
Finally, they proposed, in their desperation, to send
a squad of grenadiers into each district of the capital,
to rally around them the citizens who had taken arms
on the 13th Vendémiaire.

This time it was the Corps Législatif, which, unlike
the Convention, roused Paris against the Government.

They talked much without coming to any decision,
as is always the case with those who lack strength.

Pichegru, when he was consulted, declared that it
would be impossible for him to maintain any struggle
with the slender means at his disposal.

The confusion was at its height when a message came
from the Directory, giving information as to the march
of the troops.

The message said that Hoche's troops, on their way
from Namur to Brest, to embark for Ireland, would pass
close to Paris.

Great cries then arose, and exclamations that the
Constitution of the year III. forbade troops to approach
within a radius of twelve leagues of Paris.

The messenger from the Directory intimated that he
had a reply ready for this objection: —

" The commissioner in charge was ignorant of this
article of the Constitution. His ignorance was the sole
cause of this infraction of the law. The Directory
furthermore affirmed that the troops had received an
order to retrace their steps at once."

They were obliged to be content with this explanation, in default of any other; but it satisfied no one, and the excitement which had been stirred up in the club De Clichy and the two councils spread from them all over Paris, where each citizen prepared himself for events no less serious than those which had occurred on the 13th Vendémiaire.

CHAPTER XVII.

MADEMOISELLE DE SAINT-AMOUR'S SICK-HEADACHE.

THE directors were lodged at the Luxembourg, each according to his habits and tastes rather than according to his needs.

Barras — the man of action and of display, the *grand seigneur*, the Indian nabob — had taken the whole wing which now forms the picture-gallery, and its appurtenances.

Rewbell and La Réveillère-Lepaux shared the other wing.

Carnot had taken for himself and his brother a part of the ground floor, in which he had cut off an immense room for himself and his maps.

Barthélemy, who had come last, and who was coldly received by his *confrères* because he represented the counter-revolution, had taken what was left.

On the evening when the stormy meeting at the club De Clichy had taken place, Barras returned to his rooms in a bad humor. He had invited no one, intending to pass his evening with Mademoiselle Aurélie de Saint-Amour, who, to his message, dated two hours before, had replied by a charming letter, in which she had said that, as ever, she should be happy to see him.

But when, at nine o'clock, he presented himself at her door, it was opened by Suzette on tiptoe, entreating him with hand and voice to be silent, telling him that her mistress had been attacked by one of those sick-headaches for which the faculty, persistent though they were, had as yet found no remedy, since the cause was not in the constitution but the mind of the invalid.

The director followed Suzette, walking as cautiously as if he had had a bandage over his eyes, and had been playing blind-man's-buff. As he passed the door of the boudoir, which was closely shut, he cast a suspicious glance at it before he was ushered into the sleeping apartment which we are familiar with, and which was lighted only by an alabaster lamp suspended from the ceiling, wherein perfumed oil was burning.

There was nothing to be said. Mademoiselle Aurélie was lying upon her bed of rosewood inlaid with Sèvres porcelain. She was wearing a little lace cap reserved specially for days of great suffering, and she spoke with the plaintive voice of a woman to whom it is an effort to talk.

" Ah, my dear General," she said, " how good you are to come; and how I longed to see you! "

" Was it not understood," said Barras, " that I was to come and pass the evening with you? "

" Yes; and although I was suffering from this odious headache, I said nothing about it, I wanted so much to see you. When one is suffering, one appreciates more than ever the presence of those whom one loves."

She languidly withdrew a warm, moist hand from the clothes, and held it out to Barras, who gallantly kissed it, and then seated himself upon the foot of the bed.

The pain drew a moan from the invalid.

" Ah," said Barras, " this is a severe headache, is it not? "

" Yes and no," replied Aurélie. " With a little rest it will pass away. Ah, if I could only sleep! "

The words were accompanied with a sigh which the god of sleep himself might have envied the beautiful courtesan.

It is probable that within a week of being driven out of Paradise, Eve played for Adam this little comedy of the sick-headache, which has lasted for six thousand years, and which has always had the same success. Men joke about it, women laugh about it; but when it is needed, the headache comes to the aid of whoever summons it, and always succeeds in getting rid of those who are in the way.

Barras remained for ten minutes beside the beautiful invalid, until she thought that she could decently shut her eyes, half sadly, half smilingly, and permit her chest to rise and fall with that gentle and regular breathing which indicates that while the soul may still be awake, the body has already embarked upon the calm ocean of sleep.

Barras softly laid upon the lace coverlid the hand which he had been holding, deposited a paternal kiss upon the white forehead of the sleeper, and charged Suzette to inform her mistress that his manifold occupations would perhaps prevent him from returning for three or four days.

Then he left the room on tiptoe, as he had entered it; and as he passed the boudoir, he had a strong desire to push the door open a crack, for something told him that the cause of the fair Aurélie's headache was there.

Suzette attentively followed him to the threshold of the outer door, which she took the precaution to double-lock behind him.

When he entered the Luxembourg, his valet announced that a lady was waiting for him.

Barras asked his usual question: —

" Young or old ? "

" She must be young, Monsieur," replied the valet; " but I have not been able to see her face because of her veil."

" How is she dressed ? "

" Like a woman in good society, — all in black satin; and she has the bearing of a widow."

" You had her come in ? "

" Into the rose boudoir. If Monseigneur should not care to receive her, nothing would be easier than to show her out without having her pass through the cabinet. Will Monseigneur receive her here, or will he go into the rose boudoir ? "

" I will go there," said Barras.

Then, remembering immediately that he might be about to meet a woman of rank, and that the proprieties must be observed, even in the Luxembourg, he said to the valet, —

" Announce me."

The valet went first, opened the door of the boudoir, and said, —

" The Citizen-Director, General Barras."

He drew back at once, to give place to him whom he had announced.

Barras entered, with the grand air which he had derived from the aristocratic world to which he had formerly belonged, and to which, in spite of three years of revolution and two of the Directory, he belonged still.

In one of the corners of the boudoir, where there was a sofa which had been built into the wall, was standing a lady, dressed all in black, as the valet had said, and whose bearing indicated to Barras, at a glance, that she was not one of the frail sisterhood.

Putting his hat on the table, he walked towards her, saying, —

"You wanted to see me, Madame; I am here."

The young woman, with a superb gesture, raised her veil, and disclosed a face of remarkable beauty.

Beauty is the most powerful of all fairies, and the most clever of introducers.

Barras paused a moment, as if dazzled.

"Ah, Madame," he said, "how fortunate I am, since I had intended remaining out part of the night, that a fortuitous circumstance brings me back thus early to the Luxembourg, where such good fortune awaited me! Be good enough to sit down, Madame, and tell me to what circumstances I owe the pleasure of your visit."

And he made a movement to take her hand and lead her to the sofa, from which she had risen when he was announced.

But she, keeping her hands beneath the folds of her long veil, replied, —

"Your pardon, Monsieur; I will remain standing, as befits a suppliant."

"A suppliant! — you, Madame? A lady like you does not beg, she commands, — or, at the least, she demands."

"Well, Monsieur, I demand. In the name of the town which gave birth to us both; in the name of my father, who was your friend; in the name of outraged humanity, and in the name of outraged justice, I come to demand vengeance."

"The word is a hard one," said Barras, "to come from the mouth of one so young and beautiful."

"Monsieur, I am the daughter of the Comte de Fargas, who was assassinated at Avignon by the republicans, and a sister of the Vicomte de Fargas, who has just been assassinated at Bourg, in Bresse, by the Companions of Jehu."

"Those men again!" muttered Barras. "Are you sure, Mademoiselle?"

The young girl held out her hand, and gave Barras a dagger and a paper.

"What is that?" asked Barras.

"That is the proof of what I have told you. My brother's body was found, three days ago, on the Place de la Préfecture at Bourg, with this dagger in his heart, and this paper tied to the hilt of the dagger."

Barras first examined the weapon with interest.

It was forged from a single piece of metal, in the form of a cross, like the ancient daggers of Saint Vehme. The only thing which distinguished it from them was the inscription, "Companions of Jehu," engraved upon the blade.

"But," said Barras, "this dagger alone simply raises a presumption. It might have been stolen, or forged expressly to lead the officers of justice astray."

"Yes," returned the young girl; "but here is something which should put them back on the right track. Read this postscript, written in my brother's handwriting, and signed with his name."

Barras read:—

I die because I have broken a sacred oath; consequently, I acknowledge that I deserve death. If you wish to give my body Christian burial, it will be placed to-morrow night in the market-place at Bourg. The dagger which will be found buried in my breast will indicate that I do not die the victim of a cowardly assassination, but of a just vengeance.

VICOMTE DE FARGAS.

"And this postscript was addressed to you, Mademoiselle?" asked Barras.

" Yes, Monsieur ? "

" It is assuredly in your brother's handwriting ? "

" It is his hand."

" What does he mean by writing that ' he does not die the victim of a cowardly assassination, but of a just vengeance ' ? "

" My brother himself was a Companion of Jehu. He was arrested, and he broke his oath by betraying his accomplices." Then, with a strange laugh, the young girl added, —

" I ought to have joined the association instead of him."

" Wait," said Barras. " There should be among my papers 'a report relating to this."

CHAPTER XVIII.

THE MISSION OF MADEMOISELLE DE FARGAS.

BARRAS, leaving Mademoiselle de Fargas alone for a moment, went to his study; and in a receptacle preserved for his private correspondence, he sought and found a letter from the *procureur* of the Republic at Avignon, which gave him an account of the whole affair, up to the departure of the Vicomte de Fargas for Nantua.

He gave it to Mademoiselle de Fargas to read.

She read it from beginning to end, and found that it confirmed what she had heard before she left Avignon.

"Then," she said, "you have received no news for two days?"

"No," replied Barras.

"That does not speak very well for your police; but fortunately, in this instance, I can supply their place."

And she told Barras how she had followed her brother to Nantua; how she had arrived there just in time to learn that he had been taken from the prison; how the registry office had been burned, and the documents relating to the prosecution destroyed; and, finally, how, on waking the next morning, she had found the body of her brother, naked, and pierced with the dagger of the Companions of Jehu, on the Place de la Préfecture, at Bourg.

Everything which came from the South and East was so impregnated with mystery that the cleverest agents of the police vainly endeavored to penetrate it.

Barras hoped at first that his beautiful visitor could give him information which was not generally known; but her stay at Nantua and Bourg, while it had brought her near the scene of events, and placed their results before her eyes, had taught her nothing new.

All that Barras knew and could tell her was that these events bore a close resemblance to those in Brittany and La Vendée.

The Directory knew perfectly well that these terrible robbers of diligences did not carry on the work on their own account, but turned the money of the Government over to Charette, Stofflet, the Abbé Bernier, and Georges Cadoudal.

But Charette and Stofflet had been taken and shot, and the Abbé Bernier had submitted. But breaking the word he had given, instead of going to England, he had remained concealed in the country. So that after a year or a year and a half of tranquillity, which had made the Directory feel secure enough to recall Hoche from La Vendée and send him to the army of Sambre-et-Meuse, there had come a report of a new insurrection; and by repeated blows the directors had been warned that four new leaders had appeared in the country,— Prestier, D'Autichamp, Suzannette, and Grignon. As for Cadoudal, he had never parleyed nor laid down his arms; he had never ceased to prevent Brittany from recognizing the Republican Government.

For a moment Barras seemed to have come to a resolution; but like all chance ideas, which at first appear to be impossible, it seemed to need considerable time to ripen before leaving the mind which had conceived it. From time to time he glanced from the proud young girl to the dagger, which he still held in his hand, and from that to the farewell letter of the

Vicomte de Fargas, which he had placed upon the table.

Diana grew weary of the silence.

"I have demanded vengeance at your hands," she said, "and you have not answered me."

"What do you mean by vengeance?" asked Barras.

"I mean the death of those who killed my brother."

"Tell me their names," said Barras. "We are as desirous as you are that they should expiate their crimes. Once taken, their punishment will not be slow to follow."

"If I knew their names," said Diana, "I should not have come to you; I should have used the dagger on them myself."

Barras looked at her.

The calm voice in which she uttered the words was abundant proof that her ignorance alone had prevented her from taking the law into her own hands.

"Well," said Barras, "you can search for them, and we will do the same."

"I search?" returned Diana. "Is that my business? Am I the Government? Am I the police? Is it my duty to provide for the safety of citizens? They arrested my brother and put him in prison. The prison, which belongs to the Government, must answer to me for my brother. The prison opens, and betrays its prisoner; the Government must answer to me for it. Therefore, since you are the head of the Government, I come to you, and I say, 'My brother! my brother! my brother!'"

"Mademoiselle," replied Barras, "we live in troublous times when even the keenest eye can scarcely see, when the stoutest heart hesitates, though it does not weaken, when the strongest arm bends or trembles. In the East and South we have the Companions of Jehu, who assassinate, and in the West we have the Vendeans and the Bretons, who fight.　Here we have three-quarters of Paris conspiring, two-thirds of our Chambers in opposition to us, and two of our colleagues betraying us; and in the midst of this universal confusion you desire the great machine, which in watching over its own safety watches also over that of the saving principles which will transform Europe, to close all its eyes, and open them again upon one spot, — that Place de la Préfecture where you found the lifeless body of your brother.　It is too much to ask of us, Mademoiselle.　We are simply mortals, and you cannot expect us to do the work of gods.　You loved your brother ? ”

“ I adored him! ”

“ You desire to avenge him ? ”

“ I would give my life for that of his murderer.”

“ And if you were shown some means of learning the identity of this murderer, whatever that means might be, you would adopt it ? ”

Diana hesitated a moment.

Then she said vehemently, —

“ Whatever it might be, I would adopt it.”

“ Well, listen to me,” said Barras.　“ Help us, and we will help you.”

“ What must I do ? ”

“ You are young and beautiful, — very beautiful.”

“ That is not to the point,” said Diana, without lowering her eyes.

“ On the contrary,” said Barras, “ it is straight to the point.　In this great struggle which we call life, beauty has been given to woman, not, as a simple gift from Heaven, to rejoice the eyes of a lover or a husband, but as a means of attack and defence.

"The Companions of Jehu have no secrets from Cadoudal; he is their real chief, since it is for him that they are working. He knows all their names, from the first to the last."

"Well," asked Diana, "what then?"

"Why," continued Barras, "it is very simple. Go to La Vendée or Brittany, and join Cadoudal. Wherever he may be, present yourself to him as a victim to your devotion to the royal cause, — which you really are. Gain his confidence; it will not be difficult. Cadoudal cannot see you without falling in love with you. With his love he will give you his confidence. Resolute as you are, and with your brother's memory in your heart, you need grant nothing more than it pleases you to grant.

"Then you will know the names of these men for whom we are vainly searching. Tell us the names, — that is all we ask of you, — and your vengeance shall be satisfied. Now, if your influence over the fanatic should go far enough to induce him to submit to the government, like the others, I need hardly tell you that the government would put no bounds — "

Diana extended her hand.

"Take care, Monsieur," she said. "One word more, and you will insult me. I ask twenty-four hours for reflection."

"Take as much time as you wish," said Barras. "You will always find me at your command."

"To-morrow, here, at nine o'clock in the evening," replied Diana.

And taking her dagger from Barras' hand, and her brother's letter from the table, she placed them in her breast, saluted Barras, and left the room.

The next day, at the same hour, Mademoiselle Diana de Fargas was again announced to the director.

Barras passed quickly into the rose boudoir, and found her awaiting him.

"Well, my beautiful Nemesis?" he asked.

"I have decided," she replied. "But you will understand that I need a safe-conduct which will be recognized by the republican authorities. In the life which I shall lead, it is possible that I may be taken with arms in my hands, making war upon the Republic. You shoot women and children; it is a war of extermination: that is a matter between yourselves and God. I may be taken, but I do not want to be shot before my vengeance is accomplished."

"I have foreseen your request, Mademoiselle, and have ready, not only a passport which will assure you full liberty of movement, but a safe-conduct which, in extreme cases, would force your enemies to become your defenders. I advise you, however, to conceal them both, and particularly the latter one, from the eyes of the Chouans and Vendeans. A week ago, tired of seeing this hydra of civil war continually springing up with new heads, we sent an order to General Hédouville to give no quarter. Consequently, as in the glorious prime days of the Republic, when the Convention gained victories by decree, we have sent down one of the old *noyeurs* of the Loire, a man who knows the country, named François Goulin, with a new guillotine. The guillotine will be for the Chouans if they are taken, or for our generals if they allow themselves to be beaten. Citizen Goulin is taking to General Hédouville a reinforcement of six thousand men. The Vendeans and the Bretons have no fear of musketry; they march up to it, crying, ' *Vive le Roi! vive la religion!* ' and singing hymns. We will see how they will march to the guillotine. You will meet, or rather you will overtake, these six thousand men and Citizen Goulin on the road from Angers to Rennes.

"If you are at all afraid, put yourself under their protection until you arrive in La Vendée, and learn definitely where Cadoudal is, and join him."

"Very well, Monsieur," said Diana, "I thank you."

"When shall you start?" asked Barras.

"My carriage and post-horses are waiting at the door of the Luxembourg."

"Permit me to ask you a delicate question, but one which it is my duty to put to you."

"Ask it, Monsieur."

"Do you need money?"

"I have six thousand francs in gold in this little box, which are worth more than twenty thousand francs in assignats. You see that I can make war on my own account."

Barras held out his hand to Mademoiselle de Fargas, who pretended not to perceive the act of courtesy.

She made an irreproachable courtesy, and went out.

"That is a charming viper," said Barras; "but I should not like to be the one to warm it!"

CHAPTER XIX.

THE TRAVELLERS.

As Mademoiselle de Fargas had told Barras, a carriage was waiting for her at the door of the Luxembourg; she entered it, and said to the postilion,—

"The road to Orléans!"

The postilion gathered up the reins, the little bells tinkled, and the carriage took the road towards the barrier of Fontainebleau.

As Paris was threatened with disturbances in the near future, the barriers were carefully guarded, and the gendarmerie had received orders to examine carefully every one who entered or left the city.

Whoever failed to have upon his passport either the signature of the new Minister of Police, Sothin, or the guaranty of one of the three directors, Barras, Rewbell, or La Réveillère, was obliged to explain at length his reasons for entering or leaving Paris.

Mademoiselle de Fargas was stopped at the barrier, like every one else; she was obliged to get out of her carriage and enter the office of the police commissioner, who, without paying any attention to the fact that she was young and beautiful, asked for her passport with the same unbending dignity as if she had been old and ugly.

Mademoiselle de Fargas took from her satchel the required paper and handed it to the official.

He read it aloud.

Citizeness Marie Rotrou, post-mistress at Vitré (Ille-et-Vilaine).

Signed : BARRAS.

The passport was in proper form; the commissioner returned it to her with a bow, which was intended for the signature of Barras rather than for the humble post-mistress, who also bowed slightly and retired, without even noticing that a handsome young man of twenty-six, who was about to present his passport when she entered, had, with a courtesy which indicated gentle birth, drawn back his extended arm, and allowed the beautiful traveller to pass first.

But he came immediately after her. The magistrate took the passport with the gravity which he brought to the performance of his important duties, and read, —

"Citizen Sebastien Argentan, tax-gatherer at Dinan (Côtes. du-Nord)."

The passport was signed not only by Barras, but by his two colleagues, and there was therefore even less to criticise about it than there had been about Mademoisello Rotrou's, which had been signed by Barras alone.

Receiving his passport back, together with a gracious bow from the official, M. Sebastien Argentan mounted a post-horse and trotted slowly away, while the postilion, whose duty it was to precede him and see that his relays were ready, set off at a gallop.

All night long, the tax-gatherer rode beside a closed post-chaise, in which he was far from suspecting that the attractive young person to whom he had yielded his turn was a passenger.

Day came, and one of the windows of the post-chaise was opened to admit the fresh morning air; a pretty head, which had not yet completely shaken off the traces of sleep, looked out to see the state of the weather, and to his great astonishment he recognized the post-mistress of Vitré travelling by post in a handsome carriage.

But he remembered that her passport was signed by Barras, which would explain many things in the way of luxury, particularly when a woman was in question.

The tax-gatherer bowed politely to the post-mistress, who, remembering that she had seen his face on the previous evening, graciously returned his salute.

Although he thought the young woman charming, he was too well-bred to approach the carriage or speak to her. He urged his horse to a gallop; and as if the mutual salute had satisfied his ambition, he disappeared around the first turn in the road.

But he had guessed that his travelling companion, whose destination he knew, having heard her passport read, would stop for breakfast at Étampes. He therefore stopped there himself, arriving half an hour before her.

He ordered, in the common dining-room, the ordinary breakfast at an inn; namely, two chops, half a cold chicken, a little ham, some fruit, and a cup of coffee.

He had hardly attacked his chops when Mademoiselle Rotrou's carriage stopped before the inn, which was also the post-house.

The traveller asked for a private room, crossed the common hall, bowed to her travelling companion, who had risen on perceiving her, and went upstairs.

The question to which Monsieur d'Argentan, who had already resolved to make his journey as agreeable as possible, wished an answer, was, whether Mademoiselle Rotrou was to eat in her own room or in the public dining-room.

In a moment it was answered. The maid who had accompanied the traveller upstairs came down, laid a white cloth on a table, and set a cover thereon.

Eggs, fruit, and a cup of chocolate formed the frugal repast of the traveller, who came down just as Monsieur d'Argentan was finishing his breakfast.

The young man saw with pleasure that although her toilet was simple, it was arranged with sufficient care to indicate that the instinct of coquetry was not extinguished in the heart of the pretty post-mistress.

He probably thought that he could overtake her by hard riding, for he in his turn declared that he was in need of rest, and ordered a room.

He threw himself on the bed, and slept two hours.

In the mean time, Mademoiselle Rotrou, who had had the whole night in which to sleep, got into her carriage again, and continued her journey.

About five o'clock she saw before her the church-steeple of Orléans, and at the same time she heard behind her the galloping of a horse, which, together with the sound of bells, told her that the traveller had overtaken her.

The two young people were now acquaintances.

They bowed graciously, and Monsieur d'Argentan thought that he had a right to approach the carriage door and inquire after the health of the fair occupant.

It was easy to see, in spite of the pallor of her complexion, that she was not over-fatigued.

He congratulated her politely upon the fact, and confessed that his own manner of travelling, however agreeable his horse's gait might be, would not probably permit him to make the whole journey without a break.

He added that if he could only find an opportunity to purchase a carriage, he might continue his journey in a much less wearisome fashion.

This was a roundabout way of asking Mademoiselle Rotrou if it would be agreeable to her to have him share both her carriage and the expense of it with her.

Mademoiselle Rotrou did not reply to his hint, but spoke of the weather, which was fine, and of the probability that she should herself be obliged to stop for a day either at Tours or Angers; to which the traveller on horseback made no reply at all, secretly resolving, however, to stop wherever she stopped.

After this overture and its rejection, to remain longer beside the carriage would have been discourteous. Monsieur d'Argentan set off at a gallop, telling Mademoiselle Rotrou that he would order her relay at Orléans.

Any other than the proud Diana de Fargas, any one whose heart was not encased in a triple armor of steel, would have noticed the refinement, the courtesy, and the beauty of the traveller. But whether she was destined to remain forever indifferent, or whether her heart required to be more violently stirred in order to arouse love, certain it is that none of all that which would have caught another woman's eye attracted hers.

Entirely wrapped up in her hatred, and utterly unable to dismiss the object of her journey from her thoughts, even while she smiled, she pressed, as if remorseful at having allowed herself to smile at all, — she pressed, we say, the hilt of the dagger which had opened the way for her brother's soul to precede hers to heaven.

Looking along the road to ascertain if she were indeed alone, and seeing no one as far as the eye could reach, she drew from her pocket the last note which her brother had ever written to her, and read and re-read it, as one chews impatiently, and yet persistently, a bitter root.

Then she fell back into a doze, and remained thus until her carriage stopped for fresh horses.

She looked about: the horses were ready, as Monsieur d'Argentan had promised her; but when she inquired for him, she was told that he had gone on ahead.

They stopped five minutes to change horses.

Then they took the road to Blois.

At the first turn, the young lady saw her handsome courier riding slowly, as if waiting for her; but this indiscretion, if it were one, was so excusable that it was excused.

Mademoiselle Rotrou soon overtook him.

It was she, this time, who spoke first, to thank him for the attention he had shown her.

" For my part, " replied the young man, " I thank my lucky star which, by leading me at the same time as yourself to the police commissioner, and by permitting me to yield you my turn, also permitted me to learn by your passport where you were going. And as chance will have it, my road is the same as yours; for while you are going to Vitré, I am going six or seven leagues beyond, — to Dinan. If you are not to remain in the neighborhood, I shall at least have had the pleasure of making the acquaintance of a charming person, and of having had the honor of accompanying her for nine-tenths of her journey. On the other hand, if you do remain, as I shall be only a few leagues from you, and as my occupation requires me to travel through the three departments of La Manche, Nord, and Ille-et-Vilaine, I shall ask your permission, when chance takes me to Vitré, to recall myself to your mind, unless the reminder would be disagreeable to you."

" I really do not know how long I shall remain at Vitré, " replied she, graciously rather than curtly. " In reward for services rendered by my father, I have been appointed, as you saw by my passport, post-mistress at Vitré. But I do not think that I shall fill the position myself. I was ruined by the Revolution, and I shall be obliged to take advantage in some way of this favor which the Government has bestowed upon me. I think I shall either sell or rent the position, and thus draw an income from it, without being obliged to exert myself personally."

D'Argentan bowed low upon his horse, as if this confidence were sufficient for him, and as if he were grateful for it to one who, after all, was under no obligation to bestow it upon him.

This was an opening which permitted the conversation to enter upon all those neutral regions which adjoin the private territory of the heart, but do not form part of it.

Of what could they better speak, going, as they were, the one to Vitré and the other to Dinan, than of the Chouans, who were desolating the three or four departments which make a part of the old province of Brittany?

Mademoiselle Rotrou expressed great fear of falling into the hands of the men who were called " brigands."

But instead of sharing this fear, or adding to it, D'Argentan declared that he would be the happiest man in the world if such a thing should happen to his travelling companion; for he had been a fellow-student of Cadoudal at Rennes, and this would give him an opportunity to find out whether the famous chief of the Chouans was as stanch in his friendships as people said.

Mademoiselle Rotrou became dreamy, and allowed the conversation to droop; then after a moment she uttered a weary sigh, saying, —

" Certainly, I am more fatigued than I thought I was. I believe I shall stop at Angers, if only for a night."

CHAPTER XX.

THE BEST OF FRIENDS MUST PART.

MONSIEUR D'ARGENTAN felt a twofold satisfaction when he heard that Mademoiselle Rotrou was to stop at Angers. A man had to be as well accustomed to horses, and as fine a rider as Monsieur d'Argentan was, in order to take a ride like that which he had just taken from Paris to Angers, even supposing that he had not come from a greater distance than Paris without pause. He therefore resolved to stop at Angers also, both to find needed rest and to improve his acquaintance with his new friend.

Monsieur d'Argentan, notwithstanding the fact that his passport indicated a provincial residence, was so perfect a specimen of refined manners that the Parisian stood revealed in him; and, more than that, a Parisian of the aristocratic quarter of Paris.

His astonishment, therefore, had been great, although he had not betrayed it, when, after exchanging a few words with a young and beautiful person who was travelling alone, and under the protection of a passport signed by Barras, which was in itself significant, he found that the conversation did not bring them into more intimate relations, and that the acquaintance went no farther.

When he had left the police commissioner's office and had ridden on ahead, knowing that he was going in the same direction as the young traveller, whose passport he had heard read, although he did not know how she was travelling, he had promised himself that he would make the journey in her company. But when in the morning he was overtaken by a handsome travelling carriage, and found that it served as a nest for the charming bird of passage whom he had left behind, he had repeated his promise to himself, doubly resolved to keep it.

But, as we have seen, Mademoiselle de Fargas, while replying civilly to his advances, had not permitted him to put so much as the toe of his boot upon the step of the carriage into which he had had for a moment the hope of introducing his entire body.

Angers and a night's rest came in very fortunately, therefore, to remove a little of his fatigue, and to permit him, if the thing were possible, to advance another step in the intimacy of the unapproachable post-mistress before the journey should be finished.

They reached Angers about five o'clock in the evening.

A league before they entered the city, the horseman approached the carriage, and said, bowing to his saddle-bow,—

"Would it be indiscreet to ask if you are hungry?"

Diana, who saw what her travelling companion was driving at, made a movement of her lips which resembled a smile.

"Yes, Monsieur, it would be indiscreet," she replied.

"Indeed! and why?"

"I will tell you. Because I should no sooner have replied that I was hungry than you would have asked permission to go and order my dinner; I should no sooner have given you that permission than you would have asked to have it served at the same table with your own: in other words, you would invite me to take dinner with you, which, as you see, would be an indiscretion."

"Really, Mademoiselle," said Monsieur d'Argentan, "your logic is terrifying, and, if I may say so, it bears little resemblance to the period in which we live."

"That," retorted Diana, frowning, "is because few women find themselves in a situation like mine. You see, Monsieur, that I am in deep mourning."

"Are you in mourning for a husband? Your passport describes you as unmarried, and not as a widow."

"I am unmarried and young, Monsieur, if one can remain young after five years of solitude and misfortune. My last relative, my only friend, he who was everything in the world to me, has just died. You may rest assured, sir, that in leaving Paris you have not left your fascinations behind you; but my heart is so sad that I cannot consistently recognize the merits of those who choose to address me, and who see that I am young in spite of my grief, and passably fair in spite of my mourning. And now I am as hungry as one can be who drinks tears, and lives on memory instead of hope. I will dine, as usual, in the same room with you, assuring you that under any other circumstances, were it only out of gratitude to you for your attentions to me throughout the journey, I would have dined at the same table with you."

The young man rode as near to her as the rapidly moving carriage would permit.

"Madame," he said, "after such a frank avowal, it remains for me only to say that if, in your unprotected condition, you need the help of a friend, he is here at your hand; and although he is a friend of the high-road, I promise you that he is as true a one as you will find."

And setting off at a gallop, he went, as he had offered, to order dinner for both.

But as the hour of Mademoiselle Rotrou's arrival coincided with that of the *table d'hôte*, Monsieur d'Argentan had the delicacy to say that his companion would dine in her own room, even at the risk of not seeing her again.

At the *table d'hôte* nöthing was talked about save the six thousand men who had been sent by the Directory to bring Cadoudal to terms.

During the last two weeks, Cadoudal, with the five or six hundred men whom he had collected, had dealt blows more audacious than the most adventurous generals had ever attempted in La Vendée and Brittany, in the blood‧iest times of the war in those provinces.

Monsieur d'Argentan, the tax-collector of Dinan, inquired persistently what route the little corps had taken.

The reply was that there was the utmost uncertainty on that point, because the man who appeared, although clothed with no military rank, to give orders to the column, had said at that very hôtel that the road which he should take would depend upon information which he was to receive at the little village of Châteaubriant, and that it would depend upon the whereabouts of him he was to fight whether he plunged into Morbihan or skirted the hills of Maine.

When dinner was over, Monsieur d'Argentan sent to ask Mademoiselle Rotrou whether she would do him the honor to receive him, as he wished to make a communication which he believed to be of some importance.

She replied that she would do so with pleasure.

Five minutes later, he entered her room, where she received him seated near an open window.

Mademoiselle Rotrou pointed to an arm-chair, and signed to him to be seated.

He thanked her with a slight bow, and contented himself with leaning upon the back of the chair.

" As you might think, Mademoiselle," he said, " that regret at parting from you so soon has led me to seek a pretext for seeing you again, I will tell you without delay what brings me to you. I do not know whether or not you have any reason for desiring to meet, a hundred leagues from Paris, these extra-judicial agents of Government, who become more tyrannical the farther they get from the centre of power. What I do know is that we are about to come upon a whole column of republican troops, led by one of those wretches whose business it is to look for heads for the Government. It seems that to be shot is thought too noble a death for the Chouans, and that the guillotine is to be naturalized on the soil of Brittany.

"At Châteaubriant, five or six leagues from here, the troops will have to choose between two roads, and either march straight to the sea, or go between the Côtes-du-Nord and Morbihan. Have you any reason to fear them? If so, whichever road you take, and even if you pass the entire column from beginning to end, I will remain with you. If, on the contrary, you have nothing to fear (and I hope you will not mistake the sentiment which prompts the question), as I have myself only a moderate liking for tricolored cockades, envoys extraordinary, and guillotines,—you see that I am frank,—I will avoid the column, and will take, to get to Dinan, whichever road they do not take."

"First, let me thank you with all my heart, Monsieur," said Mademoiselle Rotrou, "and assure you of my gratitude; but I am not going to Dinan, as you are, but to Vitré. If the column has taken the road to Rennes, which is that to Dinan, I shall have no fear of meeting it; if, on the contrary, it has taken the road to Vitré, it will not deter me from taking that road also. I have not much more liking than you for tricolored cockades, envoys extraordinary, and guillotines; but I have no reason to fear them. I will say more: I was told of the march of these men, and of that which they have with them; and as they were to cross a part of Brittany which was occupied by Cadoudal, I am authorized, in case of necessity, to put myself under their protection. All will therefore depend upon the decision of their leader at Châteaubriant. If they continue on the road to Vitré, I shall regret being obliged to part with you at the parting of the roads; if, on the contrary, they take the road to Rennes, and your dislike to them is so great that you are unwilling to meet them, I shall owe to that dislike the pleasure of continuing my journey with you to my destination."

Monsieur d'Argentan's explanation when he entered forbade his lingering now that his errand was done.

He bowed and went out while Mademoiselle Rotrou was rising from her chair.

The next morning, at six o'clock, they started together, after the customary greetings. At Châteaubriant they learned that the column had left there an hour before, and had taken the road to Vitré.

The two travellers were therefore obliged to separate. Monsieur d'Argentan approached Mademoiselle Rotrou for the last time, renewed his offer of service, and said farewell in a voice full of emotion.

Mademoiselle Rotrou raised her eyes to the handsome young man, and being too much a woman of the world herself not to be grateful for the respectful manner in which he had behaved, gave him her hand to kiss.

Monsieur d'Argentan mounted his horse, and said to the postilion, who was riding ahead, "Road to Rennes!" while Mademoiselle Rotrou's carriage, obedient to the direction given in a voice as calm as usual, took the road to Vitré.

CHAPTER XXI.

CITIZEN FRANÇOIS GOULIN.

MADEMOISELLE ROTROU, or rather Diana de Fargas, fell into a profound revery after leaving Châteaubriant. In the then state of her heart it was, or at least she believed it to be, insensible to all tender sentiments, particularly to love. But beauty, refinement, and courtesy will always exercise upon a woman of breeding a sufficient influence to make her dream, if not love.

Mademoiselle de Fargas therefore dreamed of her fellow-traveller, and for the first time a faint suspicion occurred to her. She began to ask herself how it was that a man so well protected by the triple signatures of Barras, Rewbell, and La Réveillère-Lepaux could feel such unconquerable repugnance towards the agent of a Government which honored him with such noteworthy confidence.

She forgot that she herself, whose sympathies were far from being with the Revolutionary Government, was travelling under its direct protection; and even supposing Monsieur d'Argentan to be an aristocrat, as some words of his in their last interview had led her to suspect, it was possible that circumstances similar to her own had made him avail himself of a protection which he might be somewhat ashamed to claim.

Then, too, Diana had noticed that Monsieur d'Argentan, when he got off his horse, always took with

him a valise whose weight was far from being pro-
portioned to its size.

Although the young man was strong and vigorous,
and although, to avert suspicion, he often carried the
valise with one hand, it was easy to see that while he
pretended to play with it, as if it contained only a
change of clothing, it taxed his strength much more
than he chose to have it appear.

Was it money that he was carrying? If so, he was
a curious kind of tax-gatherer, to be carrying money
from Paris to Vitré, instead of sending it from Vitré
to Paris.

Then, although in those days of overturning it was
not rare to see social heresies, Mademoiselle de Fargas
was too familiar with the different rounds of the ladder
of society not to know that it was contrary to the habits
of an insignificant tax-gatherer of a canton at the extremity of France to ride horseback like an English
gentleman, and to express himself with a courtesy
which had about it an indelible perfume of gentle
birth, especially towards the close of a period when
everybody had put on a varnish of vulgarity in order
to make himself agreeable to the powers that were.

She asked herself — without any flutter of the heart,
however — who the unknown could be, and what motive
could have induced him to travel with a passport which
was certainly not his own.

It was a curious coincidence that when Monsieur
d'Argentan left Diana de Fargas, he asked himself the
same questions about her.

Suddenly, when she reached the top of the hill which
was just at the entrance of the post-town of La Guerche,
and from which the road was visible for several leagues,
Diana started, dazzled by the gleam of gun-barrels, which

reflected the light of the sun. The road looked like an immense river of flashing steel.

It was the republican column, whose advance-guard had already reached La Guerche, while the remainder was half a league behind.

Everything was of importance in these troublous times; and as Diana paid her attendants well, the postilion asked her whether he should take his place in the rear of the column, or drive along the side of the road, and, without slackening his pace, reach La Guerche in this manner.

Mademoiselle de Fargas told him to put up the top of the carriage, so that she would n t become an object of curiosity, and to continue, without slackening his speed.

The postilion executed her orders, and then, remounting, resumed the smart pace at which the horses of the Department of Posts used to make their two leagues an hour.

The result w s that Mademoiselle de Fargas duly arrived at the gates of La Guerche; and when we say "gates," we mean the beginning of the street which ran into the Châteaubriant road.

There was an obstruction at this gate.

An immense machine, drawn by twelve horses, and placed upon a truck too large to pass between the gate-posts, blocked the entrance to the street.

Mademoiselle de Fargas, seeing that her carriage had stopped, and not knowing the reason, put her head out through the open window, and said, —

"What is the matter, Postilion?"

"The matter is, Citizeness," he replied, "that our streets are not wide enough for the instruments that they want to carry through them; and they will have to dig up one of the posts before Monsieur Guillotin's machine can enter La Guerche."

And, in fact, as François Goulin, commissioner-extraordinary of the government, had decided to travel for the edification of towns and villages, it happened, as the postilion had said, that the street was too narrow, not for the machine itself, but for the sort of rolling platform upon which it was set up.

Diana looked at the hideous thing which was obstructing the road, and realizing that it must be the scaffold, which she had never seen, she quickly turned her head away, exclaiming, —

"Oh, how horrible!"

"How horrible! how horrible!" repeated a voice in the crowd. "I should like to know who the aristocrat is who speaks with so little respect of the instrument which has done more for human civilization than anything else since the invention of the plough."

"It is I, Monsieur," said Mademoiselle de Fargas; "and if you have anything to do with it, I should be very much obliged to you if you would aid my carriage to enter La Guerche as soon as possible. I am in haste."

"Ah, you are in haste!" said a little dry, thin man, dressed in the ignoble *carmagnole*, or jacket, which had ceased to be worn for the last year or two. He was pale with anger. "Ah, you are in haste! Well, you will have to get out of your carriage first, Aristocrat; and you will go on foot, if we let you go at all."

"Postilion," said Diana, "lower the top of the carriage."

The postilion obeyed. The young girl threw aside her veil, disclosing her marvellous face.

"Can it be that I am talking with Citizen François Goulin?" she said mockingly.

"I believe you are making fun of me," cried the little man, darting towards the carriage, and arranging, as he went, his red cap, which had also been out of fashion for some time, but which Citizen François Goulin had resolved to bring into style again in the provinces. "Well, yes, it is I. What have you to say to Citizen Goulin?"

And he stretched out his hand towards her, as if to take her by the throat.

Diana sprang to the other side of the carriage.

"In the first place," she said, "if you must touch me, which I do not think at all necessary, put on gloves. I detest dirty hands."

Citizen Goulin called four men, probably to give them the order to seize the beautiful traveller; but in the mean time, from a secret pocket of her satchel, Diana had drawn the special safe-conduct of Barras.

"I beg your pardon, Citizen," she said, still mockingly. "Do you know how to read?"

Goulin uttered an angry exclamation.

"You do?" she continued. "Well, then, read this; but take care not to crumple the paper too much, for it may be useful to me, if I am unlucky enough to meet many such boors as you."

And she held out the paper to him.

It contained only these few words: —

In the name of the Directory, the civil and military authorities are ordered to protect Mademoiselle Rotrou in her mission, and to afford her armed assistance, if she claims it, under penalty of dismissal.

BARRAS.

Paris, the —.

Citizen François Goulin read and re-read the safe-conduct of Mademoiselle de Fargas.

Then, like a bear who is forced by his master, whip in hand, to make a bow, he said, —

" These are singular times when women — and women, too, in satin dresses and carriages — are permitted to give orders to citizens who bear the signs of republicanism and equality. Since we have only changed our king, and you have a pass from King Barras, you may go, Citizeness; but you may rest assured that I shall not forget your name, and if ever you fall into my hands — "

" Postilion, see if the road is clear," said Mademoiselle de Fargas, in her usual tone. " I have no further business with Monsieur."

The road was not yet clear, but by making a *détour*, the carriage could pass.

Mademoiselle de Fargas with great difficulty succeeded in reaching the post-house, the roads being crowded with republicans. There she was obliged to stop. She had eaten nothing since leaving Châteaubriant; and as she wished to sleep at Vitré, it was absolutely necessary that she should have something to eat at La Guerche. She asked for a room, and something to eat to be served there. Scarcely had she begun her breakfast, however, when she was told that the colonel who commanded the column asked permission to pay his respects to her.

She replied that she had not the honor of the colonel's acquaintance, and that unless he had something of importance to say to her, she begged him to excuse her if she did not receive him.

The colonel insisted, saying that he thought it his duty to warn her of something which he alone knew, and which might be of great importance to her.

She intimated that she was ready to receive him, and Colonel Hulot was announced.

CHAPTER XXII.

COLONEL HULOT.

COLONEL HULOT was a man of thirty-eight or forty. Having been a soldier for ten years, in the time of the late king, without having been able to rise to the rank even of corporal, he had, as soon as the Republic was proclaimed, earned one grade after another at the point of his sword, like the brave soldier that he was.

He had heard of the altercation which had taken place at the gates of the town between Citizen François Goulin and the pretended Mademoiselle Rotrou.

"Citizeness," he said, as he entered, "I have heard of what passed between you and our commissioner from the Directory. I need not tell you that we old soldiers have no very great affection for these guillotine fellows, who follow the armies to cut off heads, as if powder and ball, fire and sword, did not give Death sufficient feeding-ground. Hearing that you had stopped at the post-house, I came to you with the sole intention of congratulating you upon the manner in which you treated Citizen Goulin. When men tremble before such knaves, it behooves women to make them understand that they are only the fag-end of the human race, and that they are not worthy of being called *canaille* by a beautiful mouth like yours. And now, Citizeness, have you need of Colonel Hulot? If so, command him."

"Thanks, Colonel," replied Diana. "If I had anything to fear or to ask, I would accept your offer with the same frankness with which you have made it. I am going to Vitré, which is the end of my journey; and as there is only one more stage to be made, I think that nothing more will happen to me on this one than has happened on all that have gone before."

"Hum!" said Colonel Hulot. "I know that it is only five leagues from here to Vitré; but I also know that the road is a narrow pass, bordered on both sides by thickets of thorn and furze, which seem made expressly to serve as ambush for Messieurs the Chouans. My own opinion is that in spite of our more than respectable numbers, we shall not reach Vitré without being attacked. If you are as thoroughly vouched for by Citizen Barras as they say, you must be a person of some importance. Now, one who is protected by Barras has everything to fear from Master Cadoudal, who does not feel for the Directory all the respect which it deserves.

"Moreover, I have been personally notified by an official letter, and as leader of this column, in whose neighborhood you now are, that a citizeness named Mademoiselle Rotrou might perhaps claim the favor of travelling under the protection of our bayonets. When I say 'claim the favor,' I merely quote the words of the letter; for in this case the favor would be all on my side."

"I am Mademoiselle Rotrou, Monsieur, and I am grateful to Monsieur Barras for his kind remembrance; but, as I have already said, my precautions are taken; and some claims to consideration, which I may call to the attention of the leader of the Chouans himself, make me think that I run no danger. However,

Colonel, I am none the less grateful to you; and I am particularly glad that you share my antipathy for the miserable being whom they have given you for a travelling companion."

"Oh, as for us," rejoined Hulot, "we are not at all afraid of him. We are no longer in the times of Saint-Just and Lebon, which I regret with all my heart, I must confess. They were brave men, who exposed themselves to the same dangers as we; who fought with us, and who, remaining on the field of battle at the risk of being taken or shot, had the right to proceed against those who abandoned them. The soldiers did not love them, but they respected them; and when they stretched forth their hands over a head, the men understood that no one had the right to rescue that head from the vengeance of the Republic. But as for our François Goulin, who will run away with his guillotine at the first shot he hears, there is not one of the six thousand men whom I command who would let him touch with his finger the head of one of our officers."

Just then Mademoiselle Rotrou was informed that her carriage was ready.

"Citizeness," said the colonel, "it is part of my duty to clear the road along which my column is about to pass. I have with me a little corps of cavalry, composed of three hundred hussars and two hundred chasseurs, and I am about to send them — not for you, but for myself — over the road which you are to follow. If you have need to apply to the officer who commands them, he will be under orders to do his utmost to serve you, and even, if you desire it, to escort you as far as Vitré."

"I thank you, Monsieur," replied Mademoiselle de Fargas, giving her hand to the old soldier, "but I should never forgive myself if I were to compromise the precious lives of the defenders of the Republic to assure the safety of a life as humble and of as little importance as mine."

At these words Diana went down, accompanied by the colonel, who gallantly presented her his hand to assist her to enter her carriage.

The postilion was waiting on his horse.

" Road to Vitré," said Diana.

The postilion started.

The soldiers drew aside as the carriage passed; and as there was not one of them who did not know in what fashion she had treated François Goulin, compliments, expressed somewhat coarsely, to be sure, but none the less sincerely, were not spared her.

As she set out, she heard the colonel shout, —

" To horse, chasseurs and hussars! "

And from three or four different points she heard the " boots and saddles " sounded.

When they had driven through La Guerche, and were some fifty paces from the village, the postilion stopped the carriage, as if to adjust some part of the harness, and approaching the carriage door, inquired, —

" Perhaps the Citizeness has business with *them?* "

" With *them?* " repeated Diana, astonished.

The postilion winked.

" Why, yes, with *them!* "

" Whom do you mean? "

" With the friends, of course. They are there, — at the right and left of the road."

He imitated the cry of the screech-owl.

" No," replied Diana, " go on; but when you have reached the foot of the hill, stop."

" Bah! " muttered the postilion to himself, as he

remounted his horse. "You will stop all alone, little mother."

They were then at the top of a hill which descended, sloping gently, for more than half a league. On both sides of the road were thick growths of thorn and furze. In some places the bushes were dense enough to conceal two or three men.

The postilion started his horses at their ordinary pace, and went down the hill, singing an old Breton song in the Karnac dialect.

From time to time he raised his voice, as if his song contained signals, and as if the people to whom they were addressed were near enough to hear them.

Diana, who understood that she was surrounded by Chouans, looked with all her eyes, without uttering a word. This postilion might be a spy placed to watch her, by Goulin; and she did not forget his threat, if she should give him any advantage over her, and should fall into his hands.

Just as she reached the foot of the hill, where a little path crossed the road, a man on horseback sprang from the woods to stop the carriage; but when he saw that it was occupied only by a lady, he raised his hat.

The postilion, at sight of the horseman, turned around on his horse to say to her in a low tone, —

"Do not be afraid. That is General Roundhead."

"Madame," said the rider, with the greatest politeness, "I believe that you came from La Guerche, and probably from Châteaubriant."

"Yes, Monsieur," she replied, leaning forward with interest upon the side of the vehicle, without showing any fear, although she saw more than fifty riders in ambush on the cross-road.

"Do your political opinions or your conscience permit

you to give me a few details concerning the strength
of the republican column which you have left behind
you ? "

" Both my political opinions and my social conscience
permit me to do so," the fair traveller replied, with a
smile. " The column consists of six thousand men who
are returning from prisons in England and Holland.
They are commanded by a brave man named Colonel
Hulot; but they have in their train a miserable wretch
whom they call François Goulin, and an ugly machine
which they call the guillotine. When I entered the
town, I had an altercation with the aforesaid François
Goulin, who has promised me that I shall make the
acquaintance of his instrument if I ever fall into his
hands, — which made me so popular among the republican soldiers, who detest their travelling companion
neither more nor less than you and I do, that Colonel
Hulot absolutely insisted upon making my acquaintance,
and giving me an escort to Vitré, for fear I should fall
into the hands of the Chouans. Now, as I left Paris
with no other purpose than to fall into the hands of the
Chouans, I refused the escort, told the postilion to go
on ahead, and here I am, delighted to have met you,
General Cadoudal, and to express to you the admiration which I feel for your courage, and the esteem
with which your character inspires me. As for the
escort which was to have accompanied me, there it is,
just coming out of the town. It consists of three
hundred chasseurs and two hundred hussars. Kill as
few of these brave fellows as you can, and you will
please me."

" I will not conceal from you, Madame," replied
Cadoudal, " that there will be an encounter between
my men and this detachment. Will you go on as far

as Vitré, where I will come after the fight, anxious to learn more definitely the motives of a journey for which you have given me only an improbable cause ? "

" It is the true one, however," replied Diana; " and as a proof, if you will permit me, instead of continuing my journey, I will be present at the engagement. Since I have come to join your army, this will serve as my apprenticeship."

Cadoudal looked at the little column, which seemed to increase in size as it drew nearer, and addressing the postilion, said, —

" Place Madame where she will be in no danger; and if we are beaten, explain to the Blues that I, to her great despair, prevented her from continuing her journey."

Then, saluting Diana, —

" Madame," said he, " pray for the good cause while I go to fight for it."

And darting down the path, he rejoined his ambushed companions.

.

CHAPTER XXIII.

THE ENGAGEMENT.

CADOUDAL exchanged a few words with his companions, and four of them, who were not mounted, and who acted as officers to carry orders into the heather and under-growth, slipped away immediately, and passing between the thorn-bushes, reached the foot of two enormous oaks, whose sturdy branches and thick foliage made a rampart against the sun.

These two oaks stood at the extremity of the species of avenue which was formed by the road between the two slopes, coming from the town to the cross-road.

When they reached the spot, they waited, ready to execute some manœuvre, which no one who did not know the general's plan of battle could guess.

Diana's carriage had been drawn from the middle of the road into the path; and she herself, thirty paces away from the carriage, was stationed upon a little knoll crowned with small trees, from the midst of which she could see all, without being seen.

The chasseurs and hussars advanced cautiously, at a foot pace. An advance-guard of ten men preceded them by thirty paces, and, like the rest of the division, marched with the greatest caution.

When the last man had left the town, a shot was heard, and one of the men in the rear-guard fell.

This was a signal. Immediately the two crests of the ravine which formed the road blazed with fire.

The Blues sought in vain for the enemy who had attacked them.   They saw the fire and smoke, and they felt the shot, but they could distinguish neither the weapon nor the man who carried it.   Confusion soon seized them when they found themselves surrounded by this invisible danger.   Each one sought, not to escape death, but to give death for death.   Some retraced their steps, others forced their horses to climb the slope; but as soon as a man's head and shoulders appeared above the crest, he was shot at close quarters and fell backwards, overturning his horse with him, like the Amazons in Rubens' Battle of Thermodon.

Others again, and these were most numerous, pushed forward, hoping to pass the ambuscade, and thus escape the net into which they had fallen.   But Cadoudal, who seemed to have foreseen this moment, and waited for it, when he saw them put their horses to a gallop, gave his horse the spur, and followed by his forty men, dashed out to meet them.

They fought then along the road for the length of a kilometre.

Those who had attempted to turn back, had found the way barred by Chouans, who discharged their guns almost in their faces, and forced them to return.

Those who attempted to scale the slope found death there, and fell back, with their horses, falling across and obstructing the road.

Finally, those who had pushed forward met Cadoudal and his men.

But after fighting a few minutes, these last appeared to give way, and turned tail.

The greater part of the cavalry of the Blues then set off in pursuit; but scarcely had the last Chouan passed the two oaks which were guarded by the four men, when they began to push with all their strength, and the two giants, which had previously been almost separated at their bases by the axe, bent towards each other, and with crashing branches fell, with a tremendous noise, upon the road, which they closed with an impassable barrier. The Republicans were following the Whites so closely that two of their number, together with their horses, were crushed by the falling trees.

The same manœuvre was accomplished at the other end of the pass. Two trees, falling across the road and interlacing their branches, formed a barrier like that which had just closed up the other end.

Thus, men and horses were caught as in a huge arena; and each Chouan could choose his man, aim at his ease, and bring him down without fail.

Cadoudal and his forty horsemen discarded their horses, which were now useless, and, rifle in hand, were about to take part in the fight, when Mademoiselle de Fargas, who was watching the sanguinary drama with all the ardor of which her lion-like nature was capable, suddenly heard the gallop of a horse on the road from Vitré to La Guerche. She turned quickly, and recognized the man with whom she had travelled.

When he saw Georges and his companions on the point of taking part in the fight, he attracted their attention by cries of, "Stop! Wait for me!"

And no sooner had he joined them, amidst shouts of welcome, than he leaped from his horse, which he gave to a Chouan to hold, threw himself upon Cadoudal's neck, took a rifle, filled his pockets with cartridges, and, followed by twenty men, Cadoudal taking the other twenty, darted into the thicket which lined the left side of the road, while the general and his companions disappeared on the right side.

A twofold increase in the fusillade announced the reinforcement which had come to the Whites.

Mademoiselle de Fargas was too much occupied with what was passing before her to pay particular attention to Monsieur d'Argentan's conduct.   She understood simply that the pretended tax-gatherer of Dinan was really a disguised royalist, — which explained why he was bringing money from Paris to Brittany, instead of sending it from Brittany to Paris.

The heroic efforts which were now made by this little band of five hundred men would furnish matter for a whole epic poem.

Their courage was all the greater since, as we have said, they were fighting against an invisible danger, calling to it, defying it, and howling with rage that it did not stand up before them.   Nothing could make the Chouans change their deadly tactics.   Death flew whistling by, and the Blues could see nothing but the smoke, and hear nothing but the report.   A man would throw up his arms and fall backward from his horse, and the frightened, riderless animal would wildly leap the thicket and gallop until an invisible hand stopped him, and tied his bridle to the branch of a tree.

Here and there in the fields could be seen one of these horses rearing, pulling at his bridle, and trying to escape from the strange master who had just made him prisoner.

The butchery lasted for an hour.

At the end of that time drums were heard beating the charge.

It was the republican infantry coming to the help of its cavalry.

Colonel Hulot commanded it in person.

His primary care, with the infallible glance of the

veteran, was to get a correct idea of the ground, and to open an exit for the unfortunates who were shut up in the sort of tunnel which the road had become.

He had the horses unharnessed from the gun-carriages, the artillery being useless for the sort of contest that he was about to engage in. The horses were then attached to the tops of the fallen trees, which were pulled from their transverse position and made to lie alongside the road, thus opening a means of retreat for the cavalry. Then he caused five hundred men to charge upon each side of the road with levelled bayonets, just as if the enemy were in sight. Then he ordered the most expert sharp-shooters to return shot for shot, — that is to say, whenever a puff of smoke appeared, they were to fire straight at it, since it denoted that a man was in ambush at that spot. This was the only possible way to reply to the fusillade of the Whites, who, almost always shooting from some shelter, never showed themselves except at the moment of taking aim. Habit and, above all, the necessity for defence had made many of the republican soldiers exceedingly skilful at this quick exchange of shots.

Sometimes the men upon whom they retaliated thus were killed outright. Sometimes, when they fired by guesswork, they were only wounded. · In that case, they would not move. Other shots caused theirs to be for-gotten, and often the soldiers passed very near them without discovering them. The Chouans were noted for their marvellous courage in stifling groans which insufferable agony would have forced from any other soldier.

The fight lasted until the first shades of night fell. Diana, who did not lose a single incident, fumed with impatience at not being able to take part in it. She would have liked to be dressed as a man, to be armed with a gun, and to rush upon the republicans, whom she hated. But she was made helpless by her costume and by the lack of a weapon.

About seven o'clock, Colonel Hulot caused the retreat to be sounded. In this kind of warfare day is dangerous, but night is more than dangerous, — it is fatal.

The sound of the trumpets and drums announcing the retreat redoubled the ardor of the Chouans. To leave the battle-field and return to the town was an avowal on the part of the republicans that they were beaten.

They were followed by shots to the very gates of La Guerche, leaving three or four hundred dead on the battle-field, ignorant of the loss which the Chouans might have sustained, and without a single prisoner, — to the intense chagrin of François Goulin, who had succeeded in getting his machine inside the town, and had taken it to the other end, in order to be near the field of battle.

All his efforts had been useless; and François Goulin, in despair, had taken up his lodging in a house where he need not lose sight of his precious instrument.

Since they had left Paris, neither officer nor soldier had chosen to lodge in the same house with the commissioner-extraordinary. He had been given a guard of twelve soldiers, and that was all. Four men guarded the guillotine.

CHAPTER XXIV.

PORTIA.

THE day had had no material result of any great importance for Cadoudal and his men, but the moral result was immense.

All the great Vendean chiefs had disappeared: Stofflet and Charette were dead; the Abbé Bernier had submitted, as we have said; and, finally, by the genius and courage of General Hoche, La Vendée was pacified. And we have seen how Hoche himself, by offering men and money to the Directory, had disturbed Bonaparte, away off in the centre of Italy.

Of the Chouannerie and La Vendée, the Chouannerie alone remained. Cadoudal was the only one of the chiefs who had refused to bend the knee.

He had published his manifesto, and announced that he had taken up arms again. Besides the troops which still remained in La Vendée and in Brittany, six thousand more men had been sent against him.

Cadoudal, with a thousand men, had not only kept at bay six thousand veterans who had had five years experience of active warfare, but he had driven them back to the town whence they had come, and had killed three or four hundred of them.

The new Breton insurrection thus opened with a victory.

When the Blues were fairly within the town, and had posted their sentinels, Cadoudal, who meditated a new expedition for the night, also ordered a retreat.

Through the thickets of furze and brier on each side of the road, above which, now that they were marching without disguise, they towered a full head, the victorious Chouans could be seen coming joyfully back, calling to each other, and crowding around one of their number who was playing the bagpipe, as soldiers follow the trumpets in a regiment.

The bagpipe was their trumpet.

At the bottom of the slope, at the place where the overturned trees had formed a barricade which the republican cavalry had not been able to pass, and where Cadoudal and D'Argentan had separated to take part in the fight, they met again on their return.

They were overjoyed to meet again, for they had scarcely had time for a hurried greeting before.

D'Argentan, who had not fought for a long time, had gone into the battle with such good will that he had got a bayonet-thrust in his arm. He had therefore thrown his coat over his shoulder, and had his arm in a sling made of his bloody handkerchief.

Diana also came down from the little knoll, and walked up to the two friends with her firm, masculine step.

"What!" said Cadoudal, perceiving her. "Did you remain, my brave Amazon?"

D'Argentan uttered an exclamation of surprise, for he recognized Mademoiselle Rotrou, the post-mistress of Vitré.

"Permit me," said Cadoudal, still addressing Diana, and indicating his companion with his hand, "to present to you one of my best friends."

"Monsieur d'Argentan?" said Diana, smiling. "I already have the honor of his acquaintance; indeed, we are quite old acquaintances, of three days' standing. We travelled all the way from Paris together."

"Then it would have been for him to present me to you, if I had not already done it myself."

He added, addressing Diana,—

"Are you going to Vitré, Mademoiselle?"

"Monsieur d'Argentan," said Diana, without replying to Cadoudal's question, "on the journey, you offered to act as my intercessor with General Cadoudal if I had any favor to ask of him."

"I was under the impression then, Madame," replied D'Argentan, "that you did not know the general. But when one has once seen you, you do not require any intercessor; and I will answer for it that whatever you ask will be granted by my friend here."

"That, Monsieur, is pure gallantry, and a trick to escape from your promise to me. I positively summon you to keep your word."

"Speak, Madame. I am ready to second your request with all my power," replied D'Argentan.

"I want to join the general's army," replied Diana, tranquilly.

"In what capacity?" asked D'Argentan.

"In the capacity of volunteer," replied Diana, coldly.

The two friends looked at each other.

"You hear, Cadoudal?" said D'Argentan.

Cadoudal's forehead grew grave, and his whole face took a stern expression.

Then, after a moment of silence, he said,—

"Madame, the proposal is a serious one, and deserves serious reflection. I will tell you something odd. I was at first destined for the Church; and I took in my heart all my ordination vows, and I have never broken one of them.

"I do not doubt that I should have in you a charming aide-de-camp, of undoubted bravery. I believe that women are as brave as men. But in our religious country, and especially in old Brittany, there exist prejudices which often force us to discourage too great devotion. Several of my *confrères* have had in their camps the sisters or daughters of assassinated royalists; but to such are due the protection and asylum which they demand."

"And how do you know," exclaimed Diana, "that I also am not the daughter or the sister of an assassinated royalist, perhaps both, and that I have not doubly the right to be received among you, of which you spoke just now?"

"In that case," asked D'Argentan, with a mocking smile, and joining in the conversation, "how does it happen that you carry a passport signed by Barras, entitling you to a government position at Vitré?"

"Will you be good enough to show me your own, Monsieur d'Argentan?" said Diana.

D'Argentan took it laughingly from the pocket of the jacket, which was hung over his shoulder, and gave it to Diana.

She unfolded it, and read, —

Give free passage over the territory of the Republic to Citizen Sebastien Argentan, tax-collector at Dinan.

    Signed: BARRAS, REWBELL, LA RÉVEILLÈRE-LEPAUX.

"And will you be good enough to tell me, Monsieur," said Diana, "how, as a friend of General Cadoudal, and fighting against the Republic, you have the right to free passage over the territory of the Republic, in the character of tax-collector of Dinan? Let us not simply raise our masks, Monsieur, let us take them off altogether.",

"Well answered, upon my word," said Cadoudal, who was deeply interested by Diana's coolness and persistence.

" Come, speak! How did you get that passport? Explain it to Mademoiselle. Perhaps then she will deign to explain to us how she came by hers."

" Ah," said D'Argentan, laughing, " that is a secret which I dare not reveal before our prudish friend Cadoudal; however, if you insist, Mademoiselle, at the risk of making him blush, I will say that there lives in the Rue des Colonnes, at Paris, near the Théâtre Feydeau, a certain Aurélie de Saint-Amour, to whom Citizen Barras can refuse nothing, and who, for her part, can refuse me nothing."

" And furthermore," continued Cadoudal, " the name of Argentan upon his passport conceals another, which is sufficient of itself to give him free passage among all Chouans, Vendeans, and royalists who wear the white cockade at home or abroad. Your travelling companion, Mademoiselle, who has now nothing to conceal, having nothing to fear, and whom, consequently, I now present to you under his real name, is not Monsieur d'Argentan, but Coster de Saint-Victor; and had he given no pledges heretofore, the wound which he has just received in fighting for our sacred cause — "

" If it needs only a wound to prove one's devotion," said Diana, coldly, " that is a very easy matter."

" What do you mean? " asked Cadoudal.

" This! " replied Diana.

And drawing from her belt the sharp dagger which had given her brother his death-blow, she struck her arm so violently, in the same place where Coster de Saint-Victor had received his wound, that the blade entered on one side and came out on the other.

" And as for the name," she continued, addressing the stupefied young men, " although my name is not Coster de Saint-Victor, it is Diana de Fargas! ·My father was assassinated four years ago, and my brother a week ago."

Coster de Saint-Victor started, glanced at the dagger which still remained in her arm, and recognizing it as the one which had in his presence given the death-blow to Lucien, he said solemnly, —

"I can testify that this maiden told the truth when she affirmed that she was as deserving as any orphan daughter or sister of assassinated royalists to be received among us and to form one of our holy army."

Cadoudal held out his hand to her.

"From this moment, Mademoiselle," he said, "if you have no father, I will be your father; if you have no longer a brother, be my sister. I know that there was once a Roman woman who, to reassure her husband, and fearing his weakness, pierced her own right arm with the blade of a knife. Since we live in times when every one is obliged to conceal his own name under another, your name will henceforth be Portia, instead of Diana de Fargas, as in the past; and as you are one of us, and as at the first stroke you have won the rank of leader, when our surgeon has dressed your wound you will attend the council which I am about to hold."

"Thanks, General," replied Diana. "As for the surgeon, I have no more need of his services than has Monsieur Coster de Saint-Victor; for my wound is no more serious than his."

And drawing the dagger from the wound, where it had remained until then, she slit her sleeve with it from top to bottom, revealing her beautiful arm.

Then, addressing Coster de Saint-Victor, she said laughingly, —

"Comrade, be good enough to lend me your cravat."

CHAPTER XXV.

CADOUDAL'S IDEA.

HALF an hour later, the Chouans were encamped in a half circle around the town of La Guerche. They bivouacked in groups of ten, fifteen, or twenty, and had a fire for each group, and were as peacefully cooking their supper as if a gunshot had never been heard from Redon to Cancale.

The cavalry were by themselves, on the borders of a little brook which formed one of the sources of the Seiche. Their horses were saddled, but not bridled, so that the animals as well as the men might enjoy their food.

In the midst of the encampment, under an immense oak, were Cadoudal, Coster de Saint-Victor, Mademoiselle de Fargas, and five or six of the principal Chouans, who, under the pseudonyms of Cœur-de-Roi, Tiffauges, Brise-Bleu, Bénédicité, Branche-d'Or, Monte-à-l'Assaut, and Chante-en-Hiver, deserve that their *noms de guerre* should be handed down to posterity beside that of their leader.

Mademoiselle de Fargas and Coster de Saint-Victor ate with good appetites, using the hand which was not disabled.

Mademoiselle de Fargas had proposed to put her six thousand francs into the common fund, but Cadoudal refused, and received her money only as a deposit.

The six or seven Chouan leaders whom we have named, ate as if they were not sure of being able to eat on the

morrow. But the Whites did not have as many priva·
tions to endure as the republicans, although the latter
had the power to exact contributions.

The Whites, with whom the people of the neighborhood were in entire sympathy, and who paid for whatever they took, lived in comparative abundance.

As for Cadoudal, preoccupied with some thought
which seemed to be struggling for expression, he went
and came silently, having taken nothing save a glass of
water, his ordinary beverage.

He had obtained from Mademoiselle de Fargas all the
information that she could give him concerning François
Goulin and his guillotine.

Suddenly he stopped, and, turning to the group of
Breton leaders, said, —

"I want a volunteer who will go to La Guerche and
get such information as I require."

All rose spontaneously.

"General," said Chante-en-Hiver, "without wronging
my comrades, I think I am better fitted than any one
else to undertake the errand. My brother lives in La
Guerche. I will wait until it is dark, and then I will
go to him. If I am stopped, I shall appeal to him; he will
answer for me, and that will be the end of it. He
knows the town like his own pocket; we will do whatever you want done, and I will bring you your information within an hour."

"Very well," said Cadoudal. "This is what I have
decided to do. You all know that the Blues, to strike
terror among us and to intimidate us, are dragging a
guillotine around with them; and the infamous Goulin is
charged with working it. François Goulin, you will
remember, is the hero of the *noyades* at Nantes. He
and Perdraux were Carrier's tools. They have both

boasted of having drowned more than eight hundred priests. Well, this man, who left these parts and went to Paris to ask, not only impunity, but a reward for his crimes, Providence has sent back to us, that he may expiate them on the spot where they were committed. He has brought the infamous guillotine among us. Let him perish by the foul instrument that he watches over; he is not worthy of a soldier's bullet. Now, we must get possession of him, and we must also carry off the instrument; we must take them both to some place where we are masters, so that the execution may not be interfered with. Chante-en-Hiver is going to La Guerche. He will come back and tell us all about the house where François Goulin lodges, the place where the guillotine stands, and the number of men who guard it. When I know these facts, I have my plan, which I shall explain to you; if you agree to it, we will carry it out this very night."

The chiefs applauded loudly.

" *Pardieu!* " said Coster de Saint-Victor, " I never saw a man guillotined, and I have sworn that I would have nothing to do with the abominable machine until my own turn came to be beheaded; but when François Goulin is brought to book, I promise to be in the front rank of spectators."

" You hear, Chante-en-Hiver? " said Cadoudal.

Chante-en-Hiver did not wait for him to speak twice. He laid aside all his weapons, with the exception of his knife, with which he never parted; then, asking Coster de Saint-Victor to look at his watch, and learning that it was half past eight, he renewed his promise to return at ten o'clock.

Five minutes later he had disappeared.

" Now," said Cadoudal, addressing the remaining

chiefs, " how many horses were taken on the battle-field, with their saddles, and so forth ? "

" Twenty-one, " replied Cœur-de-Roi.   " I counted them myself. "

" Can we find twenty complete chasseur or hussar uniforms ? "

" General, there are nearly a hundred and fifty of the cavalry dead on the field of battle, " replied Branche-d'Or. " We have only to take our choice. "

" We must have twenty hussar's uniforms, of which one must be that of a quartermaster-general or *sous-lieutenant*. "

Branche-d'Or rose, whistled, collected a dozen men, and started off with them.

" I have an idea, " said Coster de Saint-Victor.   " Is there a printing-press at Vitré ? "

" Yes, " replied Cadoudal.   " I had my manifesto printed there day before yesterday.   The manager is a worthy man named Borel, who is entirely with us. "

" I have a good mind, " said Coster, " as I have nothing else to do, to get into Mademoiselle de Fargas' carriage, go to Vitré, and order some placards inviting the people of La Guerche, including the six thousand Blues, to witness the execution, by his own executioner and his own guillotine, of François Goulin, government commissioner.   It would be a good joke, and would amuse our people in the Paris salons. "

" Do it, Coster, " said Cadoudal, gravely.   " Too much publicity and solemnity cannot be employed when God executes justice. "

" Forward, D'Argentan, my friend ! " said Coster, — " only, some one will have to lend me a jacket. "

Cadoudal made a sign, and each one of the leaders pulled off his own to offer it to Coster.

"If the execution takes place," he said, "where will it be?"

"Faith!" replied Cadoudal, "three hundred paces from here, at the top of the hill just in front of us."

"That's all I want to know," said Coster de Saint-Victor.

And, calling the postilion, he said, —

"My friend, as you may take it into your head to object to what I am going to command you to do, I will tell you beforehand that all objections will be useless. Your horses are rested, and they have eaten; you are rested, and you have eaten. You will put the horses to the carriage; and as you cannot return to La Guerche, because the road is obstructed, you will take me to Vitré, to Monsieur Borel the printer. If you agree to do it, you shall have two crowns of six livres each, — not assignats, but crowns. If you refuse, one of these rascals here will take your place, and will naturally receive the two crowns that you would have had."

The postilion took no time for reflection.

"I will go," he said.

"Well," said Coster, "as you show a proper spirit, here is one crown in advance."

Five minutes after, the carriage was ready, and Coster was on his way to Vitré.

"Now," said Mademoiselle de Fargas, "as I have nothing to do in all these preparations, I will ask your permission to take a little rest. I have not slept for five days and nights."

Cadoudal spread his cloak on the ground, and upon it he put five or six sheep-skins; a portmanteau served for a pillow, and Mademoiselle de Fargas began her first night's bivouac, and with it her apprenticeship to civil war.

As the clock at La Guerche struck ten, Cadoudal heard a voice at his ear which said, —

"Here I am!"

It was Chante-en-Hiver, who had returned as he had promised.

He had gathered all necessary information, and he told Cadoudal what we already know.

Goulin occupied the last house in the town of La Guerche.

Twelve men, who slept in a room on the ground floor, constituted his private guard.

Four men took turns in acting as sentinel at the foot of the guillotine, relieving each other every two hours; the other three slept in the ante-room of the ground floor of the house occupied by François Goulin.

The horses which drew the machine were in the stable of the same house.

At half-past ten, Branche-d'Or also arrived. He had taken the uniforms from twenty dead hussars, and brought them with him.

"Choose for me," said Cadoudal, "twenty men who can wear these clothes without looking too much as if they were masquerading. You will take command of them. I suppose you did as I told you, and took one uniform of a quartermaster-general or a *sous-lieutenant?*"

"Yes, General."

"You will put it on, and take command of these twenty men. You will take the road to Château-Giron, so that you will enter La Guerche at the other side of the town, by the road opposite this. At the sentinel's challenge you will advance and say that you come from Rennes, from General Hédouville. You will ask for Colonel Hulot's house, and they will show it to you. You will be careful not to go there. Chante-en-Hiver, who will be your second in command, will show you the way through the town from end to end if you do not know it."

"I do know it, General," replied Branche-d'Or; "but never mind, a good fellow like Chante-en-Hiver is never in the way."

"You will go straight to Goulin's house. Thanks to your uniform, you will have no difficulty. While two men approach the sentinel and talk with him, the other eighteen will seize the fifteen Blues who are in the house. With your swords at their breasts, you will make them swear not to offer any opposition. As soon as they have sworn, you need not trouble yourself further about them; they will keep their oath.

"Masters below, you will then go up to François Goulin's room. As I have no idea that he will defend himself, I will not tell you what to do in case of resistance. As for the sentinel, you will understand how important it is that he should not cry, 'To arms!'

"He will surrender, or you will kill him. In the mean time, Chante-en-Hiver will take the horses from the stable, harness them to the machine, and, as it is on the road, all you will have to do will be to drive straight ahead in order to join us.

"When once the Blues have given you their word, you can trust them with the secret of your mission. I am firmly convinced that there is not one of them who would court death for the sake of François Goulin, and that, on the contrary, there are more than one who will give you good advice. Thus, for example, Chante-en-Hiver neglected to learn where the executioner lived, — probably because I neglected to tell him to do so. I suppose none of you would care to fill his office, therefore he is indispensable to us. I leave the rest to your intelligence.

" The attempt will be made about three o'clock in the morning. At two o'clock we shall be where we were yesterday. A rocket will tell us that you have succeeded."

Branche-d'Or and Chante-en-Hiver exchanged a few words in a low tone. One was objecting to something that the other was saying; finally, they seemed to agree, and turning towards Cadoudal, said, —

" That is enough, General. Everything shall be done to your satisfaction."

CHAPTER XXVI.

THE ROAD TO THE SCAFFOLD.

ABOUT two o'clock in the morning the sound of wheels was heard.

It was Coster de Saint-Victor returning with his handbills.

As if he had been certain of the success of the affair, he had ordered the printer to post a hundred of them in the town of Vitré.

The handbill read as follows: —

You are invited to be present at the execution of François Goulin, commissioner-extraordinary of the Directory; he will be executed to-morrow, at nine o'clock in the morning, on the high-road from Vitré to La Guerche, at a place called Moutiers, upon his own guillotine.

General Cadoudal, by whose order the execution will take place, offers the truce of God to all who shall be present at this act of justice.

From his camp at La Guerche.

GEORGES CADOUDAL.

In passing through Étrelles, Saint-Germain du Pinel, and Moutiers, Coster had left copies with the inhabitants, whom he had awakened for the purpose, and whom he had charged to inform their neighbors of the spectacle that was in store for them the next day.

No one complained of having been awakened. A commissioner of the Republic was not executed every day.

As had already been done at the other end of the road, they attached horses to the felled trees and swung them around, to make the road passable.

At two o'clock, as had been agreed, Cadoudal gave the signal to his men, who went to take their places behind the thickets where they had fought on the previous day.

Half an hour before, Branche-d'Or, Chante-en-Hiver, and their twenty men, dressed as hussars, had started off on the road to Château-Giron.

An hour passed in absolute silence.

From where they were, the Chouans could hear the cries of the sentinels as they called to one another.

At about a quarter to three, the group of disguised Chouans appeared at the end of the main street, and, after a moment's parley with the sentinel, were directed by him to the town-hall, where Colonel Hulot was lodging. But Chante-en-Hiver and Branche-d'Or were not so simple as to follow the main thoroughfares of the town; they took to the lanes, where they looked like a patrol watching over the safety of the city. They went thus to the house occupied by François Goulin.

There, also, everything took place as Cadoudal had foreseen. The sentinel at the guillotine, seeing the little troop coming from the centre of the town, was not at all disturbed, and had a pistol at his throat before he suspected that they had aught to say to him.

The republicans, taken by surprise in the house where they were deep in sleep, made no resistance. François Goulin was taken in his bed, and rolled and tied in his sheet before he had time to utter a single cry of alarm.

As for the executioner and his assistant, they lodged in a little pavilion in the garden; and as Cadoudal had foreseen, the republicans themselves, when told of the object of the expedition, pointed out to the Whites the hole where the two foul creatures were sleeping.

The Blues promised, besides, to take and distribute the bills, and to ask Colonel Hulot for permission to attend the execution.

At three o'clock in the morning a rocket from the top of the hill announced to Cadoudal and his men that the expedition was a success.

And at the same moment they heard the rumbling of the heavy wagon upon which was placed one of the finest specimens of Monsieur Guillotin's invention.

Seeing that his men were not pursued, Cadoudal called the Chouans, and they removed the corpses from the middle of the road, so that the wagon would meet no obstacle. It was not until they were half way down the hill that they heard the first blasts of the trumpets and the first drum-beats.

The fact is that no one had been in any haste to inform Colonel Hulot. The one who had been charged with the duty had not forgotten to take with him a number of the placards; and instead of beginning by telling of the audacious deed which Cadoudal's men had just committed, he thrust the bills under his eyes; and as they told him nothing, he was compelled to ask a series of questions which extorted the truth shred by shred. He finally heard it all, however, and flew into a terrible passion, ordering a hot pursuit of the Whites, and the rescue of the government commissioner at any cost.

Then the trumpets sounded and the drums beat.

But the officers so coaxed their old colonel that they finally disarmed his anger, and obtained a tacit permission to go, at their own risk and peril, and see this execution, which the colonel himself was dying to witness.

But he knew that this was impossible, and that it would put his own head in serious peril; he therefore contented himself with telling his secretary, who had not dared to ask leave, to go with the other officers and bring him an exact report.

The young man leaped for joy when he learned that he was to be compelled to go and see François Goulin's head cut off.

The man must indeed have inspired the most profound disgust, when Whites and Blues, soldiers and citizens, approved with one accord of an act which was so open to discussion from the standpoint of right.

As for François Goulin, until he was half way down the hill, and saw the Chouans join and fraternize with his escort, he had no clear idea what was wanted of him. Taken by men wearing the republican uniform, tied up in his sheet before they replied to his questions, thrown into a carriage with the executioner, his dear friend, and following in the wake of his dear guillotine, it will readily be seen that it was impossible that the truth should have dawned upon him.

But when he saw the pretended hussars exchanging jokes with the Chouans who walked along the top of the banking by the road; when, having persistently asked what they intended to do with him, and why they had violated his domicile and laid violent hands upon his person, he was presented, by way of reply, with the placard which announced his own execution, and invited the people to be present, — then indeed did he understand the full extent of his danger, and his small chance of escape from it, unless he were rescued by the republicans, or his captors should be moved to pity: two chances which were so problematical that he could not rely upon them.

His first idea was to address the executioner, and to make him understand that he was to receive orders from no one but himself, since he had been sent from Paris with the injunction to obey him in all things. But the man himself was so cast down, and looked about him with such a haggard eye, having a firm conviction that he was doomed to die at the same time as the man whose custom it was to put others to death, that the unhappy François Goulin soon saw that he had nothing to expect from that quarter.

Then he thought of crying out, appealing for help, entreating; but he saw such utter indifference upon all faces that he shook his head and said to himself,—

"No, no, no, it is useless!"

Thus they reached the foot of the hill.

There they made a halt. The Chouans had to take off their borrowed costumes and put on their own uniform, which consisted of the vest, breeches, and gaiters of the Breton peasant. A great number of curious folk were already gathered there. The bills had done wonders; from two and even four leagues around, people were hastening to the spot. Everybody knew that this was the same François Goulin who was known at Nantes and throughout La Vendée only as Goulin the Drowner.

The guillotine shared their curiosity with him. The instrument was entirely unknown at this extremity of France, which bordered upon Finistère (*finis terræ,* end of the earth). Women and men questioned each other as to how it was made to go, where the condemned man was placed, and how the knife went up and down. People who did not know that Goulin was the hero of the *fête* addressed him, and asked him for information. One of them said to him, —

"Do you believe a person dies as soon as his head is cut off? I do not. When I cut off the head of a goose or a duck, it lives more than a quarter of an hour afterwards."

And Goulin, who was no more certain than he that death was instantaneous, writhed in his bonds, and twisted himself towards the executioner, saying, —

"Did you not tell me one day that the heads of the people who had been guillotined gnawed the bottom of your basket?"

But the executioner, stupefied with fear, either did not reply at all, or only uttered vague exclamations which showed the mortal terror of him from whose lips they issued.

After a rest of a quarter of an hour, which gave the Chouans time to resume their own clothes, they started again; but they perceived the whole population of La Guerche hurrying up at their left, to witness the execution.

It was a curious thing to these men who on the previous night had been threatened with the fatal instrument, and who had looked with terror upon the man who had it in charge, — it was a curious thing to them to see this instrument, like Diomedes' horses, which were fed on human flesh, cast itself upon its master and devour him in turn.

In the midst of the multitude came a black mass, preceded by a stick, at the end of which floated a white handkerchief.

It was those of the republicans who had taken advantage of the truce of God offered by Cadoudal, and who were coming, preceded by the emblem of truce, to join the silence of their scorn to the angry outbursts of the populace, who, having nothing at stake, respected nothing.

Cadoudal ordered a halt; and after having courteously saluted the Blues, with whom, on the previous night, he and his men had exchanged death-blows, —

"Come, gentlemen," said he. "The spectacle is a grand one, and worthy to be witnessed by men of all parties. Cut-throats, drowners, and assassins have no flag; or if they have one, it is the standard of death, — the black flag. Come, we will none of us march beneath that flag."

And he went on again, mingling with the republicans, and trusting them, as they trusted him.

CHAPTER XXVII.

THE EXECUTION.

A PERSON watching from that side of the village of Moutiers the strange procession as it approached him, slowly ascending the hill, would have had difficulty in making out the meaning of the strange jumble of men on foot, men on horseback, Whites in the costume made sacred by Charette, Cathelineau, and Cadoudal, Blues in the republican uniform accompanied by women, children, and peasants, and rolling along amid these human waves, as restless as the waves of the ocean, an unknown machine,— unless, indeed, such person had seen Coster de Saint-Victor's placards.

But these placards were for a long time taken for one of the strange gasconades which parties at this period permitted themselves to indulge in ; and many persons had come, not to see the promised execution,— for that was too much to hope,— but to learn the explanation of the promise which had been made them.

The rendezvous was at Moutiers; and all the peasants in the neighborhood had been waiting since eight o'clock in the morning on the public square of the town.

Suddenly it was announced that a procession which was increasing at each step was approaching the town. Every one at once ran to the point indicated; and there, two thirds up the hill, they saw the Vendean chiefs forming the advance-guard, and holding in their hands green branches, as in the old days of expiation.

The crowd gathered at Moutiers streamed out along the road; and, like two rivers meeting, the two human floods hurled themselves against each other, and mingled their waves.

There was a moment of tumult and confusion. Every one struggled to get near the cart which drew the scaffold, and the carriage which contained Goulin, the executioner, and his assistant.

But as they were all animated by the same desire, and as the enthusiasm was perhaps greater than the curiosity, those who had had a look thought it only right that others should see too, and fell back to make room for them.

As they advanced, Goulin grew paler and paler; for he saw that they were going straight towards an end which they would surely reach. Besides, he had seen on the bill which they had put into his hands that Moutiers was to be the scene of his execution; and he knew only too well that the town which he saw before him, and which they were approaching at every step, was Moutiers. He rolled his haggard eyes over the crowd, unable to understand the mixture of republicans and Chouans, who on the previous night were waging bloody battle against each other, and yet in the morning were uniting in friendly fashion to form his escort. From time to time he shut his eyes, doubtless to make himself believe that it was all a dream; but then it must have seemed to him, by the swaying of the carriage and the roaring of the crowd, as if he were on a vessel, tossed about by a terrible tempest at sea. Then he raised his arms, which he had succeeded in disengaging from the shroud-like wrapping which enveloped him, beat the air like a crazy man, stood up, tried to cry out, and perhaps did cry out; but his voice was lost in the tumult, and he fell back again upon the seat between his two gloomy companions.

At last they reached the plateau of Moutiers, and the cry of "Halt!" was heard.

They had arrived at their destination.

More than ten thousand persons were assembled on this plateau; the nearest houses of the village were covered with curious spectators, and the trees along the road were loaded with human freight. A few men on horseback, and a woman carrying her arm in a sling, were head and shoulders above the rest of the crowd.

The men were Cadoudal, Coster de Saint-Victor, and the other leaders of the Chouans.

The woman was Mademoiselle de Fargas, who, to familiarize herself with her future emotions upon fields of battle, had come in quest of the most intense of all emotions,—that which is felt by those who witness a death upon the scaffold.

When the procession had halted, and each one had taken the place that he intended to occupy during the execution, Cadoudal raised his hand, in token that he wished to speak.

Every voice was hushed; even the breath seemed to die away in the chest. A mournful silence ensued, and Goulin's eyes were fixed upon Cadoudal, of whose name and importance he was ignorant, whom he had not yet distinguished from the others, and who, nevertheless, was the man whom he had come so far to seek, — the man who at their first meeting was to change *rôles* with him, making himself the judge, and the executioner the victim: if an assassin can be described as a victim, no matter what the death reserved for him.

Cadoudal had made a sign that he wished to speak.

"Citizens," he said, addressing the republicans,—"as

you see, I give you the title which you give yourselves, —
my brothers," he continued, addressing the Chouans,
— "and I give you the name under which God receives
you into his bosom, — your meeting to-day at Moutiers,
and the object of your meeting, prove that each of you
is convinced that this man merits the death which he
is about to suffer; and yet, republicans, whom I hope
some day to call brothers, you do not know this man
as we know him.

"One day, in the beginning of 1793, my father and
I were returning from carrying flour into Nantes; there
was famine in the town.

"It was scarcely light. Carrier, the infamous Carrier,
had not yet arrived at Nantes; therefore we must give
unto Cæsar the things that are Cæsar's, unto Goulin
the things that are Goulin's.

"It was Goulin who invented the *noyades*.

"My father and I were going along the Quai de la
Loire; we saw a boat on which they were loading priests.
A man was making them get into it two by two, and
counting them as they went aboard.

"He counted ninety-seven of them! These priests
were bound to each other in couples.

"As they got into the boat, they disappeared, for
they were taken to the hold.

"The boat left the bank, and went out to the middle
of the Loire. This man stood in front with an oar.

"My father stopped his horse and said to me, —

"'Wait and watch; something infamous is going on
here.'

"It seems that the boat had a plug. When it was
out in the middle of the stream, the plug was removed,
and the wretches who were in the hold were thrown into
the river.

" As their heads appeared at the surface of the water, this man and his miserable companions struck at the heads which already wore the crown of martyrdom, and bruised them with blows of their oars.

" That man there urged them on to the cruel work.

" Two of the condemned men, however, were too far off to be struck; they made their way towards the bank, for they had found a sandbar upon which they had footing.

" ' Quick! ' said my father to me. ' Let us save those two.'

" We sprang from our horses, slipped down the bank of the Loire, and ran to them, with our knives in our hands. They believed that we also were murderers, and tried to escape from us; but we cried out to them:

" ' Come to us, men of God! These knives are to cut your bonds, and not to strike you.'

" They came to us. In an instant their hands were free, and we were on horseback, with them behind us, riding away at a gallop.

" They were the worthy Abbés Briançon and Lacombe.

" They both took refuge with us in the forests of Morbihan. One of them died of fatigue, hunger, and thirst, as so many of us died. That was the Abbé Briançon.

" The other," and Cadoudal pointed towards a priest who tried to conceal himself in the crowd, — " the other recovered, and serves God to-day by his prayers, as we serve him with our arms. That other is the Abbé Lacombe. There he is!

" From that time," he continued, pointing to Goulin, " this man, always the same, presided at the *noyades.* In all the slaughter which took place at Nantes, he was Carrier's right arm.

" When Carrier was tried and condemned, François Goulin was tried at the same time; but he posed before the tribunal as merely an instrument who had been unable to refuse to obey the orders that were given him.

" I possess this letter, written entirely by himself."

Cadoudal drew a paper from his pocket.

" I wanted to send it to the tribunal, to enlighten its conscience. This letter, written to his worthy colleague Perdraux, describing his method of procedure, was his condemnation.

" Listen, you men of hard-fought fields, and tell me if ever a war-bulletin made you shudder as these lines do."

Cadoudal read aloud, amid solemn silence, the following letter:—

CITIZEN, — In the exaltation of your patriotism, you ask me how I make my republican marriages.

When I get ready for the baths, I strip the men and women, then I go through their clothing, to see if they have any money or jewelry. I put the clothing in a great hamper; then I tie a man and a woman together by the wrists, face to face. I bring them to the banks of the Loire; they go aboard my boat two by two, and two men push them from behind and throw them head first into the water; then, when they try to save themselves, we have great clubs with which we beat them back.

That is what we call the civil marriage.

FRANÇOIS GOULIN.

" Do you know," continued Cadoudal, " who prevented me from sending that letter? It was the pity of good Abbé Lacombe.

" He said to me, ' If God has given this miserable man a chance to save himself, it is that he may have an opportunity to repent.'

"Now, how has he repented? You see him. After having drowned perhaps fifteen hundred persons, he seizes the moment when terror revives, and asks the favor of returning to this same region where he was executioner, in order to make fresh executions.

"If he had repented, I also would have pardoned him; but since, like the dog in the Bible, he has turned to his own vomit, since God has permitted him to fall into my hands, after having escaped those of the revolutionary tribunal, God means that he shall die."

A moment of silence followed Cadoudal's last words. Then the condemned man rose in his carriage, and in a stifled voice cried, —

"Mercy! mercy!"

"Well, so be it," said Cadoudal. "Since you are standing there, look around you. There are ten thousand men here who have come to see you die. If among them a single one asks for mercy for you, you shall have it."

"Mercy!" exclaimed Lacombe, holding out his arms.

Cadoudal stood up in his stirrups.

"You alone of us all, Father, have no right to ask for mercy for this man. You extended mercy to him on the day when you prevented me from sending his letter to the revolutionary tribunal. You may help him to die, but that is all that I can grant you."

Then, in a voice which was heard by all the spectators, he asked, for the second time, —

"Is there any one among you who asks mercy for this man?"

Not a voice replied.

"You have five minutes in which to make your peace with Heaven," said Cadoudal to François Goulin; "and unless it were a miracle from Heaven, nothing can save you. Father," he added, addressing Lacombe, "you may give your arm to this man, and accompany him to the scaffold."

Then to the executioner he said, —

" Do your duty ! "

The executioner, who now saw that his only part in the execution was to perform his ordinary functions, rose and put his hand on Goulin's shoulder, as a sign that he belonged to him.

The Abbé Lacombe approached the condemned man.

But the latter pushed him back.

Then ensued a frightful struggle between this man, who would neither pray nor die, and the two executioners.

In spite of his cries, his bites, and his blasphemies, the executioner took him in his arms as if he had been a child; and while the assistant prepared the knife, he carried him from his carriage to the platform of the guillotine.

The Abbé Lacombe went up first, with a ray of hope, and waited there for the culprit; but his efforts were vain, and he could not even put the crucifix to his lips.

Then there took place upon the frightful stage a scene which is beyond description.

The executioner and his assistant succeeded in stretching the condemned man upon the fatal plank. It rocked. Then the on-lookers saw a flash, as of lightning; it was the descending knife. They heard a dull sound; it was the falling head.

Deep silence followed; and in the midst of it Cadoudal's voice was heard, saying, —

" God's justice is done ! "

CHAPTER XXVIII.

THE SEVENTEENTH FRUCTIDOR.

LET us leave Cadoudal to continue his desperate struggle against the republicans, victor and vanquished by turns, and, with Pichegru, — the last remaining hope of the Bourbons in France, — let us cast an eye upon Paris, and pause at the pile erected by Marie de Médicis, where the citizen-directors still abide in the respective apartments we have mentioned.

Barras had received Bonaparte's message, which Augereau had brought to him.

On the eve of the latter's departure, the young commander-in-chief, choosing the anniversary of the 14th of July, which corresponded to the 26th Messidor, had given a *fête* to the army, and had had addresses drawn up, in which the soldiers of Italy protested their attachment to the Republic, and their willingness to die for it, if necessary.

On the grand square at Milan there had been erected a pyramid, surrounded by trophies taken from the enemy, — flags and cannon.

This pyramid bore the names of all the soldiers and officers who had died during the campaign in Italy.

Every Frenchman in Milan was urged to be present at this *fête*, and more than twenty thousand men presented arms to the glorious trophies and the pyramid covered with the immortal names of the dead.

While twenty thousand men formed a square, and presented arms to their brothers who lay stretched upon the battle-fields of Arcola, Castiglione, and Rivoli, Bonaparte, with uncovered head, said, as he pointed to the pyramid, —

"Soldiers, to-day is the anniversary of the 14th of July. You see before you the names of those of your companions who have died on the field of honor for liberty and their country; they have set you an example. You belong absolutely to the Republic. In your hands is the happiness of thirty millions of Frenchmen; in your hands is the glory of that name·which has received new brilliancy by your victories.

"Soldiers, I know that you are deeply grieved by the evils which threaten the Fatherland; but the Fatherland cannot be in any real danger. The same men who are responsible for its triumph over allied Europe are still there. Mountains separate us from France. You would cross them with the speed of the eagle, if it were necessary, in order to preserve the Constitution, defend liberty, and protect republicans.

"Soldiers, the Government watches over the trust which is confided to it. The royalists, as soon as they appear, will forfeit their lives. Have no fear; and swear by the spirits of the heroes who have died beside us for liberty, swear by our flags, implacable war upon the enemies of the Republic and of the Constitution of the year III."

Then there was a banquet, and toasts were offered.

Bonaparte gave the first.

"To the brave Steingel, La Harpe, and Dubois, who died on the field of honor! May their shades watch over us, and preserve us from the snares of our enemies!"

Masséna proposed a toast to the re-emigration of the *émigrés.*

Augereau, who was to start next day, with full
authority from Bonaparte, exclaimed as he raised his
glass, —

"To the union of all French republicans! To the
destruction of the club of Clichy! Let conspirators
tremble! From the Adige and the Rhine to the Seine,
it is but a step. Let them tremble! Their iniqui-
ties are known, and the price is at the end of our
bayonets!"

As the last word was uttered, trumpets and drums
sounded the charge. Each soldier sprang to his weapon,
as if he were obliged to start on the instant; and the
men could scarcely be induced to resume their places at
the table.

The members of the Directory had received Bonaparte's message with widely differing emotions.

Augereau exactly suited Barras, who, always ready
to mount his horse and to call the Jacobins and the people
of the Faubourgs to help him, welcomed Augereau as the
man for the situation.

But Rewbell and La Réveillère, whose characters
were evenly balanced, and whose heads were cool, wanted
a general who was as cool and well balanced as themselves. As for Barthélemy and Carnot, it is needless
to say that Augereau was utterly out of tune with them.

And, indeed, Augereau, as we already know him, was
a dangerous auxiliary. A brave man, an excellent
soldier, with an intrepid heart, but a boasting, Gascon
tongue, Augereau betrayed too plainly the object of his
mission. But La Réveillère and Rewbell succeeded
in getting hold of him and making him understand that
it was necessary to save the Republic by an energetic
and decisive blow, and without bloodshed.

In order to keep him quiet, they gave him the

command of the seventeenth military division, which included Paris.

It was the 16th Fructidor.

The relations of the different parties were so strained that a *coup d'état* was expected at any moment, either on the part of the councils or the directors.

Pichegru was the natural chief of the royalist move-ment. If he were to take the initiative, the royalists would gather around him.

This book which we are writing is far from being a romance, — perhaps, indeed, it is not enough of a romance to suit some readers. We have already said that it was written to coast along the shores of history, from point to point. And just as we were the first to throw broad daylight upon the events of the 13th Vendémiaire and the part which Bonaparte took in it, we shall, at this period which we have now reached, show the over-calumniated Pichegru in his true light.

Pichegru, after his refusal to listen to the Prince de Condé, — a refusal whose causes we have detailed, — entered into direct correspondence with the Comte de Provence, who, since the death of the little dauphin, had taken the title of King Louis XVIII.

Now, when Louis XVIII. sent Cadoudal his com-mission as *lieutenant du roi* and the red ribbon, he at the same time, to show his appreciation of Pichegru's disinterestedness, who had refused honors and money, and would not attempt to bring about the Restoration except for the glory of being a second Monk without the duchy of Albemarle, wrote to Pichegru as follows:

I have long desired to express to you the feelings which you early awoke in me, and the esteem which I have for your person. I yield now to this necessity of my heart, which it really is, to say to you that for the last eighteen months it has seemed to me that the honor of restoring the French monarchy was reserved for you.

I will not speak to you of the admiration which I feel for your talents, and for the noble deeds which you have performed. History has already placed you in the ranks of great generals, and posterity will confirm the judgment which all Europe has already passed upon your victories and your virtues.

The most distinguished leaders owe their success, for the most part, to long experience in their profession; but from the very first you were what you have never ceased to be since, throughout all your campaigns. You have united the *bravery* of Marshal Saxe with the *disinterestedness* of Monsieur de Turenne, and the *modesty* of Monsieur de Catinat. And I may say that your name is indissolubly associated in my mind with those names which have made our annals so glorious.

I confirm, Monsieur, the full powers which were conferred upon you by Monsieur le Prince de Condé. I put no limit to them, and leave you entirely free to do anything which you may think necessary for my service, compatible with the dignity of my crown and in accord with the interests of the kingdom.

You know, Monsieur, my sentiments towards you. They will never change.

Louis.

A second letter followed the first. The two together furnish an exact measure of Louis XVIII.'s feelings towards Pichegru, and should influence, not only his contemporaries, but posterity.

You are aware, Monsieur, of the unfortunate events which have taken place in Italy. The necessity of sending thirty thousand men there, has indefinitely postponed the project of crossing the Rhine. Your attachment to me will cause you to readily understand my disappointment at this *contre-temps*, especially just as I saw the gates of my kingdom opening before me. On the other hand, these disasters increase, if possible, the confidence with which you have inspired me. I am sure that you will re-establish the French monarchy; and whether the war continues, or whether we have peace this summer, I count upon you for the success of this great work. I place in your hands, Monsieur, absolute power to act for me and in my name. Make such use of it as you think necessary for my service.

If the valuable sources of information which you have at your command in Paris and the provinces, if your talents, and, above all, your character, could permit me to fear an event which would oblige you to leave the kingdom, you would find your place between Monsieur de Condé and myself. In speaking to you thus, I have a heartfelt desire to prove to you my esteem and attachment.

Louis.

Therefore, on the one hand, Augereau was urging matters to a climax with letters from Bonaparte, and, on the other, Pichegru was being urged by letters from Louis XVIII.

The news that Augereau had been given the command of the seventeenth military division — that is to say, that he was at the head of the forces in Paris — had told the royalists that they had no time to lose.

Therefore Pichegru, Villot, Barbé-Marbois, Dumas, Murinais, Delarue, Rovère, Aubry, Laffon-Ladébat, — the whole royalist party, in short, — assembled for deliberation at the house of Adjutant-General Ramel, commander of the guard of the Corps Législatif.

This Ramel was a brave soldier, and had been adjutant-general in the Army of the Rhine, under the orders of General Desaix, when, in January, 1797, he received orders from the Directory to return to Paris to take command of the guard of the Corps Législatif. This corps was composed of a battalion of six hundred men, most of whom were taken from the grenadiers of the Convention, whom we saw marching so bravely under fire on the 13th Vendémiaire, under the command of Bonaparte.

At this meeting the situation was clearly explained by Pichegru. Ramel sided entirely with the two councils, and was ready to obey any orders which the presidents should give him.

Pichegru proposed to take command that very evening of two hundred men, and arrest Barras, Rewbell, and La Réveillère, and make charges against them the next day.

Unfortunately, it had been agreed that all questions should be decided by the majority. The temporizers opposed Pichegru's motion.

"The Constitution will be enough to defend us," exclaimed Lacuée.

"The Constitution can do nothing against cannon, and the cannon will reply to your decrees," retorted Villot.

"The soldiers will not be on their side," insisted Lacuée.

"The soldiers side with whoever commands them," said Pichegru. "You will not decide, and you are lost. As for me," he added sadly, "I sacrificed my life long ago. I am tired of all these discussions, which amount to nothing. When you need me, you can come for me."

And with these words, he went away.

At the very moment when Pichegru, downcast and discouraged, left Ramel's house, a post-chaise stopped at the door of the Luxembourg, and Citizen-General Moreau was announced to Barras.

CHAPTER XXIX.

JEAN-VICTOR MOREAU.

MOREAU was at this time a man of thirty-seven years, and was the only man who, with Hoche, served as an equipoise to Bonaparte, — in reputation, at least, if not in fortune.

At this time he had just joined an association, — which later became a conspiracy, and which lasted from 1797 until 1809, when it became extinct by the death of Colonel Oudet, the head of the society — which was called the " Philadelphes."

In this society his assumed name was Fabius, in memory of the famous Roman consul who was victorious over Hannibal by temporizing.

Therefore Moreau was named " The Temporizer."

Unfortunately, temporizing was not with him the result of calculation, but the effect of character. Moreau was absolutely without firmness in politics and strength of will.

If he had been gifted with more instinctive force, he might have had a greater influence upon events in France, and have marked out for himself a career comparable with the most glorious of all careers of ancient or modern times.

Moreau was born at Morlaix in Brittany. His father was a distinguished lawyer. His family was of high standing, and was rich rather than poor.

At eighteen years of age, attracted towards the military profession, he enlisted. His father, who wished to make of young Moreau a lawyer like himself, bought his discharge, and sent him to Rennes to study law.

He soon secured considerable influence over his companions, which was unquestionably due to moral superiority.

Inferior in intelligence to Bonaparte, and inferior in rapidity of thought to Hoche, he was, nevertheless, the superior of most men.

When the troubles which were the precursors of the Revolution burst out in Brittany, Moreau took the part of the parliament against the court, and carried with him the whole body of students.

Then followed between Moreau, who was henceforth called the " parliament general," and the commandant at Rennes, a struggle, in which the old soldier did not always have the advantage.

The commandant at Rennes then gave orders to arrest Moreau.

But Moreau, a part of whose genius was prudence, or rather whose whole genius was prudence, found means to elude all search, showing himself every day, now at one point and now at another, so that people should be convinced that the spirit of parliamentary opposition had not departed from the old capital of Armorica.

But later, seeing that this parliament which he was defending opposed the convocation of the States-General, and considering that such convocation was necessary for the future happiness of France, he changed sides, while still preserving his opinions, upheld the convocation of the States-General, and appeared at the head of all the mobs which were organized thenceforth in Brittany.

He was president of the Breton youth gathered at Pontivy when the procureur-général of the department, desiring to utilize the talents which were revealing themselves in him, made him commander of the 1st battalion of volunteers from Ille-et-Vilaine.

Here is what Moreau says of himself: —

" I was destined to the study of law at the beginning of this revolution which was to burst the bonds of the French people. It changed the whole course of my life ; I devoted it to the profession of arms. I did not take my place among the sol-. diers of liberty through ambition, but I entered upon a military career out of respect for the rights of the nation ; I became a warrior because I was a citizen."

Moreau owed to his calm and slightly lymphatic nature a sure insight in times of danger and a coolness which were astonishing in so young a man.   At this time men were still lacking, but were soon to come forward in crowds.   His qualities, although of the negative order, procured for Moreau the rank of brigadier-general in the army of which Pichegru was then commander-in-chief.

Pichegru, the man of genius, appreciated Moreau, the man of talent, and conferred on him, in 1794, the rank of general of division.

From that time he was in command of twenty-five thousand men, and was most frequently intrusted with the conduct of siege-operations.

In the brilliant campaign of 1794, which subdued Holland, Moreau commanded the right wing of the army.

The conquest of Holland had been thought impossible by all strategists,— Holland being, as every one knows, a country which lies lower than the sea, which was wrested from the sea, and which can be flooded at will.

The Hollanders risked this semi-suicide. They pierced the dikes, which held back the waters of the sea, and thought to escape invasion by inundating their country.

But suddenly cold weather, of a severity unknown in that country, in which the mercury fell to fifteen degrees, and which had not been seen there more than once in the course of a century, froze the canals and the rivers.

Then, with a daring which is peculiar to them, the French ventured out over the abyss. The infantry risked the passage first, then the cavalry, and then the light artillery; and as they saw that the ice bore this unaccustomed weight, they ventured upon it with the heavy siege-guns. They fought on ice as they were in the habit of fighting upon dry land. The English were attacked and driven back with the bayonet. The Austrian batteries were taken. That which should have saved Holland was its destruction. The cold, which was later the mortal enemy of the Empire, was now the faithful ally of the Republic.

After this there was nothing further to hinder the invasion of the United Provinces. The ramparts no longer defended the towns, for the ice was on a level with the ramparts. Arnheim, Amsterdam, Rotterdam, the Hague were taken. The conquest of Over-Yssel, Groningen, and Friesland finished the subjugation of Holland.

There remained the fleet of the Stadtholder, which was frozen in the ice in the Strait of Texel, and the different vessels of which were near the edge of the water.

Moreau brought his cannon to bear upon the artillery of the fleet. He fought the vessels as he would have fought a fortress, sending a regiment of hussars to board it; and a fleet was taken by a regiment of light cavalry, — a thing unheard of in the annals of nations or in naval history.

These were the things which had caused Pichegru and Moreau to grow in stature; but Moreau still was nothing more than the clever lieutenant of the man of genius.

Meanwhile, Pichegru was called to the command of the Army of the Rhine and Moselle, and Moreau to the command of the Army of the North.

Soon, as we have already said, Pichegru fell under suspicion, and was recalled to Paris; and Moreau was appointed to replace him as commander-in-chief of the Army of the Rhine and Moselle.

At the opening of the campaign, some skirmishers had taken a wagon which formed part of the equipage of the Austrian General Klinglin. In a little chest which had been sent to Moreau he had found the whole correspondence between Fauche-Borel and the Prince de Condé. This correspondence fully exposed the relations that had existed between Fauche-Borel, posing as a travelling wine-merchant, and Pichegru.

In this matter every one has the right to judge Moreau's conduct in his own way and according to his own conscience.

Ought Moreau — the friend, the debtor, the lieutenant of Pichegru — simply to have examined the contents of the chest, and have then sent it back to his former chief, saying, " Take care! " or ought he, putting his country before his affections, the Stoic before the friend, to have done what he did do, — that is to say, spend six months in deciphering or having deciphered all the letters, which were written in cipher, and then, with his suspicions justified, but with Pichegru's guilt unproved, take advantage of the preliminaries of the treaty of Léoben, and when the tempest was ready to burst over Pichegru's head, go to Barras and say, "Behold me; I am the thunder-bolt!"

Now, that was what Moreau did say to Barras. Just such proofs as these, not of treason, but of negotiations, were what the Directory needed in order to accuse Pichegru; and these proofs Moreau supplied.

Barras passed two hours *tête-à-tête* with Moreau, satisfying himself that he held weapons which were so much the more deadly because they were poisoned.

Then, when he was convinced that there were grounds, if not for condemnation, at least for trial, he rang.

An usher entered.

"Go and summon the Minister of Police and my two colleagues, Rewbell and La Réveillère-Lepaux," said Barras.

Then, drawing out his watch, he added, —

"Ten o'clock; we have six hours before us. Citizen-General, you have come in time," he said, holding out his hand to Moreau.

And with his inscrutable smile, he added, —

"We will reward you for this."

Moreau asked permission to retire. It was granted. He would have embarrassed Barras as much as Barras would have embarrassed him.

The three directors remained in consultation until two o'clock in the morning. The Minister of Police joined them at once, and they sent him for Merlin (of Douai) and Augereau, one after the other.

Then they sent off to the government printer, about

one o'clock in the morning, an address, conceived in these terms: —

The Directory, attacked about two o'clock in the morning by the troops of the two councils, under the command of Adjutant-General Ramel, was obliged to meet force with force.

After an hour's fighting, the troops of the two councils were beaten, and the government remained victorious.

More than a hundred prisoners remained in the hands of the directors ; to-morrow will be given a list of their names and more ample details of this conspiracy, which almost succeeded in overturning the established power.

18th Fructidor, four A. M.

This curious production was signed by Barras, Rewbell, and La Réveillère-Lepaux. Sothin, the Minister of Police, had suggested it, and had drawn it up.

" They will not believe in your placard," said Barras, shrugging his shoulders.

" They will believe in it in the course of to-morrow," replied Sothin, "and that is all we need. It is no matter what they believe day after to-morrow; the trick will be done."

The directors separated, giving orders to arrest, first of all, their two colleagues, — Carnot and Barthélemy.

CHAPTER XXX.

THE EIGHTEENTH FRUCTIDOR.

WHILE Sothin, the Minister of Police, was drawing up his placards and proposing to have Carnot and forty-two deputies shot, while the directors were annulling the appointment of Barthélemy, the fifth director, and promising his place to Augereau if they had reason to be satisfied with him when the evening of the next day arrived, two men were quietly playing backgammon in a corner of the Luxembourg.

One of these two men, the younger by three years only, had started by being an officer of engineers, and had published mathematical essays which had won him admittance to several learned societies. He had also composed a eulogy upon Vauban, which had been crowned by the Academy of Dijon.

At the beginning of the Revolution he was captain of engineers, and had been appointed chevalier of Saint-Louis. In 1791 he had been elected deputy to the Legislative Assembly by the department of Pas-de-Calais. His first speech there had been directed against the *émigré* princes at Coblentz, against the Marquis de Mirabeau, against Cardinal de Rohan, and against Monsieur de Calonne, who was intriguing with foreign kings to induce them to declare war upon France. He proposed that non-commissioned officers and sergeants should take the places of the officers belonging to the nobility, who had emigrated. In 1792 he asked for the demolition of all the bastiles in the interior of France, and presented measures for doing away with the passive obedience which had been exacted from soldiers and officers.

In the days when the Revolution was threatened by foreign powers, he had asked for the manufacture of three hundred thousand pikes, to arm the people of Paris. Chosen deputy to the National Convention, he had unhesitatingly voted for the death of the king. He had brought about the addition of the principality of Monaco and a part of Belgium to France.

Sent to the Army of the North in March, 1793, he had, upon the battle-field of Wattignies, degraded General Gratien from his rank because he fell back before the enemy, and, placing himself at the head of the French column, he had won back the ground which we had lost.

In the month of August in the same year, being chosen a member of the Committee of Public Safety, he had displayed extraordinary talent, which has become proverbial, by organizing fourteen armies and forming plans of campaign, not only for each army by itself, but for operations including them all. It was then that our armies obtained that astonishing succession of victories, from the recovery of Toulon to the surrender of the four strongholds of the North.

This man was Lazare-Nicolas-Marguerite Carnot, the fourth director, who, not having been able to agree with Barras, Rewbell, and La Réveillère-Lepaux, had just been condemned to death by them, being thought too dangerous to be allowed to live.

His partner, who was shaking the dice with a nonchalance equal to Carnot's energy, was the Marquis François Barthélemy, the last of the directors to be appointed, who had no other merit than that of being the nephew of the Abbé Barthélemy, author of the "Voyage du Jeune Anacharsis."

As minister from France to Switzerland during the Revolution, he had concluded at Basle the treaties of peace with Prussia and Spain, two years before the period of which we are speaking, which had put an end to the first coalition.

He had been chosen because of the well-known moderation of his opinions; and it was this very moderation which had justly led to his dismissal by his colleagues, and which was about to lead to his incarceration.

It was one o'clock in the morning when Carnot, by a brilliant play, ended his sixth game of backgammon.

The two friends shook hands at parting.

"*Au revoir*," said Carnot.

"*Au revoir?*" repeated Barthélemy. "Are you sure, my dear colleague? In these times I am never sure, when I part from a friend at night, that I shall see him again in the morning."

"What the deuce do you fear?" asked Carnot.

"Oh," replied Barthélemy, "a stroke of the dagger is soon given."

"Nonsense!" said Carnot; "you need not worry about that. I am the one whom they will assassinate, and not you. You are too good-natured for them to think of fearing you. They will treat you like a *roi fainéant;* you will be shaved, and shut up in a cloister."

"But if you fear that," replied Barthélemy, "why do you prefer defeat to victory? For after the propositions which have been made to us, it depends only upon ourselves to overthrow our three colleagues."

"My dear friend," said Carnot, "you cannot see beyond your own nose, which unfortunately is not as long as that of your uncle. Who are the men who have made these propositions to us? Royalists. Now, do you think the royalists would ever pardon me for the part I have taken against them? It is only a choice of deaths: with the royalists I should be hanged as a regicide; with the directors, assassinated as a royalist. I would rather be assassinated."

"And with those ideas," said Barthélemy, "you will go to bed in your own rooms?"

"Where should I go to bed?"

"In some place, no matter where, where you would be safe."

"I am a fatalist: if the dagger is to strike me, it will find me. Good-night, Barthélemy. My conscience is clear; I voted for the death of the king, but I saved France. It is for France to take care of me."

And Carnot went to bed as composedly as he always did.

He was not mistaken; the order had been given to a German to arrest him, and if he made the least resistance, to assassinate him.

At three o'clock in the morning the German and his satellites presented themselves at the door of Carnot's apartments, which he shared with a younger brother.

Carnot's servant, when he saw the men and heard their leader ask in bad French where Citizen Carnot was, took them to the bed of the younger brother, who, knowing that he had nothing to fear for himself, left them in error at first.

Then the valet ran to warn his master that they had come to arrest him.

Carnot, almost naked, escaped through one of the doors of the Luxembourg garden, to which he had a key.

Then the servant came back. When he saw him, the prisoner knew that his brother had escaped, and he made himself known.

The soldiers, in a rage, ran through the rooms; but they found only Carnot's empty bed, which was still warm.

Once in the gardens of the Luxembourg, the fugitive paused for an instant, not knowing where to go. He finally went to a lodging-house in the Rue d'Enfer, but was told that there was not a vacant room in the house.

He set off again, seeking shelter at random, when suddenly the alarm-guns were heard.

At the sound, several doors and windows were opened. What would become of him, half-naked as he was? He would certainly be arrested by the first patrol, and from all directions troops were marching towards the Luxembourg.

While he was deliberating, a patrol appeared at the corner of Rue de la Vieille-Comédie.

A porter half opened his door, and Carnot sprang inside.

The man happened to be a worthy fellow, who kept him concealed until he had time to prepare another hiding-place.

As for Barthélemy, although Barras sent warning to him twice, during the day, of the fate which awaited him, he took no precautions.

An hour after he left Carnot, he was arrested in his bed. He did not even ask to see the warrant, and the words, "O my country!" were the only ones which he pronounced.

His servant, Letellier, who had been with him for twenty years, asked to be arrested with his master.

This singular favor was refused; we shall see how he obtained it later.

The two councils had named a committee which was to sit permanently.

This committee had Siméon for president. He had not yet arrived when the alarm-guns sounded.

Pichegru had passed the night with this committee, together with those of the conspirators who were determined to meet force with force; but no one thought that the moment was so near when the Directory would dare to attempt a *coup d'état*.

Several members of the committee were armed, among others Rovère and Villot, who, learning suddenly that they were surrounded, undertook to go out, pistol in hand.

But Pichegru opposed it.

" Our colleagues assembled here are not armed," he said. " They would be massacred by these wretches, who are only waiting for an excuse; let us not abandon them."

Just then the door of the room occupied by the committee opened, and a member of the councils named Delarue rushed in.

" Ah, my dear Delarue," exclaimed Pichegru, " what on earth have you come here for? We are all going to be arrested."

" Well, then, we will all be arrested together," replied Delarue, composedly.

And, in fact, Delarue, in order that he might undergo the same treatment accorded to his companions, had had the courage to force his way past the guard three times in order to reach the committee. He had been warned at his own house of the danger he ran, but he refused to escape, although it would have been easy for him; and after kissing his wife and children, without waking them, he had come, as we have seen, to join his colleagues.

In the preceding chapter we said that Pichegru, who had offered to bring the three directors bound to the bar of the Corps Législatif if they would give him two hundred men, was not able to obtain them.

They were now eager to defend themselves, but it was too late.

Scarcely had Delarue exchanged these few words with Pichegru when the door was forced open, and a crowd of soldiers, led by Augereau, entered the room.

Augereau found himself near Pichegru. He put out his hand to seize him.

Delarue drew a pistol from his pocket, and attempted to fire upon Augereau; but as he made the motion a bayonet was thrust through his arm.

"I arrest you," said Augereau, seizing Pichegru.

"Wretch!" exclaimed the latter. "All you needed was to become a satellite of Citizen Barras!"

"Soldiers!" cried a member of the committee, "will you dare to lay a hand upon Pichegru, your general?"

Without replying, Augereau flung himself upon him, and, with the help of four soldiers, succeeded, after a violent struggle, in bending his arms and binding them behind his back.

When Pichegru was arrested, the conspiracy had no longer a head, and no one attempted to make any resistance.

General Mathieu Dumas, the same who was Minister of War at Naples under Joseph Napoleon, and who has left such interesting memoirs, was with the committee when it was surrounded; he wore the uniform of a general officer. He left through the door which had given entrance to Augereau, and went down-stairs.

In the vestibule a sentinel put his bayonet in front of him. "No one is allowed to go out," he said.

" I know it, " said the general, " for it was I who just gave the order. "

" I beg your pardon, General, " replied the sentinel, raising his weapon.

And the general passed without further hindrance.

To assure his safety, he had to leave Paris.

Mathieu Dumas took his two aides-de-camp, put them on horseback, galloped to the barrier, gave his orders to the guard, passed outside the walls to go, as he said, to another post, and disappeared.

CHAPTER XXXI.

THE TEMPLE.

THIS is what had happened.

When a great event takes place, like the 13th Vendémiaire or the 18th Fructidor, it prints upon the book of history an indelible date. Everybody knows this date; and when the words "13th Vendémiaire" or "18th Fructidor" are pronounced, every one knows the results which followed the great events commemorated by these dates, but very few know the secret springs which prepared the way for the accomplishment of these events.

This is why we have particularly imposed upon ourselves the task, in our historical romances, or romanticized histories, of telling things which no one has told before, and of relating matters which we know, but of which very few persons share the knowledge with us.

Since friendly indiscretion has revealed the method by which we obtained possession of the priceless volumes and original and rare manuscripts upon which we have drawn, this is the proper place for us to acknowledge our indebtedness for the communication of these interesting documents, which it is so hard to coax down from their shelves. They have been to us the torch which has guided us through the arcana of the 13th Vendémiaire; and we had only to light it again, to penetrate into those of the 18th Fructidor.

It is, then, with the certainty of telling the truth, the whole truth, and nothing but the truth that we repeat the phrase with which we began this chapter: This is what had happened.

On the evening of the 17th, Adjutant-General Ramel, after he had visited his posts, went to take his orders from the members of the committee, who were to remain in session during the night. He was present at the time when, as we have said, Pichegru, prevented by his colleagues from taking the aggressive, had predicted to them what would happen, and with his habitual indifference, although he might have fled, and thus have escaped the persecution he had foreseen, had allowed himself to drift down the current of his destiny.

When Pichegru was gone, the other deputies were strengthened in their conviction that the Directory would not dare to attempt anything against them, or if it did, that it would not be at once, and that for several days they had nought to fear. He even heard, before his departure, some of the deputies, and among others, Émery, Mathieu Dumas, Vaublanc, Tronçon du Coudray, and Thibaudeau speak indignantly of this supposition, and of the terror with which it inspired the public.

Adjutant-General Ramel was therefore dismissed without any new orders; he was merely instructed to do that day what he had done the day before, and what he would do on the morrow.

Consequently, he returned to his quarters, and contented himself with ascertaining that in case of alarm the grenadiers would be ready to take up arms.

Two hours later, at one o'clock in the morning, he received from the Minister of War an order to report to him.

He hastened to the hall of the committee, where there

remained only one of the inspectors, named Rovère, who was asleep. He told him of the order which he had received, and begged him to note its importance at that hour of the night.

Ramel added that he had been notified that several columns of troops had entered Paris. But all these threatening probabilities had no effect upon Rovère, who declared that he was very comfortable, and had excellent reasons for remaining so.

Ramel, when he left the hall, met the commander of the cavalry post, whose duty, like his own, was to guard the councils. The latter announced that he had withdrawn his pickets, and caused his troop, as well as the two pieces of artillery which were in the great courtyard of the Tuileries, to cross the bridges.

"How could you do such a thing," asked Ramel, "when I told you to do just the contrary?"

"General, it was not my fault," he replied; "the commander-in-chief, Augereau, gave the order, and the cavalry officer positively refused to obey yours."

Ramel went back, and again begged Rovère to warn his colleagues, telling him what had passed since he left him.

But Rovère was obstinate in his confidence, and replied that all these movements of troops signified absolutely nothing; that he had known of them beforehand, and that several corps were to go upon the bridges at an early hour, in order to practise manœuvring.

Ramel might therefore be perfectly easy, for Rovère's sources of information were reliable, and he could count upon them; and Ramel could without any hesitation obey the order of the Minister of War.

The fear of being separated from his force prevented Ramel from obeying. He went home, but did not go to bed, and remained ready dressed and armed.

At three o'clock in the morning a former member of the body-guard, with whom he had been very intimate in the Army of the Pyrenees, named Poinçot, announced himself as a messenger from General Lemoine, and gave Ramel a note, in these words, —

"General Lemoine, in the name of the Directory, summons the commander of the grenadiers of the Corps Législatif to give passage across the swing-bridge to a column of fifteen hundred men, charged with executing the orders of the government."

"I am surprised," said Ramel, "that an old comrade, who ought to know me better, should bring me an order which I cannot obey without dishonoring myself."

"Do as you like," replied Poinçot, "but I warn you that all resistance will be useless. Eight hundred of your grenadiers are already covered by four pieces of artillery."

"I receive no orders except from the Corps Législatif," exclaimed Ramel.

And hastening from his house, he started to run to the Tuileries.

An alarm-gun sounded so near him that he thought it was the signal for attack.

On the way he met two of his chiefs of battalion, Ponsard and Fléchard, both excellent officers, in whom he had every confidence.

He immediately went once more to the committee-room, where he found Generals Pichegru and Villot. He at once sent notices to General Mathieu Dumas and the presidents of the two councils, Laffon-Ladébat, president of the Council of the Ancients, and Siméon, president of the Council of the Five Hundred. He also sent to warn the deputies whose lodgings were known to him to be near the Tuileries.

Just then, the iron gate of the swing-bridge being forced, the divisions of Augereau and Lemoine were united. The garden was filled with the soldiers of the two armies; a battery was directed upon the hall of the Council of the Ancients, all the avenues were closed, and all the posts were doubled, and covered by superior forces.

We have told how the door opened, how a throng of soldiers entered the hall of the committee, with Augereau at its head, and how, when no one dared lay a hand on Pichegru, Augereau himself committed the sacrilege, and threw down and bound the man who had been his general; and finally, how, after Pichegru was taken, no further resistance was offered, and the order was given to take all the prisoners to the Temple.

The three directors were waiting, together with the Minister of Police, who, after his placards were posted, had returned to them.

The Minister of Police advised that the prisoners should be instantly shot in the Luxembourg garden, upon the pretext that they had been taken with arms in their hands.

Rewbell agreed with him; the gentle La Réveillère-Lepaux, the man of peace, who had always advised merciful measures, was ready to give the fatal order, saying, like Cicero of Lentullus and Cethegus, —

"They have lived."

But Barras, we must do him the justice to say, opposed this measure with all his strength, saying that unless they put him in prison during the execution, he should throw himself between the victims and the bullets.

Finally, a deputy named Guillemardet, who had made himself the friend of the directors by joining their faction, proposed banishment to Cayenne, " to be done with it."

The amendment was put to vote, and enthusiastically carried.

The Minister of Police thought it his duty to take Barthélemy to the Temple himself.

We have said that Barthélemy's servant, Letellier, asked to go with him. They refused at first, but finally granted his request.

"Who is this man?" asked Augereau, who did not recognize him as one of the exiles.

"He is my friend," replied Barthélemy; "he asked to follow me, and — "

"Bah!" said Augereau, interrupting him. "When he finds out where you are going, he will not be so eager."

"I beg your pardon, Citizen-General," replied Letellier, "but wherever my master goes, I will go with him."

"Even to the scaffold?" asked Augereau.

"Above all, to the scaffold," he replied.

By dint of insistence and entreaties, the doors of the prison were opened to the wives of the exiles.

Each step which they took in the courtyard, where a queen of France had suffered so bitterly, was fresh agony for them. Drunken soldiers insulted them constantly.

"Are you coming to see those beggars?" they asked, pointing to the prisoners. "Make haste and say farewell to them to-day, for they will be shot to-morrow."

As we have already said, Pichegru was not married. When he came to Paris he did not choose to supplant poor Rose, for whom, as we have seen, he bought from his savings an umbrella which delighted her so. When he saw the wives of his colleagues, he went up to them and took in his arms Delarue's little son, who was crying.

"Why are you crying, my child?" asked Pichegru, with tears in his own eyes as he kissed him.

" Because," replied the child, " wicked soldiers have arrested my poor father."

" You are right, poor little fellow," said Pichegru, casting a look of scorn at those who were watching him; " they are wicked soldiers. Good soldiers would not allow themselves to be made executioners."

The same day Augereau wrote to Bonaparte,—

At last, General, my mission is accomplished ; the promises of the Army of Italy were fulfilled last night.

The Directory determined upon a bold stroke ; the moment for it was still undecided, and the preparations incomplete, when the fear of being forestalled precipitated measures. At midnight I sent orders to all the troops to march upon designated points. Before daylight all those points and all the principal squares were occupied by artillery ; at daybreak the halls of the councils were surrounded, the guards of the Directory fraternized with our troops, and the members whose names I send you were arrested and taken to the Temple.

A large number are still being pursued.

Carnot has disappeared.

Paris is calm, marvelling at a crisis which should have been terrible, but which has gone off like a *fête*.

The robust patriot of the Faubourgs proclaims the safety of the Republic, and the black collars are downcast.

Now it is for the wise energy of the Directory and for the patriots of the two councils to do the rest.

The place of the sessions is changed, and the first proceedings promise well. This event is a long stride towards peace ; it is for you to cross the intervening space which still separates us from it.

Do not forget the bill of exchange for twenty-five thousand francs, for it is urgent.

AUGEREAU.

Then followed the list, containing seventy-four names.

CHAPTER XXXII.

THE EXILES.

THE Temple had associations which were not precisely without remorse for the political consciences of most of those who had just been taken there.

Some of them, after they had sent Louis XVI. to the Temple, — in other words, after they had closed the prison doors upon him, — had opened them again only to send him to the scaffold, — which means that several of the prisoners were regicides.

Allowed their liberty in the interior of the prison, they had rallied around Pichegru, as being the most eminent personality among them. Pichegru, who had nothing with which to reproach himself as far as Louis XVI. was concerned, but who, on the contrary, was being punished for the pity with which the Bourbons had inspired him, — Pichegru, the archæologist, historian, and man of letters, led the group which asked permission to see the apartments in the tower.

Lavilleheurnois, former Master of Requests under Louis XVI., secret agent of the Bourbons during the Revolution, and a participant with Brotier Deprèle in a conspiracy against the republican government, acted as their guide.

" Here is the chamber of the unfortunate Louis XVI.," he said, opening the door of the apartment in which the august prisoner had been confined.

Rovère, the same to whom Ramel had applied, and who had assured him that there was nothing to fear from the movements of the troops, — Rovère, the former lieutenant of Jourdan Coupe-tête, who had apologized to the Legislative Assembly for the massacre in the Glacière, could not bear the sight of that room, and retreated, striking his forehead with his hands.

Pichegru, who was once more as calm as he would have been at the head of the Army of the Rhine, deciphered the inscriptions written in pencil on the woodwork, and with a diamond on the window-panes.

He read this one: —

" O God, pardon those who have killed my parents!

" O my brother, watch over me from heaven !

" May the French be happy! "

He had no doubt as to the hand which had traced these lines, but he wished to assure himself of the truth.

Lavilleheurnois said that he recognized the handwriting as that of Madame Royale; but Pichegru sent for the concierge, who assured him that it was indeed the august daughter of King Louis XVI. who had in such a Christian spirit written these petitions. Then he added, —

" Gentlemen, I beg of you not to efface those lines as long as I am here. I have vowed that no one shall touch them."

" Well done, my friend! You are a fine fellow," said Pichegru, while Delarue wrote below the words, " May the French be happy! "

" Heaven will hear the prayers of innocence."

Meanwhile, although they were separated from the world, the prisoners had the satisfaction of learning on several occasions that they were not forgotten.

On the very evening of the 18th Fructidor, as the wife of one of the prisoners was leaving the Temple, where she had obtained permission to see her husband, she was accosted by a man whom she did not know.

"Madame," he said, "you doubtless are connected with one of the unfortunate men who were arrested this morning?"

"Alas! yes, Monsieur," she replied.

"Well, permit me to send him, whoever he may be, this slight loan, which he can repay when times are better."

As he spoke, he put three rolls of louis into her hand.

An old man, whom Madame Laffon-Ladébat did not know, came to her house on the morning of the 19th Fructidor.

"Madame," he said, "I feel for your husband all the esteem and friendship which he deserves. Be good enough to give him these fifty louis; I regret exceedingly that just now I have only this small sum to offer him."

Then, seeing her hesitation and guessing its cause, he added, "Madame, your delicacy need not suffer. I am only lending this money to your husband; he can repay it when he returns."

Almost all the men who were condemned to exile had for a long time occupied the first offices in the government, either as generals or ministers; and it is a remarkable fact that on the 18th Fructidor, when they were about to be exiled, they were all poor.

Pichegru, the poorest of all, when he learned that he was not to be shot, as he had at first supposed, but only exiled, was very much disturbed about his sister and brother, whose sole support he had been.

As for poor Rose, we know that she was able to support herself with her needle, and was richer than any of them. If she had known of the trouble which had befallen her friend, she would certainly have hastened to him from Besançon, with open purse.

That which most disturbed the man who had saved France on the Rhine, who had conquered Holland, the richest of all provinces, who had handled millions, and refused to sell himself for millions, was not married, and consequently while he was accused of having received nine hundred louis d'or, of having exacted a promise of the principality of Arbois, with an income of two hundred thousand livres and reversion to his wife and children, and the château of Chambord, with twelve pieces of artillery taken by him from the enemy, — that which most disturbed this man, who had neither wife nor children, who had given himself for nothing when he might have sold himself at a great price, was a debt of six hundred francs which was not paid !

He sent for his brother and sister, and said to the latter, —

"You will find in the lodgings which I occupied, the coat, hat, and sword which I wore when I conquered Holland. Put them up for sale with the inscription, 'Coat, hat, and sword of Pichegru, exiled to Cayenne.'"

His sister obeyed, and the next day she came and told him that a pious hand had given her the six hundred francs in exchange for the coat, hat, and sword, and that his debt was paid.

Barthélemy, one of the most prominent men of the time, politically speaking, since he had negotiated with Spain and Prussia the first treaties of peace which the Republic had signed, and who could have compelled each of these powers to give him a million, had for his sole property a farm which brought him in an income of eight hundred livres.

Villot, when he was arrested, possessed only a thousand francs. A week before, he had lent them to a man who called himself his friend, but who failed to return them to him at his departure.

Laffon-Ladébat, who since the proclamation of the Republic had forgotten his own interests for those of the country, and who had possessed an immense fortune, could scarcely gather together five hundred francs when he heard of his condemnation. His children, charged with settling his affairs, paid all his creditors, only to find themselves in penury.

Delarue supported his old father and all his family. Rich before the Revolution, but ruined by it, he owed to friendship the help which he received at his departure. His father, an old man of sixty-nine, was inconsolable; but grief could not kill him.

He lived in the hope of seeing his son again some day.

Three months later, he was told that an officer of the navy who had arrived in Paris had met Delarue in the deserts of Guiana.

He at once desired to see and talk with him. The officer's story would interest the whole family, and they were all assembled. The officer entered. Delarue's father rose to go and meet him; but just as he was about to throw his arms around his neck, joy killed him, and he fell dead at the feet of the man, who said,—

" I have seen your son! "

As for Tronçon du Coudray, who had nothing but his salary on which to live, he was deprived of everything when he was arrested, and went away with two louis for his whole fortune.

Perhaps I am wrong, but it seems to me that it is well, since the historian neglects this duty, for the romance writer to follow after revolutions and *coups d'état*, and teach posterity that it is not always those men to whom statues are raised who are most worthy of their respect and admiration.

Augereau, after having been charged with the duty of making the arrest, was appointed to guard the prisoners.

He gave them for their immediate keeper a man who, it was reported, had been, until within a month, at the galleys in Toulon, where he had been sent, after a trial by court-martial, for theft, murder, and incendiarism committed in La Vendée.

The prisoners remained at the Temple from the morning of the 18th Fructidor until the evening of the 21st.

At midnight the jailer woke them, telling them that they were about to start, and that they had a quarter of an hour in which to get ready.

Pichegru, who still preserved the habit of sleeping with his clothes on, was ready first, and went from room to room to hasten his companions.

He went down first, and found ex-Director Barthélemy between General Augereau and Minister of Police Sothin, who had brought him to the Temple in his own carriage.

Sothin had treated him well; and as Barthélemy thanked him, the minister replied, —

"We know what revolutions are. Your turn to-day, perhaps ours to-morrow."

As Barthélemy, anxious about the state of the country rather than about himself, asked if no harm had come of it, and if the public peace had not been disturbed, —

"No," replied the minister. "The people swallowed the pill; and as the dose was a good one, they took it without any trouble."

Then, seeing all the exiles at the foot of the tower, he said, —

"Gentlemen, I wish you a pleasant journey."

And getting into his carriage, he went away.

Then Augereau ordered the roll of the prisoners to be called. As fast as they were named, a guard led them to the carriages, past a line of soldiers, who insulted them as they went along.

Some of these men — miserable curs, always ready to insult those who are down — tried to reach across the others and strike the exiles in the face, to tear away their clothing, or throw mud on them.

"Why do they let them go?" they cried. "They promised us that they should be shot."

"My dear *General*," said Pichegru as he passed Augereau, and he emphasized the title, "if you promised that to these worthy people, it is very wrong of you not to keep your word."

CHAPTER XXXIII.

THE JOURNEY.

FOUR carriages, or rather four boxes on wheels, forming cages, enclosed on all sides by iron bars, which at the least jolt bruised the prisoners, received the sixteen exiles.

Four of them were placed in each cage, and no attention was paid to their weakness or their wounds. Some of them had received sabre-cuts; others had been wounded, either by the soldiers who arrested them or by the mob, whose opinion always will be that those who are conquered do not suffer enough.

For each wagon and each group of four men there was a keeper, who had the care of the key to the padlock which locked the grating that served for a door.

General Dutertre commanded the escort, which consisted of four hundred infantry, two hundred cavalry, and two pieces of artillery.

Every time the exiles got in or out of their cages, the two cannon were trained diagonally, each upon two wagons, and the gunners, holding lighted matches, stood ready to fire upon those who should attempt to escape, as well as those who did not.

The 22d Fructidor (8th of September), at one o'clock in the morning, the condemned men began their journey, in the midst of a terrible storm.

They had to cross the whole of Paris, starting from the Temple, and, leaving the city through the Barrière d'Enfer, to take the road to Orléans.

But instead of following Rue Saint-Jacques, the escort, after crossing the bridge, turned to the right and led the procession to the Luxembourg.

There was a ball in progress, given by the three directors, or rather by Barras, who was in himself the three.

Barras, upon being notified, hastened to the balcony, followed by his guests, and pointed out to them Pichegru (the man who, three days before, had been the rival of Moreau, Hoche, and Bonaparte); and with him Barthélemy (his own former colleague), Villot, Delarue, Ramel, — in short, all those whom the turn of Fortune's wheel or the forgetfulness of Providence had put in his power. Amid bursts of laughter and noisy demonstrations of joy, the exiles heard Barras enjoin Dutertre, Augereau's man, "to take good care of these gentlemen." To which Dutertre replied, —

" Never fear, General."

We shall soon see what Barras meant when he said, " Take good care of these gentlemen."

In the mean time, the people who were coming out of the club of the Odéon surrounded the wagons; and as they were refused permission to do what they urgently requested, — tear the exiles to pieces, — they consoled themselves by throwing fireworks, which enabled them to see the prisoners without any trouble.

Finally, in the midst of fierce cries for their death and howls of rage, the procession passed through Rue d'Enfer, and left Paris.

At two o'clock in the afternoon they had made only eight leagues, and reached Arpajon. Barthélemy and

Barbé-Marbois, the weakest among the exiles, were lying on their faces, apparently exhausted.

On hearing that the day's journey was finished, the prisoners hoped to be conducted to some suitable place where they could take a little rest. But the commander of the escort took them to the prison for thieves, eagerly examining their faces, and manifesting delight when they showed repulsion and disgust.

Unfortunately, the first wagon to be opened was that of Pichegru, whose impassive face did not betray the least expression. He merely said, as they approached a sort of hole, —

"If that is a staircase, give me a light; if it is a well, tell me so at once."

It was a staircase, several steps of which were missing.

This calmness exasperated Dutertre.

"Ah, rascal," he said, "you think you can defy me; but we shall see, one of these days, whether I can find the end of your insolence."

Pichegru, who reached the bottom first, called to his companions that some one had had the thoughtfulness to spread straw for them, and thanked Dutertre for the attention. But the straw was soaking wet, and the cell was foul.

Barthélemy came next, gentle, calm, but exhausted, and feeling that he could not expect a moment's repose. Half lying down in the icy water, he raised his hands, murmuring, —

"*Mon Dieu! mon Dieu!*"

Then came Barbé-Marbois; they supported him by the arms. At the mephitic odor which arose from the cell, he drew back, saying, —

"Shoot me, and spare me the horror of such agony."

But the jailer's wife, who was following, said, —

"You are very particular. Better men than you are have not made such a fuss at going down there."

And with a vigorous push she sent him, head-first, from top to bottom of the stairs.

Villot, who was coming next, heard Barbé-Marbois' cry as he fell, and that uttered by the two exiles as they saw him, and darted forward to receive him; and seizing the woman by the neck, he said, —

"Upon my word, I have a good mind to strangle her. What do you all say?"

"Let her alone, Villot," said Pichegru, "and come down here with us."

They had raised Barbé-Marbois. His face was bruised, and his jaw-bone broken.

The three exiles who were safe and sound began to shout, —

"A surgeon! a surgeon!"

There was no answer.

Then they asked for water to wash their companion's wounds; but the door was closed, and it was not opened until two hours later, and then only to pass in their dinner, consisting of a loaf of bread and a pitcher of water.

They were all very thirsty; but Pichegru, accustomed to all sorts of privation, immediately offered his portion of the water to wash Barbé-Marbois' wounds. The other prisoners, however, would not permit this sacrifice. The necessary amount of water was taken from the general fund; and as Barbé-Marbois could not eat, his ration was divided among the others.

The next day, 23d Fructidor (9th September), they started again, at seven o'clock in the morning. No inquiries were made as to how the exiles had passed the night, and no surgeon was brought to visit the wounded man.

At noon they reached Étampes.   Dutertre ordered
a halt in the middle of the square, and exposed his
prisoners to the insults of the crowd, who were permitted to surround the wagons, and who took advantage
of the permission to hoot, curse, and throw mud upon
men, of whose crime they were ignorant, and who
were criminals in their eyes simply because they were
prisoners.

The exiles demanded to go on, or to be allowed to
get out of the wagons.   Both requests were refused.
One of the exiles, Tronçon du Coudray, was the deputy
for the department of Seine-et-Oise, which includes
Étampes, and was now in the very canton of which
the inhabitants had supported his candidacy with the
greatèst enthusiasm.

He therefore resented all the more keenly the ingrati-
tude and desertion of his people.   Rising suddenly, as
if he had been in the Tribune, and replying to those
who called him by name, he said, —

"Yes, it is I, — I, myself, your representative!   Do
you recognize him in this iron cage?   It is I, whom
you intrusted with upholding your rights, which are
violated in my person.   I am dragged to punishment
without having been tried, without having even been
accused.   My crime is, that I have protected your liberty, your property, your persons; that I have wished
to give peace to France, and, by so doing, to give back
to you your children, who are being slaughtered by the
enemy's bayonets.   My crime is, that I have been faithful to the Constitution to which we have sworn alle-
giance; and to-day, as the reward of my zeal in serving
and defending you, you join the ranks of our executioners!   You are wretches and cowards, unworthy of
being represented by a man of heart."

And he relapsed into apparent indifference once more.

The crowd were for a moment crushed and awed by this vehement attack; but they soon renewed their insults, which became more outrageous than ever when dinner was brought to the condemned men, — consisting of four loaves of bread and four bottles of wine.

This exhibition lasted three hours.

That evening they stopped for the night at Anger-ville, and Dutertre wished to put the prisoners together in one cell, as he had done on the previous night.

But an adjutant-general, who, by an odd coincidence, was named Augereau, took it upon himself to lodge them in an inn, where they passed a comfortable night, and where Barbé-Marbois was able to secure the services of a surgeon.

On the 24th Fructidor (10th September), they reached Orléans early, and passed the rest of that day and the following night in a house of confinement which had formerly been an Ursuline convent.

This time the deputies were not guarded by their escort, but by gendarmes, who, while obeying orders, treated them with great consideration.

They quickly recognized beneath the disguise of two servants, who were sent to wait upon them, two ladies of rank, who had assumed coarse clothing in order to gain access to them and to offer help and money.

They even proposed to Villot and Delarue to aid them to escape. They could facilitate the escape of two prisoners, but no more.

Villot and Delarue refused, fearing by their flight to aggravate the fate of their companions.

The names of these two angels of charity have never been known. To name them at that time would have been to denounce them.

The next day the party reached Blois.

On the outskirts of the town a crowd of boatmen were waiting for the wagons, in the hope of breaking them open and assassinating those who were in them.

But the captain of cavalry who commanded the detachment, and who was named Gauthier, — history has preserved his name, as it has preserved that of Dutertre, — made a sign to the exiles that they had nothing to fear.

He took forty men, and routed the rabble.

But insults were, none the less, lavished upon them. The names of rascals, regicides, and forestallers were hurled blindly at them by the furious crowd, through the midst of which they passed on their way to a damp little church, on the pavement of which was spread a small quantity of straw.

As they entered the church, the people crowded near enough to the condemned men for Pichegru to feel a little note slipped into his hand.

As soon as they were alone, Pichegru read the note. It contained these words: —

"General, it only depends upon yourself to leave your prison, mount a horse, and escape under an assumed name, by means of a passport. If you consent, as soon as you have read this note, approach the guard, who is watching you, and take care to have your hat on your head; this will be a sign that you consent. Then from midnight until two o'clock be dressed and on the alert."

Pichegru walked towards the guard, bare-headed.

The man who had sought to save him cast a look of admiration at him, and walked away.

CHAPTER XXXIV.

THE EMBARKATION.

THE preparations for departure from Blois took so long that the prisoners feared that they were to make a stay there, and that during their stay some harm would come to them. They were the more convinced of this when the adjutant-general who was in command of their escort under Dutertre — one Colin, well known in the province for having caused the massacres of the 2d of September — and one of his companions, named Guillet, who had no better reputation, entered the prison about six o'clock in the morning.

They seemed much excited, grumbling as if to spur themselves on, and looking at the exiles with baleful smiles.

The municipal officer who had accompanied the prisoners from Paris had an inspiration.

He went straight up to them, and looking fixedly at them, said, —

" Why do you delay the departure? Everything has been ready for a long time. The crowd increases, and your conduct is more than suspicious. I have seen and heard you both, stirring up the people and urging them to acts of violence towards the prisoners. I declare to you that if any accident happens when they go out, I will place my deposition upon the register of the municipality, and you will be the ones whom it will accuse."

The two knaves stammered some excuse. The wagons were brought out, and the prisoners were accompanied with the same shouts, threats, and imprecations which had greeted them on the previous night; but no one was hit by the blows which were aimed at them, nor by the stones which were thrown.

At Amboise they passed the night in a room so small that there was not room for them to lie down upon the straw. They were obliged either to stand up or sit down.

They hoped to get some rest at Tours, but they were cruelly disappointed.

The town authorities had just been subjected to a weeding-out process, and were still terror-stricken.

The prisoners were put in the prison occupied by the galley-slaves. They were compelled to mingle with them, and some of the deputies asked for a place by themselves.

" There is your apartment," said the jailer, pointing to a little cell which was damp and dirty.

Thereupon the men from the galleys showed more humanity than the new magistrates of Tours; for one of them, approaching the exiles, said humbly,—

" Gentlemen, we are very sorry to see you here. We are not worthy to approach you; but if, in the unhappy state to which we are reduced, there is any service that we can render you, we pray you to be good enough to accept it. The cell which has been prepared for you is colder and damper than ours; we beg you to take ours, which is larger and drier."

Pichegru thanked the poor wretches in the name of his companions, and shaking hands with the one who had spoken, he said, —

" So it is among you that we must now look for human hearts! "

The exiles had not eaten for more than thirty hours, and each one now received a loaf of bread and a bottle of wine.

It was a gala day for them.

The next day they stopped at Saint-Maure. Lieutenant-General Dutertre, having found in this little town a flying column of the National Guard, composed of peasants, took advantage of the opportunity to give some rest to his troop, who were scarcely able to put one foot before the other. He consequently ordered this column to guard the exiles, under the responsibility of the municipal body, which, fortunately, had not been weeded out.

These worthy peasants took pity on the unfortunate prisoners. They brought them bread and wine in such quantities that they could for the first time eat and drink in proportion to their hunger and thirst. Besides this, they were less strictly guarded; and so negligent were these worthy people, most of whom were armed only with pikes, that the prisoners were permitted to go as far as the causeway, and from there they could see a forest, which seemed put there expressly to afford them refuge.

Ramel ventured to propose an attempt at escape; but some opposed it because they thought flight would be a confession of their guilt, and others refused because their escape would have cruelly compromised their keepers, and would have brought punishment upon the first of their kind who had shown compassion for their distress.

Day came, and they had scarcely slept; for the whole night had slipped away in the discussion, and they were obliged to re-enter the iron cages, and become once more the property of Dutertre.

They crossed the dense forest at which, on the previous night, they had gazed so eagerly. The roads were frightful. Some of them obtained permission to walk between four of the cavalry. Barbé-Marbois, Barthélemy, and Du Coudray, wounded, and almost at the point of death, could not take advantage of the permission. Lying upon the floor, at every jolt they were thrown against the iron bars, which bruised them, and, in spite of their stoicism, drew from them cries of agony. Barthélemy was the only one who did not utter a single groan.

At Châtellerault they were shut up in a cell that was so foul that three of them fell down asphyxiated as they entered. Pichegru pushed open the door which the keepers were about to shut, and pulling a soldier towards him, he threw him to the farther end of the cell, where the man almost fainted. He reported that it was impossible to live in such an atmosphere; and the door was left open, and sentinels placed before it.

Barbé-Marbois was very ill. Du Coudray, who was taking care of him, was seated on the straw beside him. A man who for three years had been in irons in a neighboring cell obtained leave to visit them, brought them fresh water, and offered his bed to Marbois, who felt a little better after having had two hours' sleep.

"Have patience," said this man to them. "One can get accustomed to anything, in time. I am an example of the truth of this, for I have lived for three years in a cell like this one of yours."

At Lusignan the prison was too small to contain the sixteen exiles. It poured in torrents, and a cold wind was blowing from the north. Dutertre, who stopped at nothing, ordered the cages to be closed, had the horses unharnessed, and cages and prisoners remained

on the public square. They had been there about an
hour when the mayor and the commander of the National
Guard came and offered to be responsible for them if
they were allowed to pass the night at an inn. The authorities gained their point, not without difficulty. The
prisoners were no sooner established in three rooms, with
sentinels at the doors and beneath the windows, than
they saw a courier ride up and stop at the same inn to
which they had been taken. Some of them, more
hopeful than the others, were sure that the courier was
the bearer of good news. All were of opinion that he
came on some errand of importance.

As a matter of fact, he brought an order to arrest
General Dutertre for extortions and knaveries committed since the departure of the exiles, and to take
him back to Paris.

They found upon Dutertre the eight hundred louis
d'or which he had received for the expenses of his
convoy, and which he had pocketed, levying contributions instead upon the different towns through which
he passed.

The exiles heard the news with joy. They saw the
carriage approach which was to take him; and Ramel,
who carried his curiosity so far as to desire to observe
his expression, opened the window.

The sentinel in the street fired instantly, and the
ball broke the window-frame.

Dutertre once arrested, the conduct of the convoy fell
to his second in command, — Guillet.

But, as we have said, Guillet was not much better
than Dutertre. On the following day the mayor of
Saint-Maixant, where they had halted, approached the
exiles, and was so ill-advised as to say to them, " Gentlemen, I sympathize deeply with your situation, and

all good citizens share my feeling." Guillet himself
seized the mayor, pushed him towards two soldiers,
and ordered them to take him to prison.

But this act of brutality so revolted the inhabitants
of the town, by whom the good man seemed to be much
beloved, that they rose in a body and forced Guillet to
return their mayor to them.

That which most disturbed the exiles was the fact
that they were completely ignorant of their destination.
They had heard Rochefort named, but in the vaguest
manner. Deprived of all communication with their
families, they could obtain no information as to the
destiny which awaited them.

At Surgères the secret was revealed. The mayor
had insisted that all the prisoners should be lodged at
the inn, and had gained his point.

Pichegru, Aubry, and Delarue were lying upon mat-
tresses spread on the floor in a room on the first floor,
separated from the room below by planks which were
so poorly joined that they could see all that passed.

The leaders of the escort, not suspecting that they
were both watched and overheard, were in the room at
supper. A naval officer had just joined them. Every
word that they said was of moment to the unfortunate
exiles, and they listened.

The supper, which was long and abundant, was a
very lively meal. The torture which they inflicted
upon the exiles formed the theme of their gayety.
But when the supper was over, at about half-past twelve,
the naval officer remarked that it was nearly time to
begin operations.

This word "operations," as can readily be understood,
riveted the attention of the listeners.

A man who was unknown to them, and who served

as Guillet's secretary, brought pens, ink, and paper, and began to write, at the officer's dictation.

He dictated a report to the effect that, in conformity with the last orders of the Directory, the exiles were to leave their cages only to go aboard the "Brillant," — a brigantine fitted out at Rochefort to receive them.

Pichegru, Aubry, and Delarue, although thunder-struck by the tenor of his report, — made a day ahead of time, and leaving no doubt as to their deportation, — said nothing about it to their companions.

They thought that it would be soon enough for them to learn the sad news when they reached Rochefort.

They arrived there on the 21st of September, between three and four o'clock in the afternoon. The convoy left the main street of the town and went along below the fortification, where an immense crowd was awaiting them, turned the corner of the square, and went towards the bank of the Charente.

There was no longer any doubt, not only for those who had overheard the fatal secret, but for the thirteen who until now had been ignorant of it. They were about to be sent on shipboard, launched upon the ocean, deprived of the barest necessaries of life, and exposed to the risks of a voyage whose end was unknown to them.

At last the wagons stopped. Some hundreds of sailors and marines, disgracing the uniform of the navy, placed themselves in line as the exiles left their cages, — which they fairly regretted, to such a pass were they reduced. Ferocious cries welcomed them: —

"Down with the tyrants! Into the water! into the water with the traitors!"

One of these men stepped forward, doubtless to put his threat into execution. The others pressed after

him.   General Villot walked straight up to him, and,
folding his arms, said, —

"Villain!   You are too much of a coward to do me
such a service!"

A boat drew near, an official called, and one after the
other, as they were named, the exiles got into the boat.

The last, Barbé-Marbois, was in such a desperate
condition that the official declared that if they took
him aboard like that, he would not live two days.

"What is that to you, you fool?" said Guillet.
"You will not be responsible for anything but his
bones."

A quarter of an hour later the exiles were on board
a two-masted vessel lying at anchor in the middle of
the river.

It was the "Brillant," — a little privateer taken from
the English.   They were received there by a dozen
soldiers, who seemed to have been chosen especially
for the position of executioners.   The exiles were
thrust into a little place between decks, so narrow that
scarcely half of them could sit down, so low that the
others could not stand upright; and they were obliged
to take turns in the two positions, between which there
was not much choice.

An hour after they had been put there, some one
remembered that they ought to have something to eat.

Two buckets were sent down, — one of them empty,
and the other containing half-cooked beans swimming
in a reddish water which was even more disgusting than
the vessel which contained it.   A loaf of bread and
some water, the only things of which the prisoners par-
took, completed the foul repast which was served to
men whom their fellow-citizens had chosen as the most
worthy among them to be their representatives.

The exiles did not touch the beans in the bucket, although they had not had anything to eat for thirty-six hours, — either because they were disgusted at their appearance, or because their guards had thought fit to give them neither spoons nor forks.

And as they were obliged to leave the door open, in order to admit air, they had to submit to the jeers of the soldiers, who finally grew so offensive in their language that Pichegru, forgetting that he no longer had the right to command, ordered them to hold their tongues.

" You will do well to hold your tongue yourself," replied one of them. " You had better take care; you are not out of our hands yet! "

" How old are you? " asked Pichegru, seeing that he looked very young.

" Sixteen," replied the soldier.

" Gentlemen," said Pichegru, " if we ever return to France, we must not forget this child; he promises well."

CHAPTER XXXV.

ADIEU, FRANCE!

FIVE hours passed before the vessel got under way; she did so at last, however, and after sailing for an hour, came to anchor in the open roadstead.

It was nearly midnight.

Then there was great commotion on deck. Among the innumerable threats which greeted the exiles on their arrival at Rochefort, cries of "Into the water!" and "Drink out of the great cup!" had distinctly reached the prisoner's ears. No one of them then expressed his secret thought, but they all expected to find the end of their tortures in the bed of the Charente. The vessel to which they were to be transferred was doubtless one of those which had a movable plug, — an ingenious invention of Nero to get rid of his mother, and of Carrier to drown the royalists.

They heard the order to put two of the ship's long-boats into the water; an officer in a loud voice commanded every one to stand at his post; then, after a moment's silence, the names of Pichegru and Aubry were pronounced.

They embraced their companions, and then went on deck.

A quarter of an hour passed.

Suddenly the names of Barthélemy and Delarue were called.

An end had doubtless been made of the two others, and now it was their turn. They embraced their companions, as Aubry and Pichegru had done, and went on deck, from which they passed to a little boat where they were made to sit side by side upon a thwart. A sailor placed himself upon another thwart opposite; the sail was hoisted, and they were off like a shot.

The two exiles kept feeling the planks with their feet, fancying that they could see the hole through which their companions had probably passed, open and swallow them up.

But this time their fears were without foundation; they were being transported from the brigantine " Brillant " to the corvette " Vaillante," whither two of their companions had preceded them, and where the others were to follow.

They were received by Captain Julien, upon whose face they sought in vain to read the destiny which awaited them.

He affected to look severely at them, but when he was alone with them he said, —

" Gentlemen, it is easy to see that you have suffered terribly; but have patience. While executing the orders of the Directory, I shall neglect nothing which can relieve your discomfort."

Unhappily for them, Guillet had followed them; he overheard the last words, and an hour later, Captain Julien was replaced by Captain Laporte.

Strange freak of fate! The " Vaillante," a corvette carrying twenty-two guns, which the exiles were now boarding, had been recently built at Bayonne; and Villot, who was general in command of the district, had been chosen to christen her. He himself had named her the " Vaillante."

The exiles were sent between decks; and as it occurred to no one to give them anything to eat, Dessonville, who suffered more than any of the others from lack of nourishment, asked, —

"Do they really propose to let us die of hunger?"

"No, no, gentlemen," said an officer of the corvette, laughing. "Do not be uneasy; you will be served at supper-time."

"Only give us some fruit," said the dying Barbé-Marbois; "something to cool our mouths."

A fresh burst of laughter welcomed this petition, and from the deck some one threw the poor famished wretches two loaves of bread.

"What an exquisite supper," exclaimed Ramel, "for poor devils who have eaten nothing for forty hours! And yet we have often thought of it with regret, for it was the last time that bread was given us."

Ten minutes later, hammocks were distributed to twelve of the prisoners; but Pichegru, Villot, Ramel, and Dessonville received none.

"And where are we going to sleep?" asked Pichegru.

"Come," replied the voice of the new captain, "and you will be told."

Pichegru and the others who had not received hammocks obeyed.

"Put these men into the Lions' Den," said Captain Laporte; "that is the lodging set aside for them."

Every one knows that the Lions' Den is the cell in which the sailor condemned to death is confined.

When the exiles between decks heard this order, they uttered angry cries.

"No separation!" they exclaimed. "Put us with those gentlemen in that horrible cell, or leave them with us."

Barthélemy and his faithful Letellier — that brave servant who, in spite of everything, had refused to leave his master — dashed up on deck; and seeing their four companions being dragged by the soldiers towards the hatchway which led to the Lions' Den, they slid rather than climbed down the ladder, and found themselves in the hold with them.

" Here! " cried the captain, from the top of the hatchway; " come back here, or I will have you driven up at the point of the bayonet."

But they lay down.

" There is neither first nor last among us," they said. " We are all guilty, or we are all innocent. You must treat us alike."

The soldiers advanced upon them, with their bayonets pointed at them, but they did not move; and it was only when Pichegru and the other three insisted upon it that they returned to the deck.

The four were then left in the deepest darkness in the horrible cell, which was foul with exhalations from the hold. They had neither hammock nor covering, could not lie down, for there was no room, nor stand up, for the ceiling was too low.

The twelve others, crowded together between decks, were not much better off, for the hatches were closed; and, like their comrades in the Lions' Den, they had no air, and could not move about.

About four o'clock in the morning the captain gave the order to set sail; and amidst the shouts of the crew, the creaking of the rigging, and the roaring of the waves as they broke against the bow of the corvette could be heard, like a sob from the sides of the vessel itself, the last cry, —

" Adieu, France! "

And, like an echo, from the entrails of the hold the same cry was repeated, almost unintelligibly, on account of the depth from which it came,—

" France, adieu! "

The reader may perhaps wonder that I have dwelt so long upon this melancholy tale, which would become more melancholy still, were we to follow the ill-fated exiles to the end of their voyage of forty-five days. But the reader would probably not have the courage which I owe to the necessity, not of rehabilitating them,— I leave to history the task of rehabilitation,— but of directing the compassion of future generations upon the men who sacrificed themselves for France.

It has seemed to me that the saying of the old pagans, " Woe to the vanquished! " has always been brutal, and is nothing less than impious in these modern days; and, by some instinctive impulse of my heart, I always turn towards the vanquished, and my sympathies are ever with them.

They who have read my books know that I have described with the same degree of sympathy and absolute impartiality the demise of Jeanne d'Arc at Rouen, and the passing of Mary Stuart at Fotheringay, the appearance of Charles I. upon the scaffold at Whitehall, and of Marie-Antoinette upon the Place de la Révolution.

But there is one peculiarity of historians which I have noticed with regret, and that is that they marvel at the tears which the eyes of a king can shed, without studying as carefully the burden of agony which this poor human machine can endure without dying, when it is supported by the conviction of its innocence and integrity, whether it belongs to the middle, or even to the lower, classes of society.

Such were these men, whose sufferings I have tried to describe, for whom we find no historians expressing a single regret, and who, by the clever expedient adopted by their persecutors of confusing them with men like Collot-d'Herbois and Billaud-Varennes, were first despoiled of the sympathy of their contemporaries, and then cheated of their inheritance of the compassion of posterity.

THE EIGHTH CRUSADE.

WHEN we announced to you, dear readers, the importance in the matter of size alone of our romance of "The Whites and the Blues," — that is to say, when we warned you that it would comprise a considerable number of volumes, — we said at the same time that it was the sequel to "The Companions of Jehu."

But as it was our plan to describe the great events of the end of the last century and the beginning of this one, from 1793 to 1815, — or, in other words, to put before your eyes as in a panorama twenty-two years of our history, — we have filled nearly three volumes with a description of the principal crises of our Revolution, and have only reached the year 1799, in which our story of "The Companions of Jehu" begins.

As some of the actors who play parts in that book also appear in "The Whites and the Blues," it will not be surprising if, at five or six points of the fresh episode upon which we are about to enter, the two narratives coincide, and if some of the chapters of our first book are repeated naturally enough in the second, since the events not only run side by side, but are sometimes identical.

When we have once passed the execution of Morgan and his companions, our story will be in reality a sequel to "The Companions of Jehu," since the third and only remaining brother of the family of Sainte-Hermine becomes the hero and the principal personage of the volumes which remain to be published, under the title of "The Empire."

We give this explanation, dear readers, so that you may not be surprised at this coincidence between the two works; and if we dared ask so much at your hands, we would beg you to read again " The Companions of Jehu," at the same time that you read this episode of " The Eighth Crusade."

Do I need to add, dear readers, that this new work, the most strictly historical of all that I have yet undertaken, was conceived, composed, and written in pursuance of a great object, — that, namely, of coaxing the perusal of ten volumes of history under the disguise of ten volumes of romance ? The events related in " The Whites and the Blues " are the most important of our age; and it is essential that our people, who have played such a leading *rôle* for the last seventy years in European affairs, and who are called upon to play a still greater one, should know these grand pages of our annals as they ought to be known.

Then, when restorations follow revolutions, and, *vice versa*, revolutions follow restorations, when each party raises at the moment of triumph a statue to the one who represents it, — a statue destined to be cast down by the opposite party, only to give place to another, — feeble minds and short-sighted eyes falter before all these great men of a moment, who become traitors, and whom their contemporaries find no more difficulty in dishonoring than they did in exalting. It is therefore well for a keener eye and a more impartial mind to say, —

" This is plaster, and this marble ; this is lead, and this gold."

There are statues which are thrown from their pedestals, and which rise again of themselves.

There are, on the contrary, those which fall of themselves, and which break as they fall.

Mirabeau, after having been carried in great pomp to the Panthéon, has no monument to-day.

Louis XVI., after having been thrown into the common ditch, has his memorial chapel.

Perhaps posterity has been rather severe on Mirabeau. Perhaps it has been rather indulgent towards Louis XVI. But we must bow before its severity and its indulgence alike.

And yet, without envying Louis XVI. his memorial chapel, we should like to see a monument erected to Mirabeau.

The more guilty of the two, in our opinion, was not he who sold, but he who bought.

CHAPTER I.

SAINT-JEAN-D'ACRE.

ON the 7th of April, 1799, the promontory on which is built Saint-Jean-d'Acre, the ancient Ptolemaïs, seemed to be wrapped in as much thunder and lightning as was Mount Sinai on the day when the Lord gave the law to Moses from the burning bush.

Whence came these reports which shook the coast of Syria as if with an earthquake?

Whence came that smoke which covered the Gulf of Carmel with a cloud as thick as though Mount Elias had become a volcano?

The dream of one of those men who with a few words change the destiny of nations was accomplished.

We are mistaken; we should have said, had vanished.

But perhaps it had vanished only to give place to a reality of which this man, ambitious though he was, had not dared to dream.

On the 10th of September, 1797, when the conqueror of Italy learned at Passeriano of the 18th Fructidor, and of the promulgation of the law which condemned two directors, fifty-four deputies, and a hundred and forty-eight private individuals to exile, he fell into a deep revery.

He was doubtless measuring in his imagination the influence which would accrue to him from this *coup d'état* which his hand had directed, although Auge-reau's alone had been visible.

He was walking with his secretary Bourrienne in the beautiful park of the palace.

Suddenly he raised his head, and said, without apparent reference to anything that had gone before, —

"Certainly, Europe is only a mole-hill. There has never been a great empire or a great revolution except in the East, where there are six hundred millions of men."

Then, as Bourrienne, totally unprepared for this out-break, looked at him in astonishment, he seemed to lose himself again in revery.

On the 1st of January, 1798, Bonaparte, who had been recognized in his box at the theatre, in which he was trying to conceal himself, upon the first representa-tion of "Horatius Cocles," and saluted by an ovation and by cries of "Long live Bonaparte!" which thrice shook the building, returned to his house in Rue Chan-tereine (newly named in his honor Rue de la Victoire), wrapped in melancholy, and said to Bourrienne, to whom he always confided his gloomy thoughts, —

"Believe me, Bourrienne, nobody at Paris remembers anything. If I should do nothing for six months, I should be lost. One reputation in this Babylon replaces another; they will not see me three times at the theatre before they will cease to look for me."

Again, on the 29th of the same month, he said to Bourrienne, returning unceasingly to the dream of his thoughts, —

"Bourrienne, I will not stay here; there is nothing to do. If I do stay, I am done for; everything goes to seed in France. I have already exhausted my glory. This poor little Europe cannot furnish enough; *I must go to the East.*"

Finally, when, a fortnight before his departure, on the 18th of April, 1798, he was walking down Rue Sainte-Anne beside Bourrienne, to whom he had not spoken a word since they left Rue Chantereine, the secretary, in order to break the silence, which annoyed him, said, —

"Then you have really decided to leave France, General?"

"Yes," replied Bonaparte. "I asked to be one of them, and they refused me. If I stay here, I shall have to overthrow them and make myself king. The nobles would never consent to that; I have sounded the ground. The time has not yet come, and I should be alone. I must dazzle these people. We will go to Egypt, Bourrienne."

Therefore it was not to communicate with Tippoo-Sahib across Asia, and to attack England in India, that Bonaparte left Europe.

"*I must dazzle these people.*" In those words lay the true cause of his expedition to Egypt.

On the 3d of May, 1798, he ordered all the generals to embark their troops.

On the 4th he left Paris.

On the 8th he arrived at Toulon.

On the 19th he went on board the admiral's vessel, the "Orient."

On the 25th he sighted Leghorn and the Isle of Elba.

On the 13th of June he took Malta.

On the 19th he set sail again.

On the 1st of July he landed near Marabout.

On the 3d he took Alexandria by assault.

On the 13th he won the battle of Chébreïss.

VOL. II. — 20

On the 21st he crushed the Mamelukes at the Pyramids.

On the 25th he entered Cairo.

On the 14th of August he learned of the disaster of Aboukir.

On the 24th of December he started with the members of the Institute to visit the remains of the Suez Canal.

On the 28th he drank of the fountains of Moses, and, like Pharaoh, was almost drowned in the Red Sea.

On the 1st of January, 1799, he planned the campaign of Syria.

Six months before, he had conceived the idea.

At that time he wrote to Kléber, —

" If the English continue to overrun the Mediterranean, they will perhaps force us to do even greater things than we intended."

There was a vague rumor of an expedition which the Sultan of Damascus was sending against the French, in which Djezzar Pacha, surnamed the " Butcher," because of his cruelty, led the advance-guard.

The rumor had taken definite shape.

Djezzar had advanced by Gaza as far as El-Arich, and had there massacred the few French soldiers who were in the fortress.

Bonaparte, among his young ordnance officers, had the two brothers Mailly, of Château Renaud.

He sent the younger with a flag of truce to Djezzar, who, in defiance of international law, took him prisoner.

This was a declaration of war.

Bonaparte, with his usual rapidity of execution, resolved to destroy this advance-guard of the Ottoman Porte.

In case of success, he had hopes which he himself will tell later. If repulsed, he would at least destroy the fortifications of Gaza, Jaffa, and Acre, ravage the country, and destroy all the supplies, making it impossible for an army, even a native one, to cross the desert.

On the 11th of February, 1799, Bonaparte entered Syria at the head of twelve thousand men.

He had with him that galaxy of gallant men who gravitated around him during the first and the most brilliant period of his life.

He had Kléber, the handsomest and the bravest horseman in the army.

He had Murat, who disputed this twofold title with Kléber.

He had Junot, who was such a remarkable shot with a pistol that he could split a dozen bullets in succession on the blade of a knife.

He had Lannes, who had already earned his title of Duc de Montebello, but had not yet assumed it.

He had Reynier, who was destined to have the honor of deciding the victory of Heliopolis.

He had Caffarelli, who was destined to lie in the trench which he had caused to be dug.

And in subordinate positions he had, for aide-de-camp, Eugène de Beauharnais, our young friend of Strasburg, who had made the marriage between Josephine and Bonaparte by coming to ask the latter for his father's sword.

He had Croisier, gloomy and taciturn ever since, in an encounter with the Arabs, he had faltered, and the word "coward!" had escaped Bonaparte's lips.

He had the elder of the two Maillys, who was determined to deliver or avenge his brother.

He had the young Sheik of Aher, chief of the

Druses, whose name, if not his power, extended from the Dead Sea to the Mediterranean.

And, finally, he had an old acquaintance of ours, — Roland de Montrevel, — whose customary intrepidity had, since the day he was wounded and taken prisoner at Cairo, been increased twofold by that strange desire for death which we have seen him display throughout the whole of our romance of "The Companions of Jehu."

On the 17th of February the army arrived before El-Arich.

The soldiers had suffered greatly from thirst during the journey. At the end of only one stage did they find both amusement and refreshment.

It was at Messoudiah, or the "Fortunate Spot," on the shore of the Mediterranean, at a place composed of small dunes of very fine sand. Chance had led a soldier to imitate the miracle of Moses. As he thrust a stick into the sand, the water gushed up as from an artesian well. The soldier tasted it, and found it excellent. He called his comrades, and shared his discovery with them.

Every one then punched his own hole, and had his own well.

Nothing more was needed to restore to the soldiers all their cheerfulness.

El-Arich surrendered at the first summons.

On the 28th of February the green and fertile plains of Syria at last came in sight. At the same time, through a light rain, — a rare thing in the East,— could be discerned valleys and mountains which recalled those of Europe.

On the 1st of March they camped at Ramleh, — the ancient Rama, where Rachel gave way to her great despair, which the Bible describes in this nobly poetical verse: —

"In Rama was there a voice heard, lamentation and weeping and great mourning; Rachel weeping for her children, and would not be comforted because they were not."

Jesus, the Virgin Mary, and Joseph passed by Rama on their way into Egypt. The church, which was given up to Bonaparte by the monks for a hospital, was built on the very spot where the Holy Family stopped to rest.

The well whose fresh and pure water slaked the thirst of the whole army was the same which seventeen hundred and ninety-nine years before had slaked the thirst of the holy fugitives. He also was from Rama, — that disciple Joseph, whose pious hand wrapped in the shroud the body of our Lord Jesus Christ.

Perhaps in the whole vast multitude not one man knew the sacred tradition. But one thing they did know, and that was that they were not more than six leagues from Jerusalem.

As they walked beneath the olive-trees, which are perhaps the most beautiful in all the East, and which the soldiers ruthlessly cut down, to make their bivouac fires, Bourrienne asked Bonaparte, —

"General, shall you not go to Jerusalem?"

"Oh, no," he replied carelessly. "Jerusalem is not within my line of operations. I do not care to get into trouble with the mountaineers in these bad roads; and on the other side of the mountain I should be attacked by a large body of cavalry. I have no ambition for the fate of Crassus."

Crassus, it will be remembered, was massacred by the Parthians.

It is a strange fact concerning Bonaparte that although he was at one time within six leagues of Jerusalem (the cradle of Christ), and at another within six leagues of Rome (the capital of the Papacy), he had no desire to see either Rome or Jerusalem.

CHAPTER II.

THE PRISONERS.

Two days before, within a quarter of a league of Gaza (which means in Arabic, "treasure," and in Hebrew, "strong"), — the same Gaza whose gates were carried away by Samson, who died, with three thousand Philistines, beneath the ruins of the temple which he had overthrown, — they had met Abdallah, Pacha of Damascus.

He was at the head of his cavalry.

That was in Murat's department.

Murat took a hundred men from the thousand whom he commanded, and with his riding-whip in his hand — for when opposed to this Mussulman, Arab, and Maugrabin cavalry he rarely deigned to draw his sabre — he charged them vigorously.

Abdallah turned and rode through the town. The army followed him, and took up its position on the other side.

It was the day after this skirmish that they arrived at Ramleh.

From Ramleh they marched upon Jaffa. To the great satisfaction of the soldiers, for the second time the clouds gathered over their heads, and the rain fell.

A deputation was sent to Bonaparte, in the name of the army, asking permission to take a bath.

Bonaparte granted permission, and ordered a halt. Then each soldier pulled off his clothes, and revelled

ın the luxury of feeling the cool rain upon his burning
body.

Then the army started on again, refreshed and joyous,
singing as with one voice the "Marseillaise."

Abdallah's Mamelukes and cavalry no more dared
wait for the French than they had dared at Gaza.
They returned to the city, firm in their belief that
every Mussulman who is behind a rampart is safe.

A singular medley was the collection of individuals
who formed the garrison of Jaffa, and who, drunken
with fanaticism, were about to set at defiance the first
soldiers in the world.

There were representatives there from all parts of the
East, — from the extremity of Africa to the uttermost
point of Asia. There were Maugrabins, with their
black and white cloaks. There were Albanians, with
their long guns mounted in silver and inlaid with coral.
There were Kurds, with their long lances ornamented
with a bunch of ostrich plumes. There were Aleppians,
who all wore, either on one cheek or the other, the
mark of the famous button of Aleppo. There were
men of Damascus, with curved swords of such finely
tempered steel that they would cut a silk handkerchief
floating in the air. There were Natolians, Karamanians,
and negroes.

On the 3d they arrived before the walls of Jaffa;
on the 4th the city was invested. On the same day
Murat made a reconnoissance around the ramparts, to
determine on which side it would be best to make the
attack.

On the 7th everything was ready to bombard the
place.

Bonaparte, before beginning the bombardment, wished
to try conciliatory measures. He knew what a struggle,

even if he were victorious, against such a population would be.

He dictated the following summons: —

" God is merciful and pitiful.

"General Bonaparte, whom the Arabs have surnamed the 'Sultan of Fire,' charges me to inform you that Djezzar Pacha commenced hostilities in Egypt by taking the fortress of El-Arich; that God, who is always on the side of justice, gave the victory to the French army, who re-captured the fort; that General Bonaparte has come into Palestine, from which he desires to drive the troops of Djezzar Pacha, who ought never to have entered it; that Jaffa is surrounded on all sides; that the batteries will in two hours proceed to batter down the walls with shot and shell, and destroy the defences; that his heart is touched at thought of the harm that would be done to the city and its inhabitants, should it be taken by assault; that he offers a safe-conduct to the garrison and protection to the inhabitants of the city, and that he will consequently postpone the bombardment until seven o'clock in the morning."

The summons was addressed to Abou-Saib, governor of Jaffa.

Roland held out his hand to take it.

" What are you doing? " asked Bonaparte.

" Do you not need a messenger? " replied the young man, laughing. " It may as well be I as any one else."

" No," replied Bonaparte; " on the contrary, it had better be some one else than you, and better a Mussulman than a Christian."

" Why so, General? "

" Because, while Abou-Saib may perhaps cut off the head of a Mussulman, he would certainly cut off that of a Christian."

" So much the more reason," said Roland, shrugging his shoulders.

" Enough! " said Bonaparte.   " I do not wish it. "

Roland went off into a corner, pouting like a spoiled child.

Then said Bonaparte, addressing his dragoman, —

" Ask whether there is any Turk or Arab, or, in fact, any Mussulman who will undertake to deliver this despatch."

The dragoman repeated the question aloud.

A Mameluke from the dromedary corps came forward.

" I," he said.

The dragoman looked at Bonaparte.

" Tell him what he risks," said the commander-in-chief.

" The Sultan of Fire wishes you to know that you risk your life by taking charge of this message."

" What is written is written," replied the Mameluke; and he held out his hand.

A white flag and a trumpeter were given him.

They approached the town on horseback, and the gates opened to receive them.

Ten minutes later there was great commotion on the ramparts just in front of the general's camp.

The trumpeter appeared, dragged roughly along by two Albanians.   They ordered him to sound his trumpet, to attract the attention of the French camp.

He sounded the *diane*.

At that instant, when all eyes were fixed upon that portion of the wall, a man approached, holding in his hand a severed head wearing a turban.   He extended his arm over the ramparts; the turban fell off, and the head dropped to the foot of the wall.

It was the head of the Mussulman who had carried the summons.

Ten minutes later, the trumpeter came out of the

same gate through which he had entered, but he was alone.

The next day, at seven o'clock in the morning, as Bonaparte had said, six pieces of artillery began to thunder, one after the other. At four o'clock the breach was practicable, and Bonaparte ordered the assault.

He looked around for Roland, in order to give him the command of one of the regiments which were to enter the breach.

Roland was not there.

The carabineers of the 22d Light Brigade and the chasseurs of the same brigade, supported by the artillery and engineers, rushed forward to the assault, commanded by General Rambeau, Adjutant-General Nethervood, and Vernois.

They all mounted to the breach; and in spite of the fusillade which met them in front, and the showers of grape from a few cannon which had not been silenced, and which took them from behind, a terrible fight was waged over the remains of the fallen tower.

. The struggle lasted for a quarter of an hour, and the besiegers had not been able to enter at the breach, nor had the besieged succeeded in forcing them back.

All the efforts of both sides seemed to be concentrated upon that spot, when suddenly, upon the dismantled walls, Roland appeared, holding a Turkish standard, and followed by about fifty men. He waved the standard, crying, —

"The city is taken!"

This is what had happened : —

That morning, about six o'clock, which is the hour of daybreak in the East, Roland, going down to the sea for his bath, had discovered a sort of breach at the angle made by one of the walls and a tower. He had assured himself that the breach led into the city, and then he had taken his bath, and returned to the army just as the bombardment began.

There, as he was well known to be one of Bonaparte's privileged favorites, and at the same time one of the most recklessly daring officers in the army, cries of, " Captain Roland! Captain Roland! " were heard.

Roland knew what that meant.   .

It meant, " Have n't you something impossible to attempt ?   Here we are! "

" Fifty volunteers," he said.

A hundred offered themselves.

" Fifty," he repeated.

And he selected the fifty, taking every other man, in order not to hurt any one's feelings.

Then he took two drummers and two trumpeters, and himself led the way, through the hole he had found, into the city.

His fifty men followed him.

They met a party of about a hundred men, carrying a flag.   They fell upon them, and put them to the bayonet.   Roland took possession of the flag, which was the one that he waved from the wall.

He was saluted by the shouts of the whole army; but he thought the time had now come to utilize his drums and trumpets.

The whole garrison was at the breach, not expecting to be attacked elsewhere, when suddenly they heard drums beside them, and French trumpets behind them.

At the same time there were two discharges of musketry, and a hailstorm of bullets fell among the besieged.   They turned, only to see, in every direction, gun-barrels reflecting the rays. of the sun and tricolored plumes waving in the wind. The smoke, drifting towards them upon the sea-breeze, concealed the small number of French. They believed that they had been betrayed. A frightful panic seized them, and they abandoned the breach.

But Roland had sent ten of his men to open one of the gates. General Lannes' division poured in through this gate, and the besieged found French bayonets where they had thought to find the road clear for their flight.

By a reaction natural to ferocious people, who, never giving quarter, do not expect any, they seized upon their arms with renewed fury, and the combat began again with all the appearance of a massacre.

Bonaparte, ignorant of what was passing in the city, seeing the smoke which rose above the walls, and hearing the continued rattle of musketry, while no one came back, not even the wounded, sent Eugène de Beauharnais and Croisier to see what was going on, telling them to return at once and report to him.

They both wore on their arm the scarf of an aide-de-camp, — the emblem of their rank. They had been impatiently waiting for a word which would permit them to take part in the fight. They entered the town at a run, and penetrated to the very heart of the carnage.

They were recognized as envoys of the commander-in-chief; and as they were supposed to be the bearers of a message, the firing ceased for a moment.

A few of the Albanians could speak French. One of them cried, —

" If our lives shall be spared, we will surrender; if not, we will fight till the last one of us is killed."

The two aides-de-camp had no means of knowing Bonaparte's secrets. They were young, and the sentiments of humanity were strong in their hearts. With-out authority, they promised the poor fellows that their lives should be spared. The firing ceased, and the prisoners were taken to the camp.

There were four thousand of them.

As for the soldiers, they knew their rights. The town had been taken by assault. After the massacre came the pillage.

CHAPTER III.

THE CARNAGE.

BONAPARTE was walking in front of his tent with Bourrienne, waiting impatiently for news, and having no other of his intimates at hand, when he saw two troops of unarmed men leaving the town by two different gates.

One of them was led by Croisier, and the other by Eugène Beauharnais.

Their young faces shone with joy.

Croisier, who had not smiled since he had had the misfortune to displease the commander-in-chief, was smiling now, for he hoped that this fine prize would bring about a reconciliation.

Bonaparte understood the whole thing. He grew very pale, and said sorrowfully, —

" What do they suppose I am going to do with those men? Have I food to give them? Have I ships, to send the wretched creatures to France or Egypt?"

The two young men stopped ten paces from him.

They saw by the sternness of his face that they had made a mistake.

" What have you there?" he asked.

Croisier dared not reply, and Eugène spoke for both.

" As you see, General, prisoners."

" Did I tell you to take any prisoners?"

" You told us to stop the carnage," replied Eugène, timidly.

"Yes," replied the general, "of women and children and old men, I did; but not of armed soldiers. Do you know that you have made it necessary for me to commit a crime?"

The young men understood, and retired in dismay. Croisier was weeping. Eugène tried to console him; but he shook his head, saying,—

"It's all over with me. The first chance I see, I shall let myself be shot."

Before deciding upon the destiny of the unfortunate prisoners, Bonaparte determined to call a council of the generals.

But soldiers and generals had bivouacked inside the town. The soldiers did not stop until they were weary of slaughter. Besides the four thousand prisoners, there were nearly five thousand dead.

The pillage of the houses lasted all night.

From time to time shots were heard. Dull cries of anguish were incessant in the streets, the houses, and the mosques.

They were uttered by soldiers who had been dragged from their places of concealment and murdered; by inhabitants who were trying to defend their treasures; by fathers and husbands who were endeavoring to preserve their wives or daughters from the brutality of the soldiers.

But the vengeance of Heaven was hidden beneath all this cruelty.

The plague was in Jaffa, and the army carried the germs of it away with them.

The prisoners, in the first place, were made to sit down all together in front of the tents. Their hands were tied behind their backs. Their faces were gloomy, more from fear of what was to come than from anger.

They had seen Bonaparte's face darken at sight of them; and they had heard, although they had not understood it, the reprimand which he had bestowed upon the two young men. But what they had not understood they had guessed at.

Some of them ventured to say, " I am hungry; " others, " I am thirsty."

They brought water to all of them, and each one had a piece of bread, taken from the soldiers' rations.

This reassured them a trifle.

As fast as the generals returned, they received the order to go at once to the tent of the commander-in-chief.

They deliberated for a long time, without arriving at any decision.

On the following day the daily reports of the generals of division came in. All complained of insufficient rations. The only ones who had eaten and drunk as much as they wanted were those who had entered the town during the fight, and hence had the right to take part in the pillage.

But these were scarcely a fourth of the army. All the rest murmured at having to give their bread to enemies who had been rescued from legitimate vengeance; since, according to the laws of war, Jaffa having been taken by storm, all the soldiers who were within it should have perished by the sword.

The council assembled once more.

Five questions were proposed for its deliberation.

" Should the men be sent into Egypt ? "

But to do this would require a large escort, and the army was already over weak to defend itself against the deadly hostility of the country.

Besides that, how could they and their escort be fed

until they reached Cairo, travelling through an enemy's country, which the army had just laid waste as it passed, when they had no food to give them to start with?

"Should they put them on shipboard?"

Where were the ships? Where could they be found? The sea was like a desert, — or, at least, no friendly sail was to be seen.

"Should their liberty be restored to them?"

But in that case they would instantly go to Saint-Jean-d'Acre, to reinforce the pacha, or else would go into the mountains of Nabloos; and then in every ravine they would have to put up with a fusillade from invisible sharpshooters.

"Should they incorporate them, disarmed as they were, in the republican army?"

But the provisions, of which the supply was already small for ten thousand men, would be still more scanty among fourteen thousand. And then there was great danger from such comrades in a hostile country. At the first opportunity they would deal out death in return for the life we had left them. What is a dog of a Christian to a Turk? Is it not a pious and meritorious act in the eyes of the Prophet to kill an infidel?

Bonaparte rose as they were about to propose the fifth question.

"Let us wait until to-morrow," he said.

He did not himself know what he expected to gain by waiting.

It was for one of those strange chances which sometimes prevent a great crime, and which, when they come, are called interpositions of Providence.

He waited in vain.

On the fourth day the question which they had not dared to ask on the previous day had to be answered.

" Should the prisoners be shot ? "

The murmurs were increasing, and the evil was growing. The soldiers might at any moment throw themselves upon the prisoners, and thus give an appearance of revolt and assassination to that which was really demanded by necessity.

The sentence was unanimous, with the exception of a single vote. One of those present did not vote at all.

The miserable wretches were to be shot.

Bonaparte hastened from his tent, and looked searchingly out over the sea. A tempest of human feeling was rising within his heart.

He had not at this period acquired the stoicism born of numerous battle-fields. The man who afterwards looked upon Austerlitz, Eylau, and Moscow without moving a muscle was not yet sufficiently familiarized with Death to throw so considerable a prey to him, at one fell swoop, without remorse. On board the vessel which had carried him to Egypt, his pity, like that of Cæsar, had astonished everybody. It was impossible that there should not be some accidents during such a long journey, and that a few men should not fall into the sea.

This accident happened several times on board the " Orient."

It was only at such times that all the human feeling which was in Bonaparte's heart could be understood.

As soon as he heard a cry of " Man overboard! " he darted up on deck, if he were not already there, and ordered a boat to be lowered. From that moment he could not rest until the man was found and saved. Bourrienne received orders to liberally reward the men who had undertaken the task of rescue; and if there was among them a sailor who had incurred punishment for neglect of duty, he pardoned him, and rewarded him with money besides.

One dark night the sound of a body falling into the water was heard. Bonaparte, as usual, rushed from his room, went on deck, and ordered the boat to be lowered. The sailors, who knew that they would not only be doing a good deed, but would be rewarded for it afterwards, threw themselves into the boat with their usual activity and courage. At the end of five minutes Bonaparte's ceaseless question, "Is he saved? is he saved?" was answered by loud shouts of laughter.

The man who had fallen into the water was a quarter of beef from the ship's store-room.

"Double the reward, Bourrienne," said Bonaparte. "It might have been a man, and the next time they might think it was a quarter of beef."

The order for the execution must come from him. He delayed giving it, and time was passing. Finally, he called for his horse, leaped into the saddle, took an escort of twenty men, and rode away, crying, —

"Do it!"

He dared not say, "Fire!"

A scene like the one which then took place cannot be described.

Those great massacres which occurred among the nations of antiquity have no place in modern history. Out of the four thousand, a few escaped, because, having thrown themselves into the water, they succeeded in reaching reefs out of musket range.

Until they reached Saint-Jean-d'Acre, and duty compelled them to take orders from Bonaparte, neither Eugène Beauharnais nor Croisier dared show themselves before him.

On the 18th the French were before Saint-Jean-d'Acre. In spite of the English frigates lying in the port, some of the young men, among whom were the Sheik of Aher, Roland, and the Comte de Mailly, asked permission to go and bathe in the roadstead.

The permission was granted them.

When they were diving, Mailly found a leather sack, which was floating under water. The bathers were curious to know what was in it, and swam with it to the bank.

It was tied up with a cord, and seemed to contain a human body.

The cord was unfastened, and the sack emptied on the sand, and Mailly recognized the head and the body of his brother, who had been sent with a flag of truce a month before, and whom Djezzar had beheaded when he saw the dust thrown up by the horses of the advance-guard of the French.

CHAPTER IV.

FROM ANCIENT DAYS TO OUR OWN.

SINCE we are fortunate enough to have readers who are sufficiently intelligent to encourage us to write a book in which romance is given the second place, we shall doubtless be permitted to give, not only the modern, but the ancient history of the localities visited by our heroes. There is a great charm for the philosopher, the poet, and even the dreamer in treading upon soil composed of the ashes of past generations; and nowhere more than in the region we are traversing do we find traces of those great historical catastrophes which, becoming less substantial and fainter in outline with the lapse of years, finally disappear like ruins and the spectres of ruins amidst the ever-thickening shadows of the past.

This is true of the city which we have just left, alive with shrieks of anguish, overflowing with carnage and blood, with its walls battered to pieces, and its houses in flames. The swift movement of our narrative, and the wish to enter modern Jaffa with the young conqueror, have hitherto prevented us from telling you in a few words what manner of place the Jaffa of old days was.

Jaffa, in Hebrew, signifies *beauty*. Joppa, in Phœnician, means *height*.

Jaffa is to the eastern gulf of the Mediterranean what Jiddah is to the centre of the Red Sea.

The city of pilgrims.

Every Christian pilgrim who goes to Jerusalem to visit the tomb of Christ takes Jaffa on his way.

Every Mussulman *hadji* who goes to Mecca to visit Mahomet's tomb takes Jiddah on his way.

When we read to-day great works on Egypt, — works upon which the most learned men of the age have united their efforts, — we are astonished to find so few of those luminous points which, placed in the dark night of the past, light and attract the traveller like beacons.

We are about to try to do what they have not done.

The author who assigns to Jaffa (the Joppa of the Phœnicians) the most ancient place in history, is Pomponius Mela, who affirms that it was built before the Deluge.

Est Joppe ante diluvium condita.

And Joppa must have been built before the Deluge, since the historian Josephus, in his " Antiquities," says, with Berosus and Nicolas of Damascus, not exactly that the Ark was built at Joppa, for that would be in contradiction of the Bible, but that it stopped there. They assure us that in their time fragments of it were still shown to incredulous travellers, and that they used, as a remedy which was efficacious in all cases, as a universal panacea, the dust of the tar which was used to coat the Ark.

It was at Joppa, if we may believe Pliny, that Andromeda was chained to the rocks to be devoured by the sea-monster; and there she was delivered by Perseus, mounted upon the Chimera, and armed with the head of Medusa, which turned the beholder to stone.

Pliny affirms that in the reign of Adrian the holes through which Andromeda's chain passed could still be seen; and Saint Jerome — a witness who cannot be accused of partiality — declares that he saw them.

The skeleton of the sea-monster, forty feet long, was thought by the people of Joppa to be that of their divinity, Ceto.

The water of the fountain in which Perseus bathed after killing the monster, remained tinged with his blood. Pausanias tells us so, and says that he saw the rose-colored water with his own eyes.

Ceto, a goddess of whom Pliny speaks (*colitur fabulosa Ceto*), and who is called Derceto by historians, was the name given by tradition to the unknown mother of Semiramis.

Diodorus of Sicily relates the pretty fable of this unknown mother, with the quaint charm which makes poetry of the fable without taking away the element of sensuousness.

"There is," he says, "in Syria a city called Ascalon, overlooking a large deep lake, in which fish abound, and near which is a temple dedicated to a celebrated goddess whom the Syrians call Derceto.

"She has a head and face like a woman's; all the rest is fish-like. The learned men of the nation say that Venus, having been offended by Derceto, caused her to feel for a young priest a passion as intense as she had inspired in Phedrus and Sappho. Derceto had a daughter by him; but she repented so bitterly of her fault that she caused the young man to disappear, abandoned the infant in a desert place full of rocks, and threw herself into the lake, where her body was changed to that of a siren. For this reason the Syrians worship the fish as gods, and abstain from eating them.

"But the little girl was saved and fed by doves, which came in great numbers to make their nests among the rocks where she had been left to die.

"A shepherd found her, and brought her up with as

much affectionate care as if she had been his own child, and named her Semiramis, or, 'the daughter of the doves.' "

If we may believe Diodorus, it is to this daughter of the doves, the haughty Semiramis, the wife and murderess of the Ninus who fortified Babylon and laid out at its highest point those magnificent gardens which were the admiration of the ancient world, that the Orientals owe the splendid costume which they wear to this day.

When she had reached the topmost height of power, having conquered Arabia in Egypt, a part of Ethiopia, Lybia, and all Asia as far as the Indus, she felt the need of inventing for her travels a costume at once convenient and elegant, in which she could not only perform the ordinary duties of life, but also ride horseback and fight. This costume was adopted by all the peoples whom she conquered.

"She was so beautiful," says Valerius Maximus, "that one day, when an insurrection broke out in her capital just as she was at her toilet, she had only to show herself, half naked and with unbound hair, to restore things at once to order."

Perhaps we may find in Higin the explanation of Venus's hate for Derceto.

"The Syrian goddess who was worshipped at Hierapolis," he says, "was Venus. An egg fell from heaven into the Euphrates; the fishes brought it to the bank, where it was hatched by a dove. Venus issued from it, and became the goddess of the Syrians, while Jupiter, at her request, placed the fishes in the sky; and she, in gratitude to her nurses, harnessed the doves to her chariot."

The famous temple of Dagon, where a statue of the

god was found overturned in front of the ark with both hands broken, was situated in the city of Azoth, between Joppa and Ascalon.

Read the Bible, that great treasure-house of history and poetry, and you will see that the cedars of Lebanon for the building of Solomon's temple were brought to the gates of Joppa. You will see that the prophet Jonah came to the gates of Joppa to embark for Tarsus, when he was flying from the face of the Lord.

Then, passing from the Bible to Josephus, whose writings may be called a continuation of it, you will see that Judas Maccabæus, to avenge the deaths of two hundred of his brethren who had been treacherously slain by the inhabitants of Joppa, came with a sword in one hand and a firebrand in the other, and set fire to the ships anchored in the port, and put to death with the sword all those who had escaped the fire.

We read in the Acts of the Apostles, as follows, —

"There was at Joppa a certain disciple named Tabitha, which by interpretation is called Dorcas : this woman was full of good works and almsdeeds which she did.

"And it came to pass in those days, that she was sick, and died : whom when they had washed, they laid her in an upper chamber.

"And forasmuch as Lydda was nigh to Joppa, and the disciples had heard that Peter was there, they sent unto him two men, desiring him that he would not delay to come to them.

"Then Peter arose and went with them. When he was come, they brought him into the upper chamber : and all the widows stood by him weeping, and showing the coats and garments which Dorcas made, while she was with them.

"But Peter put them all forth, and kneeled down, and prayed ; and turning him to the body said, 'Tabitha, arise!' And she opened her eyes: and when she saw Peter, she sat up.

"And he gave her his hand, and lifted her up, and when he had called the saints and widows, presented her alive.

"And it was known throughout all Joppa; and many believed in the Lord.

"And it came to pass, that he tarried many days in Joppa with one Simon a tanner."

It was there that the servants of the centurion Cornelius found him when they came to beg him to go to Cæsarea. It was in Simon's house that he had the vision commanding him to carry the Gospel to the Gentiles.

At the time of the rising of the Jews against Rome, Sextus besieged Joppa, took it by storm, and burned it.

Eight thousand of the inhabitants perished; but it was soon rebuilt. As the new city constantly sent forth pirates who infested the coasts of Syria, and made expeditions as far.as Greece and even to Egypt, the Emperor Vespasian took it again, razed it to the ground, from the first house to the last, and built a fortress upon the spot.

But in his Jewish Wars, Josephus relates that a new city soon sprang up at the foot of the fortress of Vespasian, which was the seat of a bishopric, or rather of a bishop, from the reign of Constantine, A. D. 330, until the invasion of the Arabs, in 636.

This bishopric was established during the First Crusade, and made subject to the metropolitan see of Cæsarea. Finally, the place was made into a countship, and embellished and fortified by Baldwin I., Emperor of Constantinople.

Saint Louis also came to Jaffa, and Joinville, his naif historian, tells of the sojourn which he made with the Comte de Japhe, as the good chevalier Frenchifies the name.

This Comte de Japhe was Gautier de Brienne, who

did his best to clean and whitewash his town, which was in such a pitiable state that Saint Louis was ashamed of it, and took it upon himself to raise the walls and beautify the churches.

Saint Louis while there received the news of his mother's death.

"When the sainted king," writes Joinville, "saw the Archbishop of Tyre and his confessor entering his apartments with expressions of great sorrow, he asked them to go with him into his chapel, which was his refuge from all the ills of the world.

"Then, when he had heard the fatal news, he fell on his knees, and with clasped hands he exclaimed, weeping,—

"'I thank thee, O God, for that thou didst lend my mother to me while it seemed best to thee, and for that in thy good pleasure thou hast now taken her to thyself again. It is true that I loved her above all other creatures, and she deserved it; but since thou hast taken her from me, may thy holy name be blessed for evermore.'"

The works erected by Saint Louis were destroyed in 1268 by the Pacha of Egypt, Bibas, who levelled the citadel with the ground, and sent the wood and precious marbles of which it was composed to Cairo, to build his mosque.

Finally, when Monconys visited Palestine, he found at Jaffa only a castle, and three caves hollowed out of the rock.

We have told in what state Bonaparte found it, and in what state he left it.

We shall return once more to this town, which to Bonaparte was neither Jaffa the Beautiful, nor Joppa the Lofty, but "Jaffa the Fatal."

CHAPTER V.

SIDNEY SMITH.

On the 18th, at daybreak, while the army was crossing the little stream of Kerdaneah, on a bridge thrown over it during the night, Bonaparte, accompanied only by Roland de Montrevel, the Sheik of Aher, and the Comte de Mailly, whom he was utterly unable, do what he would, to reconcile to the death of his brother, ascended a little hill not far from the town to which he had laid siege.

From the top of this little hill he could see the whole country, including not only the two English vessels "Tiger" and "Theseus," rocking upon the sea, but also the troops of the pacha, occupying all the gardens around the city.

" Let all that *canaille* be dislodged from those gardens, " he said, " and driven back into the town."

As he addressed no one in particular, the three men started off together, like three hawks in pursuit of the same prey.

But with his harsh voice he cried, —

" Roland! Sheik of Aher!"

The two young men, when they heard their names, stopped their horses, which were tugging at their bits, and returned to their places beside the commander-in-chief. Mailly went on, with a hundred sharpshooters, a like number of grenadiers and of voltigeurs, and urging his horse to a gallop, charged at their head.

Bonaparte had great confidence in the omens of war. That was why, at the first engagement with the Bedouins, he had been so much displeased at Croisier's hesitation, and had reproached him so bitterly for it.

Through his glass, which was an excellent one, he could see the movement of the troops from where he stood. He saw Eugène Beauharnais and Croisier, who had not dared to speak to him since the affair of Jaffa, take command, the former of the grenadiers and the latter of the sharpshooters, while Mailly, with the utmost deference to his companions, led the voltigeurs.

If the commander-in-chief was hoping for a speedy omen, he should have been content. While Roland was impatiently biting the silver handle of his riding-whip, and the Sheik of Aher, on the contrary, was watching the fight with the calmness and patience of an Arab, Bonaparte could see the three detachments pass through the ruins of a village, a Turkish cemetery, and a little wood which, by its freshness, showed that it concealed a spring, and hurl themselves upon the enemy, in spite of the brisk firing of the Arnauts and the Albanians, whom he recognized by their magnificent gold-embroidered costumes and their long silver-mounted rifles, and rout them at the first contact.

The firing on the part of the French began vigorously, and continued with increasing vigor; while above it could be heard the loud explosions of the hand-grenades, which our soldiers threw with their hands, and with which they tormented the fugitives.

They all arrived at about the same time at the foot of the walls; but the posterns being shut behind the Mussulmans, and the walls being enveloped in a girdle of fire, the three hundred Frenchmen were forced to beat a retreat, after having killed about a hundred and fifty of the enemy.

The three young men had shown marvellous gallantry; in emulation of each other, they had performed prodigies of valor.

Eugène, in a hand-to-hand fight, had killed an Arnaut who was a head taller than he; Mailly, who had approached within ten paces of a group which was making a stand, had emptied both his pistols at them, and with one bound rejoined his own men. Croisier, for his part, had sabred two Arabs who had attacked him at once, cutting open the head of the first one, and breaking the blade of his sabre in the breast of the second, and had returned with the bloody hilt dangling from his wrist.

Bonaparte turned to the Sheik of Aher: —

" Give me your sword in exchange for mine," he said. And he detached his own sword from his belt and handed it to the sheik.

The latter kissed its handle, and made haste to give his own in return.

" Roland," said Bonaparte, "go and present my compliments to Mailly and Eugène; as for Croisier, you will give him this sword, simply saying, —

" Here is a sword which the commander-in-chief sends you; he has been watching you."

Roland set off at a gallop. The young men to whom Bonaparte had sent congratulations leaped in their saddles for joy, and embraced one another.

Croisier, like the Sheik of Aher, kissed the sword which had been sent him, threw away the scabbard and broken hilt of the old one, and put at his belt the one Bonaparte had given him, saying, —

" Thank the commander-in-chief for me, and say to him that he will have reason to be content with me at the first assault."

The entire army had gradually ascended the hill, where Bonaparte was standing like an equestrian statue. The soldiers uttered shouts of delight when they saw their companions driving the Maugrabins before them as the wind drives the sand of the sea. Like Bonaparte, the army saw no great difference between the fortifications of Saint-Jean-d'Acre and those of Jaffa; and like Bonaparte, it did not doubt that the city would be taken at the second or third assault.

The French were still ignorant that there were in Saint-Jean-d'Acre two men who were worth more in themselves than a whole army of Mussulmans, —

Sidney Smith, the English admiral, who commanded the "Tiger" and the "Theseus," which were gracefully rocking on the waters of the Gulf of Carmel;

And Colonel Phélippeaux, who was in charge of the defensive works and the fortress of Djezzar the Butcher. Phélippeaux had been the friend and schoolfellow of Bonaparte at Brienne, his rival at college and in his mathematical successes. Fortune, chance, or an accident had now cast his lot among Bonaparte's foes.

Sidney Smith, whom the exiles of the 18th Fructidor had met at the Temple, had, by a strange freak of destiny, escaped from his prison, and reached London to resume his place in the English navy at the moment of Bonaparte's departure from Toulon.

It was Phélippeaux who had undertaken the rescue of Sidney Smith, and had succeeded in his daring enterprise. False orders had been prepared, on the pretext of removing the captive to another prison. A stamped fac-simile of the signature of the Minister of Police was purchased at a heavy price. From whom? From himself, perhaps; who knows?

Under the name of Loger, and in the uniform of an

adjutant-general, Sidney Smith's friend presented himself at the prison and exhibited his order to the clerk.

He examined it minutely, and was forced to acknowledge that it was correct in every point.   .

But he said,—

"For a prisoner of such importance you will need a guard of at least six men ? "

The pretended adjutant replied,—

"For a man of such importance I need only his word."

Then, turning to the prisoner, he added,—

"Commodore, you are a military man, and so am I; your parole that you will not try to escape will be enough for me.   If you will give it, I shall need no escort."

And Sidney Smith, who, like the honorable Englishman that he was, would not lie, even to assist his escape, replied, —

"Monsieur, if this will satisfy you, I will swear to follow you wherever you go."

And Adjutant-General Loger escorted Sir Sidney Smith to England.

These two men were let loose upon Bonaparte.

Phélippeaux undertook the defence of the fortress, as we have said; Sidney Smith was to provide arms and soldiers.

And there, where Bonaparte had expected to find only a stupid Turk in command, as at Gaza and Jaffa, he found all the science of a compatriot, and all the hate of an Englishman.

That same evening Bonaparte ordered the chief of the engineering brigade, Sanson, to reconnoitre the counterscarp.

The latter waited until it was very dark.   It was a moonless night, well suited to such operations.

He set out alone, and traversed the ruined village, the cemetery, and the gardens from which the Arabs had been dislodged and driven into the town in the morning. Seeing a mass of still blacker darkness in front of him, which could be nothing less than the fortress, he got down on his hands and knees to feel the ground step by step. Just as he perceived, by groping, a more rapid incline, which made him think that the moat was without facing, he was seen by a sentinel whose eyes were probably accustomed to the darkness, or who had that faculty which certain men, in common with certain animals, possess, of seeing plainly at night.

The cry, "Qui vive?" rang out in the darkness.

Sanson did not reply. The cry was repeated a second and a third time; a shot followed: the ball shattered the extended hand of the general of engineers.

In spite of the terrible pain, the officer did not utter a sound; he crawled back again, thinking that he had studied the moat sufficiently, and made his report to Bonaparte.

On the following day the trench was begun. They took advantage of the gardens, which were the moats of ancient Ptolemaïs, whose history we will relate, as we have related that of Jaffa. They took advantage of an aqueduct which crossed the glacis; and, in ignorance of the fatal assistance which Djezzar Pacha possessed, to our discomfiture, they gave their trench scarcely three feet of depth.

When the giant Kléber saw the trench, he shrugged his shoulders, and said to Bonaparte, —

"That is a fine trench, General. It will not come up to my knees."

On the 23d of March, Sidney Smith captured the two vessels which were bringing to Bonaparte the heavy artillery and to the army its supplies.

The French looked on at the capture of the two ships, without being able to prevent it, and found themselves in the strange position of besiegers who were being fought with their own weapons.

On the 25th they made a breach and attempted an assault, but were stopped by a counterscarp and a ditch.

On the 26th of March the besieged, led by Djezzar in person, attempted a sortie to destroy the works which had been begun; but, being charged with the bayonet, they were at once repulsed, and obliged to retreat within the walls.

Although the French batteries consisted only of four twelve-pounders, eight eight-pounders, and four howitzers, on the 28th this feeble battery was unmasked, and made a breach in the tower against which the principal attack was directed.

Although of a heavier caliber than those of the French, Djezzar's cannon were silenced by ours, and at three o'clock in the afternoon the tower offered a practicable breach.

When they saw the wall crumbling, and could look through to the other side, a cry of joy burst from the French army. The grenadiers who had been the first to enter Jaffa, excited by the memory, and thinking that it would be no more difficult to take Acre than it had been to take Jaffa, asked with one voice to be permitted to storm the breach.

Ever since morning Bonaparte, with his staff, had been in the trench; yet he hesitated to give the order for the assault. However, urged by Captain Mailly, who told him that he could no longer restrain the grenadiers, Bonaparte decided almost in spite of himself, and let the words escape him: —

" Well, go then! "

At once the grenadiers of the Sixty-ninth Brigade, led by Mailly, dashed towards the breach; but to their great astonishment, where they had expected to find the slope of the moat, they found an escarpment twelve feet high. Thereupon they raised a cry of "Ladders! ladders!"

Ladders were thrown into the ditch, the grenadiers leaped to them from the top of the counterscarp, and Mailly seized the first ladder and raised it to the breach; twenty others were at once placed beside it.

But the breach was filled with Arnauts and Albanians, who fired at close quarters, and rolled down the very stones from the wall upon the assailants. Half the ladders were broken, and in breaking carried down with them those who were upon them. Mailly, severely wounded, fell from top to bottom of his. The fire of the besieged redoubled; the grenadiers were obliged to retreat, and to use for mounting the counterscarp the ladders with which they had thought to scale the breach.

Mailly, who was wounded in the foot and could not walk, begged his grenadiers to take him with them. One of them put him upon his shoulders, carried him ten feet, and fell, with a bullet through his head; a second took up the wounded man and carried him to the foot of the ladder, where he fell with a broken thigh. Eager to secure their own safety, the soldiers left him; and they could hear his voice crying out, while no one stopped to reply to it, —

"At least make an end of me with a bullet, if you cannot save me!"

Poor Mailly had not long to suffer. The moats were no sooner evacuated by the French grenadiers than the Turks went down into them and cut off the heads of all who remained there.

Djezzar thought to bestow an acceptable gift upon

Sidney Smith; he had all these heads put in a sack and taken to the English commodore.

Sidney Smith looked sadly at the ghastly trophy, and merely said, —

" This is what it is to be allied with barbarians."

CHAPTER VI.

PTOLEMAÏS.

However indifferent Bonaparte may have been with regard to Jerusalem, having passed within seven leagues without tarrying to visit it, he was none the less interested in the history of the ground on which he stood. Having been unable, or not having cared, to do what Alexander did at the time of his conquest of India, and go out of his way to visit the high-priest at Jerusalem, he looked upon it as some compensation to stand upon the site of ancient Ptolemaïs, and to set up his tent where Richard Cœur-de-Lion and Philippe-Auguste had set up theirs.

Far from being indifferent to the historical environment, his pride rejoiced in it; and he had chosen for his headquarters the little hill from which, on the first day, he had watched the fight, confident that the heroes who had preceded him must have placed theirs upon the same spot.

But he, the first of the leaders of a political crusade, following the banner of his own fortune and leaving behind him all the religious ideas which had led millions of men to the spot, from Godefroy de Bouillon to Saint Louis, — he, on the contrary, brought in his train the science of the eighteenth century, of Volney and Dupuis; or, in other words, scepticism.

Caring little for Christian tradition, he was, on the other hand, very deeply interested in historical legend.

The very evening of the unsuccessful assault, in which poor Mailly had perished by the same death which his brother had died, he assembled his generals and officers in his tent, and ordered Bourrienne to take from his boxes the few books which composed his library.

Unfortunately, it contained very few historical works which treated of Syria. He had only Plutarch, — the lives of Cicero, Pompey, Alexander, and Antony; and in the way of political literature he had only the Old and New Testaments and the mythology.

He gave each of the books which we have just named to the most literary of his generals or his young friends, and then called upon the historical reminiscences of the others, which, added to his own, furnished the only information which he could obtain in that desert country.

Thus his information was very incomplete. We who, more fortunate than he, have under our eyes the literature of the Crusades, can raise for our readers the veil of centuries, and tell them the history of this little corner of the earth, from the day when it fell to the share of the tribe of Asher in the distribution of the Promised Land, until the time when another Cœur-de-Lion essayed to take it for the third time from the Saracens.

Its ancient name was Acco, meaning "burning sand;" and the Arabs still call it Acca.

Made tributary to Egypt by the kings of the Greek dynasty of Ptolemy, who had inherited Alexandria at the death of the conqueror of the Indies, it took the name of Ptolemaïs about one hundred and six years before Christ.

Vespasian, while preparing his expedition against Judæa, remained three months at Ptolemaïs, and held court there for the kings and princes of the neighboring countries.

It was there that Titus saw Berenice, daughter of Agrippa I., and fell in love with her.

But Bonaparte had nothing relating to this period save the tragedy of Racine, fragments of which he so often made Talma declaim.

The Acts of the Apostles says: "From Tyre we came to Ptolemaïs, where our voyage ended, and having saluted the brethren, we abode one day with them." As you know, Saint Paul says that, and it was he who came from Tyre to Ptolemaïs.

The first siege of Ptolemaïs by the Crusaders began in 1189. Boah-Eddin, an Arab historian, says, in speaking of the Christians, that they were so numerous that God alone could number them. But, on the other hand, a Christian author, Gauthier Vinisauf, chronicler of Richard Cœur-de-Lion, assures us that the army of Saladin was more numerous than that of Darius.

After the battle of Tiberius, of which we shall have occasion to speak in describing the battle of Mount Tabor, Guy de Lusignan, having escaped from captivity, laid siege to Jerusalem, whose fortifications had just been rebuilt; strong towers defended it on the side towards the sea.

One was called the Tower of Flies, because it was there that the pagans offered up their sacrifices, and the flies were attracted by the flesh of the victims; the other was called the Cursed Tower, because, says Gauthier Vinisauf in his "Itinerary of King Richard," it was in this tower that the pieces of silver were struck for which Judas sold our Saviour.

It was by this same tower, a "cursed tower" in very truth, that in 1291 the Saracens made their way into the city and took it.

Although he was ignorant of this fact, it was this very tower which Bonaparte had unsuccessfully attacked.

Walter Scott, in one of his best romances, "The Talis-man," has related an incident of this famous siege, which lasted two years.

The Arab histories, much less well known than the French, contain some interesting details regarding this siege.

Ibn-Alatir, one of Saladin's physicians, has, among others, left us an interesting description of the Mussul-man camp.

"In the midst of the camp" (it is Ibn-Alatir who is speaking) "was a vast square, containing the forges of the farriers. There were a hundred and forty of them. We can judge of the rest of the camp in proportion.

"In one single kitchen were twenty-nine pots, each one large enough to hold an entire sheep. I myself counted the number of shops registered with the inspec-tor of markets. There were seven thousand. You must know that they were not like our city shops. A shop in a camp would make a hundred of ours. All were well supplied. I have heard that when Saladin changed his camp to retire to Karouba, although the distance was short, it cost a single butter-merchant seventy pieces of gold to move his shop. As for the shops for the sale of old and new clothes, they were something beyond description. There were counted in the camp more than a thousand baths. They were kept by Africans; it cost a piece of silver to take a bath.

"The camp of the Christians was like a fortified city. All the trades and all the mechanical arts of Europe had their representatives there."

The markets were supplied with meat, fish, and fruits

as completely as the capital of a great kingdom would have been. There were even churches with their bells. Therefore, it was usually at the hour of mass that the Saracens attacked the camp.

"A poor English priest," says Michaud, "built at his own expense in the plain of Ptolemaïs a chapel consecrated to the dead. There was a vast cemetery of consecrated ground around the chapel, whither, himself chanting the office of the dead, he followed the mortal remains of more than a hundred thousand pilgrims. Forty lords of Bremen and Lübeck made tents with the sails of their vessels, to receive there the poor soldiers of their nation, and to care for them in sickness. This was the origin of a celebrated order which still exists under the name of the "Teutonic Order."

Whoever has travelled in the East, in Egypt, or to Constantinople, has made the acquaintance of the famous Turkish Punchinello, called Caragous. The exploits of our Punchinello are nothing in comparison with his; and he, the cynic *par excellence*, would blush at the most innocent jokes of his turbaned colleague.

It was during this siege, in which Richard Cœur-de-Lion, Philippe-Auguste, and Saladin played such great parts, that the ancestor of the modern Caragous appeared.

He was an emir.

Another historical date, not less important to verify, is that of the first bill of exchange. Emad-Eddin speaks of an ambassador from the Caliph of Bagdad who was the bearer of two loads of naphtha and reeds, and who brought with him five persons skilled in the distillation and use of the naphtha. It is well known that naphtha and Greek fire are one and the same.

Furthermore, this same ambassador brought a note of

hand for twenty thousand pieces of gold on the merchants of Bagdad.

Thus, the bill of exchange and the note of hand are not inventions of modern commerce, as they were used in the East in the year 1191.

It was during this two-years' siege that the besieged invented the *zenbourech*, which the popes afterwards forbade the Christians to use.

It was a sort of arrow, thirty centimetres long and twelve thick. It had four sides, an iron point, and a head ornamented with feathers.

Vinisauf relates that this terrible arrow, thrown by the instrument which was used to impel it, would sometimes pass through the bodies of two men, armed with shields, at one stroke, and then bury itself in the wall.

It was towards the end of this siege that the great quarrel arose which alienated Richard of England and Leopold, Duke of Austria. Cœur-de-Lion, who sometimes returned from an assault so riddled with arrows that, as his historian says, he looked like a pincushion covered with pins, was justly proud of his courage and strength.

Leopold, who was himself exceedingly brave, caused his flag to be hoisted over one of the towers of the city, which he had entered with Richard. Richard might have put his own flag beside that of Duke Leopold, but he preferred to take away the Austrian flag and throw it into the ditch. All the Germans uprose, and wished to attack the king in his quarters; but Leopold opposed this.

A year later, as Richard did not want to return through France, on account of his differences with Philippe-Auguste, he travelled through Austria in disguise; but he was recognized in spite of his disguise.

made prisoner, and taken to the castle of Durenstein. For two years no one knew what had become of him; this thunderbolt of war had been extinguished like a meteor. There were no traces of Richard Cœur-de-Lion.

A gentleman of Arras named Blondel undertook to find him; and one day, with no idea that he was so near the English king, he sat down at the foot of an old castle, and chanced to sing the first couplet of a ballad which he had written with Richard. Richard, by the way, was a bit of a poet in his leisure moments.

When he heard the first strains of the song composed by himself and Blondel, he suspected the presence of the latter, and replied with the second couplet.

The rest of the story, which furnished Grétry with the theme for a masterpiece, is well known.

Ptolemaïs surrendered to the Christians, as we have said, after a siege of two years. The garrison were promised their lives on condition that they would give up the True Cross, which had been taken at the battle of Tiberias.

It is needless to say that, once at liberty, the Saracens forgot all about their promise.

A hundred years later Ptolemaïs was retaken from the Christians, never to be given up to them again.

This siege also had its chroniclers, its sudden turns of fortune which moved all Europe and Asia, and its devotion, which was marked by more than one instance of heroism and self-abnegation.

Saint Antoninus relates, à propos of this siege, a curious legend.

"There was," he says, "at Saint-Jean-d'Acre a celebrated monastery of nuns, belonging to the order of Sainte-Claire. When the Saracens entered the town, the abbess ordered the convent bell to be rung, and collected the whole community.

" Addressing the nuns, she said, ' My dear daughters and beloved sisters, you have promised our Lord Jesus Christ to be his spotless wives. We are at this moment in twofold danger, — danger to our lives and danger to our purity. There are close at hand those enemies of our bodies, and of our souls as well, who, after dishonoring those whom they meet, run them through with the sword. If we cannot escape them by flight, we can do so by taking a painful but invincible resolve. It is woman's beauty which oftenest attracts man. Let us despoil ourselves of this attraction. Let us use our faces as a means of preserving our moral beauty, our chastity, intact. I will set you the example. Let those who wish to appear spotless before their spotless Spouse imitate their mistress.'

" Having so spoken, she cut off her nose with a razor; and the others followed her example, and courageously disfigured themselves, in order to appear more beautiful in the eyes of Jesus Christ.

" By this means they preserved their purity; for the Mussulmans," continues Saint Antoninus, " upon seeing their bleeding faces, felt nothing but horror for them, and contented themselves with merely taking their lives."

\-

CHAPTER VII.

THE SCOUTS.

DURING this night, when Bonaparte had assembled his staff, not for a council of war or to arrange a plan of battle, but as a literary and historical committee, several messengers arrived for the Sheik of Aher, to tell him that an army, under the Pacha of Damascus, was preparing to cross the Jordan, in order to force Bonaparte to raise the siege of Saint-Jean-d'Acre.

This army, which numbered about twenty-five thousand men, according to the always exaggerated reports of the Arabs, had an immense baggage train with it, and was to cross the Jordan at Jacob's Bridge.

On the other hand, Djezzar's agents had been all through the ˌsea-coast of Saïd, and its contingent had joined those of Aleppo and Damascus with the greater feeling of security, in that the messengers of the pacha had everywhere spread the report that the French were a mere handful of men, that they had no artillery, and that it would only be necessary for the Pacha of Damascus to show himself, and unite with Djezzar, to exterminate Bonaparte and his army.

Bonaparte, at this news, threw down the volume of Plutarch that he was reading, and called for Junot, Vial, and Murat. He sent Vial north, to take possession of Sour, — the ancient Tyre. He despatched Murat northeast, to make sure of the Fort of Zaphet; and Junot south, with orders to take possession of Nazareth, and from the elevated position on which this village was built to take an observation of all the surrounding country.

Vial crossed the mountains of Cape Blanco, and on the 3d of April came in sight of the town of Sour.

From the top of a little hill, the French general could see the frightened inhabitants leaving the town in disorder, and showing signs of great terror. He entered the town without any opposition, promised peace and protection to the people who had remained, reassured them, persuaded them to go and look for those who had run away, and, at the end of two or three days, had the pleasure of seeing them all in their homes once more.

Vial returned to Saint-Jean-d'Acre on the 6th of April, leaving a garrison of two hundred men at Sour.

Murat had been equally fortunate with his expedition. He had made his way to Fort Zaphet, where a few shots had driven away half the garrison. The other half, which was composed of Maugrabins, had offered to put themselves under Murat's orders. From there he had gone to the Jordan, reconnoitered its right bank, taken a look at the Lake of Tiberias, and, leaving a French garrison, well provisioned, in the fort, he returned on the 6th of April with his Maugrabins.

Junot had taken Nazareth, — our Saviour's birthplace, — and had encamped there, half in and half out of the village, awaiting fresh orders from Bonaparte, who had told him not to come back until he was recalled.

But Murat sought in vain to reassure the commander-in-chief. His presentiments, and, above all, the persistency of the Sheik of Aher, gave him no rest respecting this invisible army which was said to be marching against him. Therefore he accepted the sheik's offer to go as a scout to the Lake of Tiberias.

Roland, who was weary of remaining in the camp, where, beneath Bonaparte's eyes, he could not risk his life as he desired, asked leave to accompany the sheik in his explorations.

On that very night they set forth, taking advantage of the coolness and darkness to reach the plain of Esdrelon, which offered them the twofold shelter of the mountains of Nabloos, to the right, and those of Nazareth, to the left.

"On the 7th of April, 1799, the promontory on which is built Saint-Jean-d'Acre, the ancient Ptolemaïs, seemed to be wrapped in as much thunder and lightning as was Mount Sinai on the day when the Lord gave the law to Moses from the burning bush.

"Whence came these reports which shook the coast of Syria as if with an earthquake?

"Whence came that smoke which covered the Gulf of Carmel with a cloud as thick as though Mount Elias had become a volcano?"

We began thus the first chapter of this new narrative. The other chapters have only served to explain what had preceded this Syrian campaign, — the eighth, and probably the last, Crusade.

Bonaparte was, in fact, beginning his second assault. He had taken advantage of the return of Murat and Vial to try his fortune once more.

He was in the trench, scarcely a hundred paces from the ramparts. Near him was General Caffarelli, with whom he was talking. The latter was standing with his hand on his hip, to help balance himself upon his wooden leg. The joint of his elbow was just visible above the trench.

The peak of Bonaparte's three-cornered hat was also in sight, and a bullet knocked it from his head.

He stooped down to pick it up. As he stooped, he noticed the general's position, and, drawing near to him, he said, —

"General, these Arnauts and Albanians are excellent marksmen, as my hat has just discovered. Take care that they do not do to your arm what they did to my hat."

Caffarelli made a disdainful movement.

The gallant general had left one of his legs on the banks of the Rhine, and he did not seem to worry at the thought of leaving some other part of his body on the banks of the Kerdaneah.

He did not move.

A moment later Bonaparte saw him start and turn around, his arm hanging lifeless at his side. A bullet had struck his elbow, and broken the joint. At the same time Bonaparte raised his eyes, and saw Croisier, not ten paces away from them, standing on the edge of the trench. It was useless bravado. Therefore Bonaparte called to him, —

"Come down, Croisier! You have no business there. Come down; I wish it."

"Did you not say in public, one day, that I was a coward?" asked the young man.

"I was wrong, Croisier," replied the general, "and you have proved to me since that I was mistaken. Come down."

Croisier started to obey, but he fell down instead.

A bullet had broken his thigh.

"Larrey! Larrey!" cried Bonaparte, stamping his foot impatiently. "Here, come here! There is work for you."

Larrey approached. They laid Croisier on some

muskets. As for Caffarelli, he walked away, leaning on the arm of the surgeon-in-chief.

Let us leave the assault, commenced under such gloomy auspices, to take its course, and cast our eyes upon the beautiful plain of Esdrelon, covered with flowers, and the river Kishon, whose course is marked by a long line of rose-laurels.

On the banks of this river two horsemen were carelessly riding along.

One of them, dressed in the green uniform of the mounted chasseurs, with his sabre at his side, and his three-cornered hat on his head, was making a breeze for himself with a perfumed handkerchief, as he might have done with a fan.

The tricolored cockade which he wore in his hat showed that he belonged to the French army.

The other wore a red cap, tied around his head with a piece of chamois skin. A head-dress of brilliant colors fell from his head over his shoulders. He was completely enveloped in a burnoose of white cashmere, which, when it opened, disclosed a rich Oriental caftan of green velvet embroidered with gold. He had a silk belt of varied colors, which shaded into each other with that marvellous taste which is found only in Eastern stuffs. In this belt were stuck on one side two pistols with silver-gilt handles, wrought like the finest lace. His sword alone was of French make. He had wide trousers of red satin, tucked into green boots embroidered like the caftan, and of the same material. Besides all this, he held in his hand a long, slender lance, light as a reed, and strong as a bar of iron, tipped at the end with a bunch of ostrich feathers.

The two young men stopped at one of the bends of the

river, in the shade of a little grove of palms; and there, laughing pleasantly together, as befitted travelling companions, they began to prepare their breakfast, which consisted of a few pieces of biscuit which the young Frenchman took from his holsters and dipped for a moment in the river.

As for the Arab, he began to look around and above him. Then, without saying anything, he attacked with his sword one of the palm-trees, whose tender and porous wood yielded rapidly to the sharp steel.

" Upon my soul, this is a good sword that the commander-in-chief gave me a few days ago," he said. " I hope to try it on something besides palm-trees before long."

" I should think so," returned the Frenchman, crushing the biscuit between his teeth. " That was a gift of Versailles manufacture. But are you destroying that poor tree just to try the temper of the blade?"

" Look!" replied the Arab, pointing up into the air.

" Faith!" said the Frenchman, " it is a date-palm, and we shall have a better breakfast than I had thought."

And just then the tree fell with a crash, bringing within their reach enough dates, fully ripe, for two or three meals.

They began to attack with the appetites of twenty-five years the manna which the Lord had sent them.

They were in the midst of the meal when the Arab's horse began to neigh.

The Arab uttered an exclamation, darted out of the little grove, and with his hand above his eyes, scanned the plain of Esdrelon, in the middle of which they then were.

" What is it ? " asked the Frenchman, nonchalantly.

" One of ours, riding a fast mare. From him we shall probably learn what we want to know. "

He returned, and seated himself near his companion without disturbing himself about his horse, which set off at a gallop to meet the advancing rider.

Ten minutes later the gallop of two horses was heard.

A Druse, who had recognized his chief's horse, stopped near the group of palms, where the presence of a second horse showed him that a party had halted there, even if there was no encampment.

" Azib! " called the Arab chief.

The Druse stopped, leaped from his horse, throwing the reins upon its neck, and advanced towards the sheik, crossing his hands upon his breast, and bowing low.

The sheik addressed a few words to him in Arabic.

" I was not mistaken, " said the Sheik of Aher, turning to his companion. " The advance-guard of the Pacha of Damascus has just crossed Jacob's Bridge. "

" We will go and see, " returned Roland, whom our readers have doubtless recognized, from his indifference to danger.

" There is no need, " replied the sheik. " Azib has seen. "

" Yes, " returned Roland; " but perhaps Azib has not seen correctly. I shall feel much more certain when I have seen it myself. This great mountain, which looks like a pie, must be Mount Tabor. The Jordan is, therefore, just beyond it. We are within a quarter of a league of it. Let us go and look, and then we shall know for ourselves what to think. "

And, without stopping to see whether the Sheik of Aher was following him, Roland leaped upon his horse, which was refreshed by the halt which they had made, and galloped swiftly away in the direction of Mount Tabor.

A minute later he heard the others galloping behind him.

CHAPTER VIII.

THE BEAUTIFUL DAUGHTERS OF NAZARETH.

HE rode for a full league over the magnificent plain of Esdrelon, — the most immense and most celebrated in all Palestine, after that of the Jordan.

In other days it was called the paradise and granary of Syria, the plain of Jezreel, the field of Esdrela, the plain of Mejiddo. It is mentioned in the Bible under all these names. It witnessed the defeat of the Midianites and the Amalekites by Gideon. It saw Saul encamped by the fountain of Jezreel to fight the Philistines, who were assembled at Aphek. It saw Saul, conquered, throw himself upon his sword, and saw his three sons perish with him. It was in this plain that poor Naboth had his vineyard, near Ahab's palace, and where the infamous Jezebel had him stoned to death as a blasphemer, in order to get possession of his heritage. It was here that Joram had his heart pierced by an arrow, hurled by the hand of Jehu. And, finally, it was on almost the same spot where the young men had breakfasted that Jezebel, by Jehu's order, was thrown from a window, and her body devoured by the dogs.

In the Middle Ages this plain, which has seen so many sights, was called the plain of Sabas. Today it is called Merdjibn-Amer, which means "Pasturage of the sons of Amer." It extends for about five leagues between the mountains of Gilboa and those of Nazareth. At its extremity rises Mount Tabor, towards which the three riders were galloping, without giving a thought to the celebrity of the ground which their horses were trampling beneath their feet.

Mount Tabor is accessible on all sides, and particularly so on the side of Fouli, by which they were approaching it.

They were obliged to climb to its summit — an easy task for their Arab horses — before they could look over the two small hills which, from any less height, obstructed the view of the Jordan and the Lake of Tiberias.

But as they ascended, the horizon broadened around them. Soon they discovered, like an immense blue cloth, framed in golden sand on one side, and hills of tawny verdure on the other, the Lake of Tiberias, joined to the Dead Sea by the Jordan, which stretches across the bare plain like a yellow ribbon sparkling in the sun. Their eyes were soon riveted in that direction by the sight of the whole army of the Pacha of Damascus, which was following the eastern bank of the lake, and crossing the Jordan at Jacob's Bridge. The whole of the advance-guard had already disappeared between the lake and the mountain of Tiberias. It was evidently on its way towards the village.

It was impossible for the young men to compute, even approximately, the number of this vast multitude. The cavalry alone, marching in the fantastic fashion of the Orientals, covered leagues of ground. Although the young men were four leagues away, they could see the weapons glistening, and flashes of gold seemed to dart through the clouds of dust thrown up by the horses' feet.

It was about three o'clock in the afternoon.

There was no time to lose. The Sheik of Aher and Azib, by resting an hour or two near the river Kishon, could reach Bonaparte's camp at daybreak, or a little before, and give him warning.

As for Roland, he undertook to go to Nazareth and put Junot on his guard, intending to remain and fight with him there, where he could have more liberty of action.

The three young men rapidly descended the mountain. At its foot they separated, the two Arabs striking directly across the plain of Esdrelon, and Roland spurring straight for Nazareth, whose white houses, lying like a nest of doves amidst the sombre verdure of the mountain, he had seen from the top of Tabor.

The traveller who has visited Nazareth will remember what abominable roads lead to it. Now on the right and now on the left the road is bordered with precipices, and the beautiful flowers which grow wherever there is earth enough to hold their roots, add to the attractions of the journey, but do not make it the less dangerous. There are white lilies, yellow narcissi, blue crocuses, and roses whose freshness and sweetness are beyond description.

Does not the Hebrew word "nezer," which is the root of Nazareth, mean "flower"?

Owing to the windings of the road, Roland obtained several glimpses of Nazareth before he finally arrived there. When he was within ten minutes of the nearest houses, he met a detachment of grenadiers of the Nineteenth Brigade; and, making himself known, he inquired whether the general was in Nazareth or in its environs.

The general was in Nazareth, and had been to visit the outposts not a quarter of an hour before.

Roland was obliged to let his horse walk.   The noble animal had just made eighteen or twenty leagues without any other rest than that afforded by the breakfast hour; but as Roland was now sure of finding the general, he had no need to force him.

At the first houses of the village he found a squad of dragoons, commanded by one of his friends, Major Desnoyers.   He left his horse in the care of a soldier, and asked where General Junot's quarters were.

It was about half-past five in the evening.

Desnoyers looked at the sun, just ready to disappear behind the mountains of Nabloos, and replied, laughing, —

"This is the hour when the women of Nazareth go to the spring for water.   General Junot is probably on his way to the spring."

Roland shrugged his shoulders.   He evidently thought that the general's place was elsewhere, and that he had others to review besides the beautiful daughters of Nazareth.   He nevertheless followed the directions given him, and soon reached the other end of the village.

The spring was situated about ten minutes' walk beyond the last house.   The avenue which led to it was lined on either side by immense cactus-trees, which . were like a wall.   A short distance from the spring, and following with his eyes the women who were going and coming, Roland espied the general and his two aides-de-camp.

Junot recognized him at once as Bonaparte's ordnance officer.   The commander-in-chief's partiality for Roland was well known, and would have been in itself a sufficient reason for everybody to smile upon him; but his courteous familiarity and his daring courage, which was proverbial in the army, would have won him friends, even though he had possessed a much smaller share of the general's favor.

Junot came to meet him, with extended hand.

Roland, a strict observer of the proprieties, saluted him as his superior officer; for he feared nothing more than that it should be thought that he attributed the commander-in-chief's kindness to him to his own merit.

"Do you bring us good news, my dear Roland?" asked Junot.

"Yes, General," replied Roland, "since I come to announce to you the presence of the enemy."

"Faith!" said Junot, "next to the sight of these beautiful girls, who carry their jugs as if each was a veritable princess Nausicaa, I know of nothing that would be more agreeable to me than the sight of the enemy. Look, Roland; see what a haughty manner the vixens have. Would you not say they were so many antique goddesses? And when shall we look for the enemy?"

"As soon as you please, General, since they are not more than five or six leagues from here."

"Do you know what they answer, when you tell them that they are beautiful? 'The Virgin Mary wills it so.' This is really the first time since we came to Syria that we have seen pretty women. Have you seen them, — the enemy, I mean?"

"With my own eyes, General."

"Where are they coming from? Where are they going? What do they want of us?"

"They are coming from Damascus, and I suppose

they want to whip us. They are going to Saint-Jean-d'Acre, if I am not mistaken, to raise the siege."

"Only that? Oh, we will cut them off! Are you going to stay with us, or return to Bonaparte?"

"I shall stay with you, General. I have a great desire to try a turn with the rascals. We are dying of ⌐ennui at the siege. Except for two or three sorties which Djezzar has had the stupidity to make, there is nothing to vary the monotony."

"Well," said Junot, "I can promise you that you will find some variety by to-morrow. By the way, I forgot to ask you how many there were."

"Ah, my dear General, I will reply to you as an Arab would: 'As well try to count the sands of the sea!' There must be at least twenty-five or thirty thousand of them."

Junot scratched his head.

"The devil!" he said. "There's not much to be done, with the few men I have here."

"How many have you?" asked Roland.

"Just a hundred men more than the three hundred Spartans. But we can do what they did, and that will not be so bad. However, it will be time enough to think of all that to-morrow morning. Would you like to see the curiosities of the town, or will you have some supper?"

"Well," said Roland, "to be sure, here we are at Nazareth, and interesting relics ought not to be scarce; but I will not conceal from you, General, that my stomach is just now more impatient than my eyes. I breakfasted this morning, near the Kishon, off some hardtack and a dozen dates, and I confess that I am both hungry and thirsty."

"If you will give me the pleasure of supping with

me, we will try to appease your appetite. As for your thirst, you will never find a better opportunity to quench it."

Then, addressing a young girl who was passing, he said in Arabic, —

"Water! Thy brother is thirsty."

And he pointed to Roland.

She drew near, tall and stern, her tunic, with its long, flowing sleeves, leaving her arms bare. She tipped the jug which she was carrying on her right shoulder until it was on a level with her left hand. Then, with a most graceful motion, she offered the water to Roland.

Roland drank deeply, not because the girl was beautiful, but because the water was fresh.

"Has my brother drunk sufficiently?" asked the girl.

"Yes," replied Roland, in the same language, "and thy brother thanks thee."

The young girl bowed, put her jug back upon her shoulder, and went on her way towards the village.

"Do you know that you speak Arabic very fluently?" said Junot, laughing.

"Was I not, for a month, wounded and a prisoner among these rascals," said Roland, "at the time of the insurrection at Cairo? I had to learn a little Arabic, in spite of myself. And since the commander-in-chief has found out that I can chatter a little in the language of the Prophet, he is determined on all occasions to take me with him as interpreter."

"Upon my word," said Junot, "if I thought I could learn Arabic in a month as well as you know it, I would pay the same price, and get myself wounded and made a prisoner to-morrow."

"Well, General," said Roland, laughing with the harsh, nervous laugh peculiar to him, "if I might offer my advice, it would be to learn some other language, and in a different manner.   Let us go to supper, General."

And Roland moved towards the village without giving another glance at the beautiful Nazarenes whom Junot and his aides stopped again and again to gaze upon.

CHAPTER IX.

THE BATTLE OF NAZARETH.

THE next day at dawn, about six o'clock in the morning, the drums beat and the trumpets sounded the *diane*.

As Roland had told Junot that the advance-guard of the Damascenes was on the way to Tiberias, Junot, not wishing to give them time to besiege him on his mountain, crossed the ravine between the hills which rise around Nazareth, and descended through the valley as far as the village of Cana.

He did not see it until he was within a quarter of a league, for a spur of the mountain hid it completely.

The enemy might be either in the valley of Batouf or on the plain which lies at the foot of Mount Tabor. But, in either case, as the French were coming down from the "high places," as Scripture has it, they were in no danger of being surprised; on the contrary, they were sure to see the enemy at a distance.

The soldiers were better versed in the miracle which Jesus performed at Cana than in any other of his miracles; and of all the places sanctified by his presence, Cana was the one which was most firmly impressed upon their memory.

For it was at the wedding in Cana that Jesus turned the water into wine. And although the soldiers were very happy on those days when they had water, it is self-evident that they would have been still happier if there had been days on which they had had wine.

It was also at Cana that Jesus performed another miracle spoken of by Saint John.

"There was a certain nobleman, whose son was sick at Capernaum.

"When he heard that Jesus was come out of Judea into Galilee, he went unto him, and besought him that he would come down, and heal his son; for he was at the point of death.

"Then Jesus said unto him, Except ye see signs and wonders, ye will not believe.

"The nobleman said unto him, Sir, come down ere my child die.

"Jesus said unto him, Go thy way; thy son liveth. And the man believed the word that Jesus had spoken unto him, and he went his way.

"And as he was now going down, his servants met him, and told him, saying, Thy son liveth."

At the entrance to the village of Cana, Junot found the Sheik El-Beled, who was coming to meet him to ask him to go no farther, since, he said, there were two or three thousand of the enemy's cavalry on the plain.

Junot had one hundred and fifty grenadiers of the Nineteenth Regiment of the Line, a hundred and fifty carabineers of the Second Light, and about a hundred cavalry, commanded by Major Duvivier, belonging to the Fourteenth Dragoons. This was exactly four hundred men, as he had said on the previous night.

He thanked the Sheik El-Beled, and, to the latter's great admiration, he continued on his way. When he reached one of the branches of a little river which has its source at Cana, he went along up its bank. As he came to the pass which separates Loubi from the mountains

of Cana, he saw two or three thousand cavalry divided
into several corps, who were galloping about between
Mount Tabor and Loubi.

To get a better idea of their positions, he put his
horse to a gallop, and went as far as the ruins of a village which crowned the hill, and which the people of
the country called Meschenah.

But just then he saw a second corps marching upon
the village of Loubi. It was composed of Mamelukes,
Turcomans, and Maugrabins.

This troop was almost as strong as the other, and
Junot, with his four hundred men, had five thousand
against him.

Moreover, this troop was marching in a compact mass,
contrary to the custom of the Orientals, at a slow pace,
and in good order. There were visible in the ranks
great numbers of standards, banners, and horses' tails.

These horses' tails, which served as ensigns for the
pachas, had been a laughing-stock for the French, until
they knew the origin of this singular standard. Then
they had been told that at the battle of Nicopolis,
Bajazet, having seen his standard taken by the soldiers of
the Cross, had with a blow of his sabre cut the tail from
his horse and put it on a pike; and not only had he
rallied his men around this novel oriflamme, but had
gained the famous battle, which was one of the most
disastrous for Christianity.

Junot was right in thinking that the troop which was
marching in good order was the only one to be feared.
He sent fifty grenadiers to keep back the cavalry whom
he had seen first, and whom he recognized as Bedouins,
who would content themselves with harassing his troops
during the fight.

But in opposition to the regular force he drew up the

hundred grenadiers and the hundred and fifty carabineers, keeping the hundred dragoons in hand, in order to use them where they might be most needed.

The Turks, seeing this handful of men stop and wait for them, supposed that they were motionless with terror. They approached within pistol-shot; but then carabineers and grenadiers, choosing each a man, fired, and the whole front rank of the Turks fell, some of the bullets ploughing their way to horses and men in the third and fourth lines.

This volley caused great confusion among the Mussulmans, and gave the carabineers and grenadiers time to reload. But this time only the front rank fired, the second rank then passing forward their loaded guns and receiving empty ones in their places.

This continuous fusillade made the Turks falter; but when they looked upon their own great number, and the insignificant number of their enemy, they charged with loud shouts.

This was the moment that Roland was waiting for. While Junot ordered his two hundred and fifty men to form a hollow square, Roland, at the head of his hundred dragoons, dashed upon the troop, which was charging in disorderly fashion, and took them in the flank.

The Turks were not accustomed to these straight sabres, which pierced them like lances at a distance at which their curved sabres were of no use. The effect of the charge was therefore terrible. The dragoons cut straight through the mass of Mussulmans, coming out on the other side. They gave the square an opportunity to discharge their rifles, and then dashed into the furrow which the bullets had ploughed; and, riding with their sabres held straight before them, they enlarged the opening in such a fashion that the mass seemed to burst, and the Turkish horsemen, instead of continuing to march with closed ranks, began to scatter over the plain.

Roland had closed with a standard-bearer of the principal chiefs. Having the curved sabre of the chasseurs, instead of the straight and pointed sabre of the dragoons, he and his antagonist were upon equal terms. Two or three times, letting the rein fall upon his horse's neck and managing him with his legs, he put his left hand to his pistols; but it seemed to him unworthy of himself to use this means of defence. He urged his horse upon that of his adversary, and seized the man about the body, and the struggle continued, while the horses, recognizing each other as enemies, bit and tore savagely at each other. For a moment those who surrounded the two combatants stopped; French and Mussulmans waited to see the end. But Roland, loosening his girths, drove the spurs into his horse, who seemed to slip out from between his legs, while Roland's weight dragged the Turkish rider from his horse, and he fell, head downwards, hanging by his stirrups. In a second Roland was up again, his bleeding sabre in one hand, and the Turkish standard in the other. As for the Mussulman, he was dead; and his horse, maddened by a blow from Roland's sabre, dragged him into the ranks of his companions, where he added to the disorder.

Meanwhile, the Arabs on the plain of Mount Tabor hastened towards the firing.

Two chiefs, who were better mounted, preceded their men by five hundred paces.

Junot rode out alone to meet them, ordering his soldiers to leave them to him.

A hundred paces in advance of the fifty men whom he had, as if in derision, sent against the Arabs of the plain, he stopped; and seeing that there was a distance of a dozen paces between the two horsemen with whom he had to do, he let his sabre hang by its knot, and took a pistol from his holster. Between the ears of the horse of one of his antagonists, who was coming at full speed towards him, he saw two flaming eyes, and (we have said that he was marvellously skilful with the pistol) put a ball straight through the middle of their owner's forehead.

The rider fell; the horse, carried on by his own impetus, was taken by one of the fifty grenadiers, while, putting his pistol back into the holster, and seizing his sabre, the general cut off his second adversary's head with a single blow.

Then each officer, inspired by the general's example, left the ranks. Ten or twelve single combats, like that which we have just described, engaged the attention of the two armies, who applauded vigorously. The Turks were defeated in all.

The battle lasted from half past nine in the morning until three o'clock in the afternoon, when Junot ordered a retreat, step by step, into the mountains of Cana.

When he came down in the morning, he had seen a large plateau which had seemed well suited for his purpose; for he knew well that with his four hundred men he might hope to make a brilliant fight, perhaps, but could not expect victory. The battle had been fought; four hundred Frenchmen had held the ground for five hours against five thousand Turks; they had laid eight hundred dead and three hundred wounded upon the field of battle.

They themselves had had five men killed and one wounded.

Junot gave orders that the wounded man should be

taken with them; and as his leg was broken, they put him on a litter, which four of his comrades took turns in carrying.

Roland had mounted his horse again. He had exchanged his curved sabre for a straight one; and he had in his holsters his pistols, with which he could, at twenty paces, cut off a pomegranate flower. With Junot's two aides-de-camp he took command of the hundred dragoons who formed the general's cavalry; and the three young men, in friendly rivalry, made of this work of death a pleasure party. Whether they were fighting the Turks hand-to-hand with swords, or whether, encouraged by the general, they contented themselves by using them as targets, they filled the day full of picturesque incidents which long furnished heroic anecdotes and amusing tales for the bivouac of the Army of the East.

At four o'clock Junot, established on his plateau, having at his feet one of the feeders of the little river which empties into the sea near Carmel, and in communication with the Greek and Catholic monks of Cana and Nazareth, was by his position sheltered from attack and sure of his supplies.

He could therefore afford to wait quietly for the reinforcements which Bonaparte, warned by the Sheik of Aher, could not fail to send him.

CHAPTER X.

MOUNT TABOR.

As Roland had expected, the Sheik of Aher had arrived at the camp at daybreak. In accordance with his maxim, "Always wake me for bad news, but never for good news," Bonaparte had been awakened.

The sheik, admitted to his presence, told him what he had seen, and how twenty-five or thirty thousand men had crossed the Jordan and had just entered the territory of Tiberias.

When Bonaparte asked him what had become of Roland, he told him that the young aide-de-camp had taken it upon himself to warn Junot, who was at Nazareth, and that there was at the foot of Tabor, between that mountain and the mountains of Nabloos, a great plain, in which twenty-five thousand Turks could sleep side by side without crowding.

Bonaparte had sent somebody to wake Bourrienne, had called for his map, and sent for Kléber.

In the presence of the latter, the sheik had the young Druse point out the exact spot at which the Mussulmans had crossed the river, the road which they had taken, and that which he and the sheik had followed in returning to the camp.

"You will take your division," said Bonaparte to Kléber; "it should consist of about two thousand men. The sheik will serve as your guide, so that you may not pass over exactly the same route that he took with Roland. You will go by the shortest route to Safarie; to-morrow morning you should be at Nazareth. Let each of your men take enough water for the day. Although I see a river marked upon the map, I am afraid that at this season of the year it will be dried up. If possible, let the battle be on the plain, either in front of or behind Mount Tabor, at Loubi or Fouli. We must take our revenge for the battle of Tiberias, won by Saladin over Guy de Lusignan in 1187. See that the Turks have lost nothing by waiting all these years. Do not be uneasy about me; I will get there in time."

Kléber assembled his division, and bivouacked that evening near Safarie, — a city which tradition says was inhabited by Saint Joachim and Saint Anne.

That same evening he was in communication with Junot, who had left an advance-guard at Cana and gone up to Nazareth, for which he had a weakness.

He learned from him that the enemy had not left their position at Loubi, and that consequently they would be found at one of the two points indicated by Bonaparte, — namely, the one in front of Mount Tabor.

A quarter of a league from Loubi was a village called Saïd-Jarra, occupied by a portion of the Turkish army, seven or eight thousand men in all. He ordered Junot to attack it with a part of his division, while with the rest of his men, formed in a square, he charged the cavalry.

At the end of two hours the pacha's infantry was driven from Saïd-Jarra, and the cavalry from Loubi.

The Turks, completely routed, fell back in disorder to the Jordan. Junot in this engagement had two horses killed under him; finding nothing at hand but a dromedary, he mounted that, and soon found himself in the midst of the Turks, among whom he seemed like a giant.

The ham-strings of the dromedary were cut, and the animal fell, or rather sank, beneath him. Fortunately, Roland had not lost sight of him; he came up with Junot's aide-de-camp Teinturier, — the same whom Roland found watching the fair damsels of Nazareth with him.

They fell like a thunderbolt upon the mass which surrounded Junot, opened a passage, and reached his side. They mounted him on the horse of a dead Mameluke, and all three, pistol in hand, pierced the living wall and reappeared in the midst of the soldiers, who had thought them dead, and who were hastening forward, with no other object than that of recovering their bodies.

Kléber had come so fast that his army wagons were not able to keep up with him; and so, for want of ammunition, they could not pursue the fugitives.

He fell back upon Nazareth, and fortified his position at Safarie.

On the 13th, Kléber sent out scouts to reconnoitre the enemy. The Mamelukes of Ibrahim Bey, the Janissaries of Damascus, the Arabs of Aleppo, and the different tribes of Syria had effected a junction with the people of Nabloos; and all these different tribes were encamped in the plain of Fouli, or Esdrelon.

Kléber immediately informed the commander-in-chief of these details. He told him that he had reconnoitred the hostile army, that it amounted to about thirty thousand men, of which twenty thousand were cavalry; and he announced that on the next day, with his twenty-five hundred men, he proposed to attack this multitude. He ended his letter with these words: —

" The enemy is exactly where you want him. Try to come to the *fête.* "

The Sheik of Aher was intrusted with the despatch; but as the plain was overrun with hostile riders, it was sent in triplicate by three different messengers on as many separate routes.

Bonaparte received two of the three despatches,—one at eleven o'clock at night, the other at one in the morning. The third messenger was never heard from.

Bonaparte fully intended to be at the *fête*. He was eager for a general action and to fight a decisive battle which should drive back the formidable host, which might eventually crush him against the walls of Saint-Jean-d'Acre.

Murat, at two o'clock in the morning, was sent forward with a thousand infantry, one piece of light artillery, and a detachment of dragoons. He had orders to march until he came to the Jordan, where he was to take possession of Jacob's Bridge, to prevent the retreat of the Turkish army. He had more than ten leagues to make.

Bonaparte started at three o'clock in the morning, taking with him every man who was not absolutely needed in order to keep the enemy within their walls. At daybreak he bivouacked on the heights of Safarie, and distributed to his men bread, water, and brandy; he had been obliged to take the longest route, because his artillery and wagons could not follow him along the banks of the Kishon.

At nine o'clock he took up his march again; and at ten o'clock in the morning he was at the foot of Mount Tabor.

There, in the vast plain of Esdrelon, about three leagues away, he saw Kléber's division, scarcely twenty-five hundred strong, face to face with the entire mass of the enemy's army, which enveloped it on all sides, and

in the midst of which it looked like a black point surrounded by fire.

More than twenty thousand cavalry were attacking it,
now twisting about it like a whirlwind, now falling upon
it like an avalanche. Never had these men, who had seen
so many things, seen such a number of horsemen in
motion, charging and galloping around them; and yet
each soldier, standing foot to foot with his neighbor,
preserved the terrible coolness which alone would insure
his safety, received the Turks at the end of his rifle, and
fired only when he was sure of his man; striking the
horses with his bayonet when they came too near, but
reserving his bullets for their riders.

Each man had received fifty cartridges; but at eleven
o'clock in the morning they were obliged to make a
second distribution of fifty more. They had fired a hundred thousand bullets; they had made around them a
breastwork of dead horses and men; and they were sheltered by this horrible heap, this bleeding wall, as by a
rampart.

This was what Bonaparte and his army saw when they
came around Mount Tabor.

At the sight, enthusiastic shouts ran along the lines:

" To the enemy! to the enemy! "

But Bonaparte cried, " Halt! " He made them take
a quarter of an hour's rest. He knew that Kléber could
hold out for hours yet, if necessary, and he wished the
day's work to be well done.

Then he formed his six thousand men in two blocks
of three thousand each, and distributed them in such
manner as to enclose the whole savage horde, cavalry
and infantry, in a triangle of steel and fire.

The combatants were in such deadly earnest that, like
the Romans and Carthaginians, who, during the battle of

Trasimene, did not feel the earthquake which overthrew twenty-two cities, neither the Turks nor the French saw the approach of the two armed masses, in whose train were rolling thunders that were mute as yet, but whose glistening weapons flashed ceaselessly in the sunlight, — precursors of the storm which was about to burst.

Suddenly they heard a single cannon-shot.

It was the signal by which Bonaparte had agreed to announce his approach to Kléber. The three squares were not more than a league from each other, and their triple fire was about to be directed upon a compact mass of twenty-five thousand men.

The fire burst forth from the three sides at once.

The Mamelukes and Janissaries, in short, all the cavalry, turned this way and that, not knowing how to escape from the furnace; while the ten thousand infantry, ignorant of all military science and theory, broke their ranks, and hurled themselves upon the three lines of fire.

All those who were fortunate enough to run between the shots succeeded in escaping. At the end of an hour the fugitives had disappeared like dust swept by the wind, leaving the plain covered with dead, abandoning their camp, their standards, four hundred camels, and an immense amount of booty.

The fugitives thought that they were safe; and those who reached the mountains of Nabloos did indeed find a refuge there; but those who tried to escape across the Jordan, as they had come, found Murat and his thousand men guarding the ford of the river.

The French did not stop until they were weary of killing.

Bonaparte and Kléber met upon the field of battle; and amidst the shouts of the three squares, they embraced each other.

It was then, according to military tradition, that the colossal Kléber, putting his hand upon the shoulder of Bonaparte, who barely reached his chest, said to him those words which have been so much disputed since:

"General, you are as great as the world!"

Bonaparte ought to have been content.

It was upon the same spot where Guy de Lusignan had been defeated that he had just conquered; it was there that, on the 5th of July, 1187, the French, "having exhausted even the sources of their tears," says the Arab author, "met in desperate combat with the Mussulmans, commanded by Saladin."

"At the beginning," says this same author, "they fought like lions; but at the end they were nothing more than scattered sheep." Surrounded on all sides, they were driven back to the foot of the Mount of Beatitudes, where our Saviour, teaching the people, said, "Blessed are the poor in spirit, blessed are they who weep, blessed are they who are persecuted for righteousness' sake," and where he also said, "When ye pray, say, 'Our Father, who art in heaven.'"

The whole action was in the neighborhood of this mountain, which the infidels call Mount Hittin.

Guy de Lusignan took refuge upon the hill, and defended the True Cross as well as he could; but he could not prevent the Mussulmans from obtaining possession of it, after they had mortally wounded the Bishop of Saint-Jean-d'Acre, who was carrying it.

Raymond opened a passage with his men, and escaped to Tripoli, where he died of grief.

So long as a single group of horsemen remained, that group returned to the charge; but it soon melted before the Saracens like wax in a furnace.

Finally, the pavilion of the king fell, to rise no more.

Guy de Lusignan was made a prisoner, and Saladin, taking the sword of the King of Jerusalem from the hands of him who brought it to him, dismounted from his horse and gave thanks to Mahomet for his victory.

Never did Christians, in Palestine or elsewhere, suffer such a defeat. "In looking upon the number of the dead," says an eye-witness, "one could not believe that there were any prisoners; in looking upon the prisoners, one could not believe that there were any dead."

The king, after having sworn to renounce his kingdom, was sent to Damascus. All the Chevaliers of the Temple and the Hospitallers lost their heads. Saladin, who feared lest his soldiers should feel the pity which he did not himself feel, and thinking that they might spare some of these soldier-monks, paid fifty pieces of gold for each one that was brought to him.

There scarcely remained a thousand men out of the whole Christian army. The Arab authors say that they sold a prisoner for a pair of sandals, and that they exposed the heads of the Christians like melons in the streets of Damascus.

Monseigneur Mislin, in his beautiful book, " Les Saints Lieux," says that a year after this horrible carnage, in crossing the fields of Hittin, he still found heaps of bones, and that the mountains and valleys around were covered with the remains that the wild beasts had dragged there.

After the battle of Mount Tabor the jackals of the plain of Esdrelon had no occasion to envy the hyænas of the mountain of Tiberias.

CHAPTER XI.

THE DEALER IN BULLETS.

SINCE Bonaparte's return from Mount Tabor, nearly a month before, there had not been a day when the batteries had ceased to thunder, or when there had been a truce between besiegers and besieged.

This was the first resistance that Fortune had put in Bonaparte's path.

The siege of Saint-Jean-d'Acre lasted sixty days; there were seven assaults and twelve sorties. Caffarelli died in consequence of the amputation of his arm, and Croisier was still on a bed of suffering.

A thousand men had been killed, or had died of the plague.

There was still plenty of powder, but no bullets.

The report spread throughout the army; things like these cannot be concealed from the soldiers. One morning when Bonaparte and Roland were in the trench, a sergeant-major approached the latter.

"Is it true, my commandant," he said, "that the commander-in-chief is in need of bullets?"

"Yes," replied Roland. "Why?"

"Oh," replied the sergeant-major, with a movement of the neck which was peculiar to him, and seemed to date back to the days when he wore a cravat for the first time, and did not like the feeling of it, "if he wants some, I can get them for him."

" You ? "

" Yes, I. And not so dear, either. Five sous. "

" Five sous ! — and they cost the Government forty ! "

" You see it would be a good bargain. "

" You are not joking ? "

" Do you think I would joke with my superior officers ? "

Roland went to Bonaparte, and told him what the sergeant-major had just said.

" These rascals have good ideas sometimes, " he said. " Call him. "

Roland made a sign to the sergeant to come forward.

He came forward with the military step, and stopped two metres away from Bonaparte, with his hand at the visor of his shako.

" Are you the dealer in bullets ? " asked Bonaparte.

" I sell them, but I do not make them. "

" And you can furnish them for five sous ? "

" Yes, General. "

" How do you do it ? "

" Ah, that is my secret! If I were to tell it, everybody would be selling them. "

" How many can you furnish ? "

" As many as thou dost wish, Citizen-General, " replied the sergeant-major, emphasizing the " thou. "

" What do you need in order to get them ? " Bonaparte asked.

" Permission to go in bathing with my company. "

Bonaparte burst out laughing, for he understood at once.

" Very well, " he said ; " go. "

The sergeant-major saluted, and went off at a run.

" Faith ! " said Roland, " that fellow is deeply attached to the republican vocabulary. Did you notice, General, the accent with which he said, 'as many as *thou* dost wish' ? "

Bonaparte smiled, but made no reply.

Almost immediately the commander-in-chief and his aide saw the company who had permission to bathe pass, with the sergeant-major at their head.

" Come and see something curious, " said Bonaparte to his aide-de-camp.

And taking Roland's arm, he walked up a little elevation, from which the whole gulf was visible.

Then he saw the sergeant-major, setting the example of rushing into the water, as he certainly would have done of rushing into the fire, remove his clothes first, and wade into the sea with a part of his men, while the others scattered along the shore.

Until then Roland had not understood.

But scarcely had the sergeant-major's manœuvre been executed, when, from the two English frigates and the ramparts of Saint-Jean-d'Acre, a storm of bullets began to fall. As the soldiers, however, both those who were in the water and those who were on the sand, took care to keep well away from each other, the bullets fell in the spaces between the men, where they were immediately picked up, without a single one being lost, — not even of those which fell into the water. The beach sloped away gradually, and the soldiers had only to stoop and pick up the bullets from the bottom.

This strange game lasted two hours.

At the end of that time there were three men killed, and the inventor of the system had collected from a thousand to twelve hundred bullets, which netted three hundred francs to the company.

A hundred francs for each man lost. The company thought it a very good bargain.

As the batteries of the frigates and the city were all of the same calibre as those of our army (16 and 12), not a bullet was useless.

The next day the company went in bathing again; and when he heard the cannonading directed upon them from the frigates and the fort, Bonaparte could not resist the temptation to witness the spectacle once more; and this time some of the principal officers of the army accompanied him.

Roland could not contain himself. He was one of those men who are driven wild by the sound of cannon, and intoxicated by the smell of powder.

With two bounds he was upon the shore; and tossing his clothes upon the sand, retaining only his drawers, he threw himself into the sea.

Twice Bonaparte called him back, but he did not seem to hear.

"What is the matter with the foolish fellow," Bonaparte murmured, "that he never lets slip a possible opportunity to be killed?"

Roland was no longer there to reply, and he probably would not have replied if he had been.

Bonaparte followed him with his eyes.

He soon passed the cordon of bathers, and swam almost within musket-shot of the "Tiger."

They opened fire upon him, and the balls made the water leap all around him.

He did not disturb himself about them, but his act looked so much like bravado that an officer on board the "Tiger" ordered a boat to be lowered.

Roland longed to be killed, but he did not long to be taken prisoner. He swam vigorously, to reach the reefs which lie along the base of the fort of Saint-Jean-d'Acre.

It was impossible for the boat to follow him among these reefs.

Roland disappeared for a moment, and Bonaparte was beginning to fear lest some accident had happened to him, when he saw him reappear at the foot of the walls of the city, under the fire of the musketry.

The Turks, seeing a Christian within rifle-shot, did not hesitate to fire at him; but Roland seemed to have made a bargain with the bullets. He walked slowly back along the edge of the sea. The sand on one hand and the water on the other were thrown up almost beneath his feet. He reached the place where he had put his clothes, dressed himself, and walked towards Bonaparte.

A *vivandière* who was one of the party this time, and who was distributing the contents of her cask to the collectors of bullets, offered him a glass.

"Ah, is it you, Goddess of Reason?" said Roland. "You know very well that I never drink brandy."

"No," she said, "but once does not make a habit; and what you have just done deserves a drop, Citizen-Commandant." And she held out to him a little silver cup full of liquor.

"To the health of the commander-in-chief, and the capture of Saint-Jean-d'Acre," she said.

Roland drank, raising his glass towards Bonaparte. Then he offered her a piece of money.

"Bah!" she exclaimed, "I sell my liquor to those who need to buy courage, but not to you. Besides, my husband will make a good thing out of this."

"What is your husband doing?"

"He is the bullet merchant."

"Well, by the sound of the cannonading, he is likely to make his fortune in a short time. Where is this husband of yours?"

" There he is," she said.

And she pointed out to Roland the sergeant-major who had proposed to Bonaparte to sell him bullets at five sous each.

As the Goddess of Reason was in the act of pointing, a shell buried itself in the sand, not four feet from the speculator.

The sergeant-major, who seemed to be familiar with all manner of projectiles, threw himself face down upon the sand, and waited.

In about three seconds the shell burst, scattering a cloud of sand.

" Upon my word, Goddess of Reason," said Roland, " I am afraid that shot has made you a widow."

But from the midst of the sand and dust the sergeant-major rose unhurt.

It was as if he rose from the crater of a volcano.

" Long live the Republic! " he shouted as he shook himself.

And, on the instant, in the water and on the beach, by all the actors and spectators, was echoed that sacred phrase, which made the very dead immortal.

CHAPTER XII.

HOW CITIZEN PIERRE-CLAUDE FARAUD WAS MADE SOUS-LIEUTENANT.

THIS collection of musket-balls lasted four days; but the English and Turks finally guessed the meaning of the performance, which they had at first taken for bravado.

A count of the balls picked up showed that there were thirty-four hundred.

Bonaparte paid for them to, the last sou, through Estève, the paymaster of the army.

"Ah," said Estève, when he recognized the sergeant, "so you are speculating in artillery again! I paid you for a cannon at Frœschwillers, and now I am to pay you for thirty-four hundred cannon-balls at Saint-Jean-d'Acre."

"Pshaw!" said the sergeant-major, "I am none the richer for it; the six hundred francs for the Frœschwillers cannon, together with the treasure of the Prince de Condé, went to pay pensions to the widows and orphans of Dawendorff."

"And what are you going to do with this money?"

"Oh, I have a use for it."

"Might I ask what it is?"

"Certainly, since I depend upon you to undertake the commission, Citizen-Paymaster. This money is destined for the old mother of our brave Captain Guillet, who was killed at the last assault. He bequeathed her to his company before he died. The Republic is not very rich, and might forget to pay her a pension. Well, in default of a pension, the company will give her a little capital. It is a great pity, though, that those devils of Englishmen and those fools of Turks should have made out our game, and declined to keep it up longer; we would have made up the sum of a thousand francs for the poor woman. But what would you have, Citizen-Paymaster? The prettiest girl in the world can give no more than she has; and the third company of the Thirty-second Brigade, although it is the prettiest girl in the army, has only eight hundred and fifty francs to offer."

"Where does Captain Guillet's mother live?"

"At Châteauroux, the capital of the Indre. Ah, it is fine to be faithful to one's old regiment, and he was just that, was brave Captain Guillet."

"Very well, the sum shall be paid to her, in the name of the third company of the Thirty-second Brigade, and of — "

"Pierre-Claude Faraud, executor of his will."

"Thanks. And now, Pierre-Claude Faraud, the commander-in-chief wishes me to say to you that he wants to speak with you."

"When he likes," replied the sergeant-major, with the movement of the neck which was peculiar to him. "Pierre-Claude Faraud is never too much embarrassed to talk."

"He will send for you."

"I await the summons!"

And the sergeant-major turned upon his heel and went to the headquarters of the Thirty-second Brigade, to wait till he was sent for.

Bonaparte was eating dinner in his tent when he was told that the sergeant-major whom he had sent for was awaiting his pleasure.

"Let him come in," said Bonaparte.

The sergeant-major entered.

"Ah, is it you?" said Bonaparte.

"Yes, Citizen-General," replied Faraud; "*didst thou* not send for me?"

"To what brigade do you belong?

"The Thirty-second."

"To what company?"

"The third."

"Captain?"

"Captain Guillet, deceased."

"Not replaced?"

"Not replaced."

"Which of the two lieutenants is the braver?"

"There is no 'braver' in the Thirty-second. They are all brave alike."

"The older, then?"

"Lieutenant Valats, who stayed at his post with a shot through his breast."

"The second lieutenant was not wounded?"

"That was not his fault."

"Very well. Valats will be captain, and the second lieutenant will take his place as first. Now, is there not an under-officer who has distinguished himself?"

"All the men distinguished themselves."

"But I cannot make them all lieutenants, stupid!"

"That's a fact; well, there's Taberly."

"Who is Taberly?"

"A brave man."

"And would his appointment be well received?"

"With applause."

"Then there will be a vacant lieutenantcy. Which is the oldest sergeant-major?"

The man whom he was questioning made a movement with his neck as if his cravat were strangling him.

"He is one Pierre-Claude Faraud," he replied.

" What have you to say about him ? "

" Nothing much. "

" Perhaps you do not know him ? "

" It is exactly because I do know him. "

" Well, I know him, also. "

" You know him, General ? "

" Yes. He is an aristocrat of the Army of the Rhine. "

" Oh! "

" A quarrelsome fellow. "

" General! "

" Whom I caught fighting a duel at Milan with a brave republican. "

" He was one of his friends, General. Friends may fight. "

" And whom I sent to the guard-house for forty-eight hours. "

" Twenty-four, General. "

" Then I cheated him out of the other twenty-four. "

" He is ready to take them, General. "

" A *sous-lieutenant* does not go to the guard-house; he is put under arrest. "

· " General, Pierre-Claude Faraud is not a *sous-lieutenant;* he is only a sergeant-major. "

" Oh, yes, he is a *sous-lieutenant.* "

" That 's a good one, upon my soul! Since when ? "

" Since this morning. You see what it is to have patrons. "

" I! Patrons ? " exclaimed Faraud.

" Oho! so it is you ? " said Bonaparte.

" Yes, it is I; and I should like to know who my patrons are. "

" I, " replied Estève, " who have twice seen you generously give away the money which you have earned. "

"And I," said Roland, " who want a brave man to second me in an expedition from which few will return."

" Take him," said Bonaparte; " but I advise you not to put him on sentry.   Go alone in a place where there are wolves."

" What, General, dost thou know that story ? "

" I know everything Monsieur."

" General," said Faraud, " thou art the one who ought to do my twenty-four hours in the guard-house."

" Why ? "

" Thou didst just say ' Monsieur.' "

" Come, come," said Bonaparte, laughing, " you are a bright fellow, and I shall remember you.   In the mean time, you shall drink a glass of wine to the health of the Republic."

" General," said Roland, laughing, " Citizen Faraud never drinks to the health of the Republic in anything but brandy."

" The deuce!   And I have none," said Bonaparte.

" I have provided for the emergency," said Roland.

Then, going to the door of the tent, he called, —

" Come in, Citizeness Reason."

Citizeness Reason obeyed.

She was still beautiful, although the sun of Egypt had darkened her complexion.

" Rose here ? " exclaimed Faraud.

" Do you know the citizeness ? " asked Roland, laughing.

" I should think so! " replied Faraud.   " She is my wife."

" Citizeness," said Bonaparte, " I saw you at work in the midst of the musket-balls.   Roland wanted to pay you for the brandy you gave him when he came out of the water, but you refused.   As I had no brandy here, and my guests desired a glass each, Roland said, 'Let us call the Goddess of Reason, and we can pay her for all at once.' So we called you. Now serve us."

Citizeness Reason tipped her little cask, and poured out a glassful for each one.

She forgot Faraud.

"When the health of the Republic is drunk," observed Roland, " everybody drinks."

" But any one who chooses is at liberty to drink water," said Bonaparte.

And, raising his glass, he cried, —

" To the health of the Republic."

. The toast was repeated, in chorus.

Then Roland, drawing a parchment from his pocket, said, —

" Here is your bill of exchange on posterity, but it is in your husband's name. You may indorse it, but he alone can use it."

The Goddess of Reason, with trembling hands, unfolded the parchment, at which Faraud was gazing with sparkling eyes.

"Here, Pierre," she said, holding it out to him, " read it! It is your commission as *sous-lieutenant,* in place of Taberly."

" Is that true ? " asked Faraud.

" Look for yourself."

Faraud looked.

" Hurrah, *Sous-lieutenant* Faraud ! " he cried. " Long live General Bonaparte ! "

"Twenty-four hours' arrest for having cried 'Long live General Bonaparte !' instead of 'Long live the Republic !' " said Bonaparte.

"I see that I cannot escape them," replied Faraud. " But I will do those twenty-four hours with pleasure."

CHAPTER XIII.

THE LAST ASSAULT.

DURING the night which followed Faraud's promotion to the rank of *sous-lieutenant*, Bonaparte received eight pieces of heavy artillery, and ammunition in abundance.

Faraud's thirty-four hundred bullets had served to repulse the sorties from the town.

The " Cursed Tower " was almost entirely destroyed, and Bonaparte resolved to make a final effort.

Then, too, circumstances made it imperative.

On the 8th of May, a Turkish fleet of thirty vessels, escorted by English ships-of-war, was sighted.

It was scarcely daylight when Bonaparte was told of it. He went up the little hill, from which he got a view of the entire harbor.

His opinion was that this fleet came from the Isle of Rhodes, and that it was bringing to the besieged a reinforcement of troops, ammunition, and provisions.

It was imperative to take Saint-Jean-d'Acre before the force of the garrison was doubled.

When Roland saw that the attack was decided upon, he asked the general for two hundred men, with *carte-blanche* to use them in any way and for any purpose that he chose.

Bonaparte asked for an explanation.

He had great confidence in Roland's courage, which amounted to rashness; but because of this very rashness, he hesitated to trust the lives of two hundred men to him.

Then Roland explained that on the day that he took his long bath in the sea, he had seen from the water a breach which could not be seen from the land, and about which the besieged evidently felt no uneasiness, defended as it was by an inside battery and by the fire from the English vessels.

Through this breach he would enter the town, and make a diversion with his two hundred men.

Bonaparte gave him the desired permission.

Roland chose two hundred men from the Thirty-second Brigade, of which number the new *sous-lieutenant*, Faraud, was one.

Bonaparte ordered a general attack.   Murat, Rampon, Vial, Kléber, Junot, generals of division, generals of brigade, chiefs of corps, — all were to charge at once.

At ten o'clock in the morning all the outer works which had been retaken by the enemy were thrown down once more.   Five flags were taken, three cannon carried off, and four more spiked.   But the besieged did not yield an inch; as fast as they were beaten down, others took their places.   Never had such audacity and valor, never had more impetuous ardor or more obstinate courage struggled for the possession and defence of a city.   Never since the epoch when religious enthusiasm put the sword in the hands of the Crusaders, and Mohammedan fanaticism the cimeter in the hands of the Turks, had such a mortal, deadly, bloody struggle struck terror to the hearts of a population, one-third of whom sympathized with the Christians, and the other two-thirds with Djezzar.   From the ramparts, which they occupied, in part, and from which already resounded cries of victory, the French soldiers could see the women running through the streets, throwing dust into the air, with invocations and maledictions, and uttering cries which resembled at once the hooting of owls and the yelping of hyænas, — cries which no one* of those who heard them could ever forget.

Generals, officers, and soldiers fought together, pell-mell, in the trench. Kléber, armed with an Albanian rifle which he had wrested from its owner, had made a club of it, and, raising it above his head, as a thresher in a barn raises his flail, at each blow a man went down. Murat, with head uncovered, and long hair floating, was flashing his sabre back and forth, its fine temper bringing death to all who came in contact with it. Junot, now with a rifle, and now with a pistol, killed a man every time he fired.

The commander of the Eighteenth Brigade, Boyer, fell in the *mêlée*, with seventeen officers and more than a hundred and fifty soldiers of his corps; but Lannes, Bon, and Vial passed on over their bodies, which served to raise them nearer to the level of the rampart.

Bonaparte, not in the trench, but upon it, himself directing the artillery, motionless, a target for all shots, was making a breach in the wall on his right, with the cannon upon the tower. At the end of an hour there was a practicable opening. They had no bushes with which to fill up the ditch; but, as they had already done at another part of the ramparts, they threw in corpses. Mussulmans and Christians, French and Turks, thrown out through the windows of the tower, where they lay heaped up, raised a bridge as high as the ramparts.

Shouts of "Long live the Republic!" were heard, mingled with cries, "To the assault! to the assault!" The bands played the "Marseillaise," and the remainder of the army took part in the fight.

Bonaparte sent one of his ordnance officers named Raimbaud to tell Roland that the time was come for him to effect his diversion; but when he knew what was to be done, Raimbaud, instead of returning to Bonaparte, asked Roland's permission to stay with him.

The two young men were friends; and when a battle is on, one does not refuse favors of that sort to a friend.

Faraud had succeeded in getting possession of the coat and epaulets of a dead *sous-lieutenant*, and he shone resplendent at the head of his company.

The Goddess of Reason, even prouder of his promotion than he was, marched in the same rank with him, with a pair of pistols at her belt.

No sooner had Roland received the order than he placed himself at the head of his two hundred men, plunged into the water with them, turned the corner of the bastion, with the water up to their waists, and presented himself at the breach, with the trumpets going before.

The attack was so unexpected, the siege having already lasted two months, that the artillerymen were not even at their guns. Roland took possession of them, and having no men to work them, spiked them.

Then, with cries of " Victory! victory! " they dashed into the winding streets of the town.

The cries were heard at the ramparts, and redoubled the energy of the besiegers. For the second time, Bonaparte believed that he was master of Saint-Jean-d'Acre, and sprang into the " Cursed Tower," which they had had such difficulty in taking.

But when he reached it, he saw, with dismay, a second enclosure, by which our troops were brought to a stand.

This was the one that Colonel Phélippeaux — Bonaparte's schoolfellow at Brienne — had had constructed behind the first.

Leaning half way out of the window, Bonaparte shouted encouragement to his soldiers. The grenadiers, furious at meeting with this fresh obstacle, attempted to mount upon one another's shoulders, for want of ladders; but suddenly, while the assailants were attacked in front by those put there to defend the enclosure, they were swept by a battery in flank. A tremendous fusillade burst forth from all sides, — from the houses, the streets, the barricades, and even from Djezzar's seraglio. A thick smoke poured up from the interior of the city. It was Roland, Raimbaud, and Faraud setting fire to the bazaar. In the midst of the smoke they appeared upon the roofs of the houses, attempting to enter into communication with those on the ramparts. Through the smoke of the fire and of the artillery, they saw the tricolored plumes waving, and from the city and the ramparts the cry of "Victory!" went up for the third time that day. It was destined to be the last.

The soldiers who were to effect a junction by way of the rampart with Roland's two hundred men, and a part of whom had already jumped or slid down into the town, while the others were fighting on the ramparts or in the ditches, being assailed by volleys from four sides, hesitated, as the bullets whistled and the cannon-balls roared about them, falling like hail, and passing like a hurricane. Lannes, wounded in the head by a musket-shot, fell upon his knees, and was carried away by his grenadiers. Kléber, like an invulnerable giant, held his own in the midst of the fire. Bon and Vial were driven back into the ditch. Bonaparte sought for some one to support Kléber, but every one was occupied. He then ordered the retreat, with tears of rage in his eyes; for he did not doubt that all who had entered the town with Roland, as well as those who had slipped over the rampart to join him, two hundred and fifty or three hundred in all, were lost. And on the next day, what a harvest of heads they would have to gather in the moat before the town.

He was the last to retreat, and he shut himself up in his tent, with orders that he was to be disturbed by no one.

In the course of three years, this was the first time that he had doubted his own fortune.

What a sublime page could be written by the historian who could tell what thoughts passed through his mind during that hour of despair.

CHAPTER XIV.

THE LAST BULLETIN.

MEANWHILE, Roland and the fifty men who had gone over into the city and joined him, having cherished for a while the hope that they were to be supported, began to think that they were abandoned.

The shouts of victory which had answered their own became fainter, and died away; then the volleys of musketry and artillery gradually grew less, until at the end of an hour it entirely ceased.

Amid the other sounds by which he was encompassed, Roland even thought that he heard the trumpets sounding and the drums beating the retreat.

Then, as we have said, all sounds ceased.

Thereupon, like a tide, rising upon all sides at once, there rushed upon the little group from all points of the compass, English, Turks, Mamelukes, Arnauts, and Albanians, — the entire garrison, in short, of some eight thousand men.

Roland formed his little troop into a square, one side of which rested on a mosque; he sent fifty of his men into the mosque, converting it into a fortress, and there, after he had made them swear to defend themselves to the death against enemies from whom they knew they could hope to receive no quarter, they waited with levelled bayonets.

The Turks, full of their usual confidence in their cavalry, hurled it upon the little square with such fury that although the double volley of the French laid low sixty men and horses, those who came behind rode up over their bodies, as they would have done over a hill, and dashed upon the still smoking bayonets.

But there they were forced to stop.

The second rank had had time to reload, and fired at close quarters.

They had no choice but to fall back ; but as they could not again pass the mountain of dead and wounded, they tried to escape to right and left.

Two terrible volleys accompanied their flight, and cut them down in swathes.

But they returned with the greater desperation.

Then a frightful struggle began, a veritable hand-to-hand fight, in which the Turkish horsemen, defying the murderous volley, rushed up to the very points of the bayonets of our troops, to discharge their pistols.

Others, seeing that the reflection of the sun upon the barrels of the guns frightened their horses, made them walk backwards, and forcing them to rear, threw themselves over with them upon the bayonets.

The wounded dragged themselves along the ground, and, like serpents, gliding under the gun-barrels, hamstrung the Frenchmen.

Roland, armed with a double-barrelled gun, as was his custom in this kind of fighting, laid low a chief at each shot that he fired.

Faraud, in the mosque, directed the fire there ; and more than one arm which held an uplifted sabre fell down helpless, struck with a bullet from some window in the gallery of the minaret.

Roland, seeing that the number of his men was diminishing, and that, in spite of the triple row of corpses which made a rampart around his little troop, he could not sustain such an unequal struggle for any length of time, caused the door of the mosque to be opened, and with the greatest coolness, and continuing his murderous fire, made his men enter, being himself the last to pass through the door. .

Then the firing began again through every opening in the mosque ; but the Turks brought up a piece of artillery, and trained it upon the door.

Roland himself was near a window, and, one after the other, the first three gunners who drew near to put a match to the touch-hole fell.

Then a horseman rode swiftly past the gun ; and before any one knew what his purpose was, he fired his pistol at the priming.

The gun was discharged, and horse and rider rolled over and over, ten feet away ; but the door was broken in.

Through this broken door, however, there came such a terrible fusillade that three times the Turks presented themselves before it, to enter the mosque, and three times were they repulsed.

Mad with rage, they rallied, and made a fourth attempt ; but this time only a few scattered shots replied to their shouts of death.

The ammunition of the little troop was exhausted.

The grenadiers waited for the enemy with fixed bayonets.

"Friends !" said Roland, "remember that you have sworn to die rather than be made prisoners by Djezzar the Butcher, who cut off our companions' heads."

" We swear it ! " exclaimed with one voice Roland's two hundred men.

"Long live the Republic!" said Roland.

"Long live the Republic!" they all repeated after him.

And each one prepared to die, but to sell his life dearly.

Just then a group of officers appeared at the door; at their head marched Sidney Smith. They all carried their swords in their scabbards.

Smith raised his hat, and made a sign that he wished to speak. There was silence.

"Gentlemen," he said, in excellent French, "you are brave men, and it shall not be said that in my presence men were massacred who have borne themselves like heroes. Give yourselves up; I will guarantee that your lives shall be spared."

"It is too much, or not enough," said Roland.

"What do you want, pray?"

"Kill us to the last man, or let us all go."

"You are exacting, gentlemen," said the commodore; "but one can refuse nothing to men like you. But you will permit me, will you not, to furnish you with an escort of Englishmen as far as the gate of the city? Otherwise, not one of you would reach it alive. Is it agreed?"

"Yes, my Lord," replied Roland; "and we can only thank you for your courtesy."

Sidney Smith left two English officers to guard the door, and he himself entered the mosque and held out his hand to Roland.

Ten minutes later, the English escort arrived.

The French soldiers, with fixed bayonets, and the officers with drawn swords, traversed the street which led to the French camp, amid the imprecations of the Mussulmans, the howling of the women, and the cries of the children.

Ten or twelve wounded, among whom was Faraud, were carried on improvised litters made of gun-barrels.

The Goddess of Reason walked by the litter of the *sous-lieutenant*, pistol in hand.

Until they were out of range of the Turkish guns, Smith and his English soldiers accompanied the grenadiers, who defiled before the double row of red-coats; these presented arms as the grenadiers passed.

Bonaparte, as we have said, had retired within his tent. He called for Plutarch, and read the biography of Augustus; and thinking of Roland and his gallant companions, who were probably being murdered, he muttered, like Augustus after the battle of Teutberg, " Varus, give me back my legions."

He, however, had no one of whom to demand his legions, for he was his own Varus.

Suddenly he heard a great uproar, and the strains of the " Marseillaise " reached his ears.

Why did they rejoice and sing, these soldiers, while their general was weeping with rage and grief?

He sprang to the door of his tent.

The first persons he saw were Roland, his aide-de-camp Raimbaud, and the *sous-lieutenant* Faraud, the latter on one leg like a heron, his other leg having been broken by a cannon-ball.

The wounded man was leaning on the shoulder of the Goddess of Reason.

Behind them were the two hundred men whom Bonaparte supposed he had lost.

" Ah, my good friend," he said, pressing Roland's hands, " I was mourning for you, for I thought you were done for. How the deuce did you get out of it?"

" Raimbaud will tell you," said Roland, who was out of humor because he owed his life to an Englishman.

"For my part, I am too thirsty to talk. I want something to drink."

And taking a glass full of water which was upon the table, he emptied it at a single draught, while Bonaparte went out to meet the group of soldiers, all the more delighted to see them, since he had never expected to see them again.

CHAPTER XV.

VANISHED DREAMS.

NAPOLEON at Saint Helena, in speaking of Saint-Jean-d'Acre, said, "That paltry town held the destiny of the East. If Saint-Jean-d'Acre had fallen, I would have changed the face of the world."

This regret, expressed twenty years later, gives some idea of what Bonaparte must have suffered when, in the face of the impossibility of taking Saint-Jean-d'Acre, he published this general order in all the divisions of the army.

As usual, Bourrienne wrote it at his dictation.

"Soldiers !

"You have crossed the desert which separates Africa from Asia with more swiftness than an army of Arabs.

"The army which was on the way to invade Egypt is destroyed. You have taken its general, its camp-equipage, its baggage, its supplies, its camels.

"You have taken all the strongholds which defended the wells in the desert.

"On the fields of Mount Tabor you have dispersed that cloud of men gathered from all parts of Asia, in the hope of pillaging Egypt.

"Finally, after having, with a handful of men, maintained the war for three months in the heart of Syria, taken forty pieces of artillery, fifty flags, made six thousand prisoners, levelled the fortifications of Gaza, Jaffa,

Kaïffa, and Acre, we are about to return to Egypt ; the season of disembarkation calls me back.

"A few days more, and you might hope to take the pacha in his own palace ; but in this season, the price of the castle of Acre is not worth the loss of a few days, and the brave men whom I should lose are now necessary to me for other operations.

"Soldiers, we have a season of fatigue and danger before us. Having made it impossible for the East to do anything against us during this campaign, we shall perhaps be obliged to repulse the efforts of a part of the West.

"You will find new opportunities for glory ; and if, in so many battles, every day is marked by the loss of a brave man, other brave men must be made every day, and take their places among the little band who set the example of daring in times of danger, and who make victory easy."

As he finished dictating this bulletin to Bourrienne, Bonaparte rose and went out of his tent, as if to breathe more freely.

Bourrienne followed him uneasily ; events did not usually leave such a deep impresssion upon that heart of bronze.

Bonaparte climbed the little hill which overlooked the camp, seated himself upon a stone, and remained for a long time with his eyes fixed upon the partly destroyed fortress and the ocean which lay before him in its vast immensity.

Finally he said, —

"The men who will write my life will not understand why I was so determined to take this wretched little place. Ah, if I had taken it, as I had hoped ! "

He let his head fall into his hands.

"What if you had taken it?" asked Bourrienne.

"If I had taken it," exclaimed Bonaparte, seizing his hand, "I should have found in the city the treasures of the pacha, and arms for three hundred thousand men; I would have aroused and armed all Syria; I would have marched upon Damascus and Aleppo; I would have increased my army with all the malcontents; I would have announced to the people the abolition of servitude and of the tyrannical government of the pachas; I would have reached Constantinople with my armed masses; I would have overthrown the Turkish Empire; I would have founded in the Orient a new and vast empire which would fix my place in history; and perhaps I should have returned to Paris by way of Adrianople and Vienna, after having humbled the House of Austria."

This, as will be seen, was nothing more or less than Cæsar's project when he fell by the assassin's dagger; it was his war begun among the Parthians, which was to end only in Germany.

As far as was the man of the 13th Vendémiaire from the conqueror of Italy, so far was the conqueror of Italy, that day, from the conqueror of the Pyramids.

Proclaimed in Europe the greatest of living generals, he sought, on the shores where Alexander, Hannibal, and Cæsar had fought, to equal, if not to surpass, the names of those captains of antiquity; and he did surpass them, since he tried to do what they only dreamed of.

"What would have become of Europe," says Pascal, speaking of Cromwell's death from calculus, "if that grain of sand had not been in his entrails?"

What would have become of Bonaparte's fortunes, if Saint-Jean-d'Acre had not stood in his path?

He was dreaming of this great mystery of the unknown,

when his eye was attracted by a black speck between two mountains of the chain of Carmel, which gradually grew larger.

As it approached, he could recognize a soldier of the dromedary corps created by him, "with which he pursued fugitives after a battle." This man was coming as fast as his beast would bring him.

Bonaparte drew his glass from his pocket, and after having looked for a moment, said, —

"Good! Now we shall have some news from Egypt."

And he stood up.

The messenger also recognized him; he immediately turned his dromedary, which was edging off towards the camp, which was a little out of the direct line, to the direction of the hill. Bonaparte went down, and seating himself upon a stone, waited.

The soldier, who appeared to be an excellent rider, put his dromedary to a gallop. He wore the uniform of a quartermaster-general.

"Whence do you come?" called Bonaparte, as soon as he thought the man could hear him.

"From Upper Egypt," was the reply.

"What news?"

"Bad, General."

Bonaparte stamped his foot.

"Come here," he said.

In a few moments the man had reached Bonaparte. The dromedary knelt down, and the man slid to the ground.

"Here, Citizen-General," he said.

And he handed him a despatch.

Bonaparte passed it to Bourrienne.

"Read it," he said.

Bourrienne read, —

To COMMANDER-IN-CHIEF BONAPARTE: —

I do not know whether this despatch will reach you, Citizen-General, or whether, if it does, you will be in a position to remedy the disaster with which I am threatened.

While General Desaix was pursuing the Mamelukes from the coast of Syout, the flotilla, composed of the "Italie" and several other armed ships, which had on board almost all the supplies of the division, some artillery, and the sick and wounded, was detained off Beyrout by the wind.

This flotilla will be attacked in a quarter of an hour by Scherif Hassan and three or four thousand men. We are not in any condition to resist, but we shall do so.

But, except by a miracle, we cannot escape death.

I am preparing this despatch, to which I shall add the details of the battle as it progresses.

Hassan attacks us with a sharp fusillade; I have ordered his fire to be returned. It is two o'clock in the afternoon.

Three o'clock. — After a horrible carnage made by our artillery, the Arabs are returning for the third time to the charge. I have lost a third of my men.

Four o'clock. — The Arabs have thrown themselves into the river and taken the small boats. I have only a dozen men; all the rest are wounded or dead. I shall wait until the Arabs have crowded aboard of the "Italie," and then I shall blow her up, with myself and them.

I am sending this despatch by a brave and clever man, who has promised me that unless he is killed, he will find you, wherever you are.

In ten minutes all will be over.

CAPTAIN MORANDI.

"And then ? " asked Bonaparte.

"That is all," replied Bourrienne.

"But Morandi ? "

"Blew himself up, General," said the messenger.

"And you ? "

"Oh, I did not wait until he blew up; I blew away before that, after I had carefully put my despatch in my tobacco-box; and then I swam under water to a place where I hid myself in the tall grass. When it was dark I came out of the water, and, crawling on all fours to the camp, I came to a sleeping Arab; I put a dagger into him, and, taking his dromedary, I started off at a gallop.

" And you have come from Beyrout? "

" Yes, Citizen-General."

" Without any accident ? "

" If you call shots fired by me or at me accidents, then I have had plenty, and my camel also. Between us, we have been hit four times, — he three times in the side, and I once in the shoulder. We have been thirsty and hungry; he has eaten nothing at all, and I have eaten horseflesh. But here we are. You are all right, Citizen-General, and that is all that is necessary."

" But Morandi ? " asked Bonaparte.

" *Dame!* as he put the match to the powder himself, I rather think it would be hard work to find a piece of him as big as a nut."

" And the 'Italie' ? "

" Oh, there isn't enough left of the ' Italie ' to make a box of matches."

" You were right, my friend, this is indeed bad news. Bourrienne, you will say that I am superstitious; did you hear the name of the vessel that was blown up? "

" The ' Italie.' "

" Well, now listen, Bourrienne. Italy is lost to France; it is beyond doubt: my presentiments never deceive me."

Bourrienne shrugged his shoulders.

" What connection do you suppose there is between a ship which is blown up eight hundred leagues away from France, on the Nile, and Italy ? "

"I have said it," replied Bonaparte, with a prophetic accent. "You will see!"

Then, after a moment of silence, he said, pointing to the messenger, —

"Take this good fellow with you, Bourrienne : give him thirty talaris, and get him to tell you the story of the battle of Beyrout."

"If instead of the thirty talaris, Citizen," said the quartermaster, "you could give me a glass of water, I should be very grateful."

"You shall have your thirty talaris and a whole pitcher of water; and you should have a sword of honor, if you had not Pichegru's already."

"He knows me!" exclaimed the quartermaster.

"Gallant fellows like you are not easily forgotten, Falou; only, do not fight a duel, if you would keep out of the guard-house."

CHAPTER XVI.

THE RETREAT.

In the evening, in order to conceal the movement from the enemy, as well as to avoid the heat of the day, the army began its retreat.

The orders were to follow the Mediterranean, in order to take advantage of the fresh air of the sea.

Before the departure Bonaparte called Bourrienne, and dictated an order to the effect that everyone who was able should go on foot, leaving the horses, mules, and camels for the sick and wounded.

An anecdote sometimes gives a better idea of a man's state of mind than any number of descriptions.

Bonaparte had just dictated the order to Bourrienne, when his personal attendant, Vigogne the elder, entered his tent, and putting his hand to his hat, inquired, —

"General, which horse do you reserve for yourself?"

Bonaparte looked him through and through, and then, striking him on the face with his riding-whip, he said, —

"Did you not hear the order, imbecile? Everybody is to go on foot, myself as well as others. Go!"

Vigogne went.

There were three men sick with the plague at Mount Carmel; they were too ill to be moved, and were left to the generosity of the Turks and the care of the Carmelite brothers.

Sidney Smith, unfortunately, was not there to save them, and the Turks put them to death. When the French had gone two leagues, the news was brought to Bonaparte.

Then Bonaparte gave full vent to a fit of passion to which the blow across Vigogne's face with the riding-whip was only the prelude. He stopped the artillery wagons and distributed torches to the army.

The order was given to light the torches, and to set fire to all the small towns, villages, hamlets, and houses.

The barley was fully ripe.

They set fire to it.

It was a terrible yet magnificent sight. The whole coast was in flames for ten leagues, and the sea, like a gigantic mirror, reflected the tremendous ocean of flame.

It seemed as if they were marching between two flaming walls, so faithfully did the sea reproduce the image of the coast. The beach, being bare sand, was the only thing which was not on fire, and seemed like a bridge thrown over the Cocytus.

This shore offered a mournful spectacle.

Some of those whose wounds were the most serious were carried on litters, and others were on mules, horses, and camels. Chance had given to Faraud, the man who had been wounded on the previous night, the horse which Bonaparte habitually rode. The latter recognized both the man and his mount.

"Ah, so that is how you are doing your twenty-four hours under arrest!" he called out to him.

"I will do them at Cairo," replied Faraud.

"Have you anything to drink, Goddess of Reason?" asked Bonaparte.

"A glass of brandy, Citizen-General."

He shook his head.

"Wait," she said; "I know what you need."

And, fumbling in the bottom of her little cart, she added, —

"Here! take this."

And she gave him a watermelon from the gardens of Carmel.

It was a royal gift.

Bonaparte stopped, and sent for Kléber, Bon, and Vial to share his good-fortune. Lannes, who was wounded in the head, was passing on a mule. Bonaparte stopped him, and the five generals finished their breakfast by emptying a pitcher of water, and drinking to the health of the Goddess of Reason.

When he took the head of the column again, Bonaparte was alarmed.

A devouring thirst, the total want of water, an excessive heat, and a fatiguing march through the burning sand-dunes, had demoralized the men, and had caused the most cruel selfishness and the most heart-rending indifference to take the place of all generous sentiments.

And this went on, day after day.

They began by getting rid of those who were sick with the plague, under the pretext that it was dangerous to carry them.

Then came the turn of the wounded.

The unfortunate men cried out, —

" I have not got the plague, I am only wounded ! "

And they showed their old wounds, or inflicted fresh ones upon themselves.

The soldiers did not even turn their heads.

" Your time has come," they said.

And they went on.

Bonaparte shivered with terror as he saw this.

He called a halt. He forced all the able-bodied men who were on horses, dromedaries, or mules to give them up to the sick.

They reached Tentoura on the 20th of May, in stifling heat. They sought in vain for a bit of grass and for a tree to give them shelter from the brazen sky. They lay down upon the sand, but the sand was fiery hot. Men were continually falling, to rise no more. A wounded man on a litter asked for water. Bonaparte went up to him.

"Whom have you there?" he asked the soldiers.

"We do not know," replied the men. "He has double epaulets, but that is all we know about him."

The moaning and asking for water had ceased.

"Who are you?" asked Bonaparte.

The wounded man was silent.

Bonaparte lifted up one corner of the cloth which shaded the litter, and recognized Croisier.

"Ah, my poor boy!" he cried.

Croisier began to sob bitterly.

"Come," said Bonaparte, "have a little courage."

"Ah," said Croisier, lifting himself up in his litter, "do you think I am weeping because I am going to die? I am weeping because you called me a coward; and I tried to get myself killed just because you called me that."

"But," said Bonaparte, "I sent you a sword since then. Did not Roland give it to you?"

"Here it is." said Croisier, seizing his weapon, which was lying beside him, and putting it to his lips. "Those who are carrying me know that I want to have it buried with me. Tell them to do it, General."

And the wounded man clasped his hands imploringly.

Bonaparte dropped the corner of the sheet which covered the litter, gave the order, and walked away.

When they left Tentoura, on the following day, they encountered a quicksand of great extent. There was no other road; the artillery was obliged to take it, and the guns sank deep in it. They laid all the sick and wounded on the edge for a moment, while they harnessed all the horses to the gun-carriages and wagons. All was useless; wagons and cannon were sunk in the sand up to their middles. The able-bodied soldiers asked to be allowed to make one last effort. They attempted it, but, like the horses, they exhausted themselves to no purpose.

They wept as they abandoned the brass which they had so often blessed, which had been so often the witness of their triumphs, and whose thunders had made Europe tremble.

On the 22d of May they slept at Cæsarea.

So many of the sick and wounded had died that horses were more plentiful. Bonaparte, who was himself far from well, had nearly died with fatigue on the previous day. He was urged so strongly that he finally consented to mount a horse. He was hardly three hundred paces from Cæsarea when, just at daybreak, a man who was hidden in a bush fired at him almost point-blank, but missed him.

The soldiers who surrounded the commander-in-chief darted into the wood and dragged out the man, a native of Nabloos, who was condemned to be shot on the spot.

Four men pushed him towards the sea with the ends of their carbines; there they pulled the triggers, but none of the carbines went off.

The night had been very damp, and the powder was wet.

The Syrian, astonished at finding himself still alive, immediately recovered his presence of mind, threw himself into the sea, and rapidly swam to a reef out of range of their muskets.

In their first stupefaction, the soldiers watched him go, without thinking to fire upon him.

But Bonaparte, who knew the bad effect it would have

upon that superstitious population if such an attempt should go unpunished, ordered a platoon to fire at him.

They obeyed, but the man was out of range; the balls fell hissing into the sea, without reaching the rock.

The man drew a dagger from his breast, and made a threatening gesture with the weapon.

Bonaparte ordered them to put a charge and a half into the guns, and to fire again.

"It is useless," said Roland; "I will go."

And instantly he had thrown off his clothes, retaining only his drawers.

"Stay here, Roland," said Bonaparte. "I do not want you to risk your life against that of an assassin."

But whether he did not hear him, or did not wish to hear, Roland had already taken a dagger from the Sheik of Aher, who was retreating with the army, and, putting it between his teeth, had thrown himself into the sea.

The soldiers, who knew the young captain to be the most adventurous officer in the army, shouted bravo.

Bonaparte was obliged to be a witness of the duel which was about to take place.

The Syrian, when he saw a single man coming towards him, did not attempt further flight, but waited.

He was a fine sight, there upon his rock. With one hand clinched, and his dagger in the other, he looked like the statue of Spartacus on its pedestal.

Roland swam towards him in a line as straight as the flight of an arrow.

The Syrian made no attempt to attack him until he had gained a footing, and he even drew back chivalrously as far as the size of the rock permitted.

Roland emerged from the water young and handsome, and dripping like a sea-god.

' They stood facing each other. The rock which was to be their arena looked liked the shell of an immense tortoise protruding from the water.

The spectators expected to see a scientific and prolonged contest, where each would be careful to give his opponent no advantage.

But it was not so.

Roland had no sooner gained his feet, and shaken off the water which blinded him as it fell from his dripping hair, than, without taking any precaution to defend himself from his adversary's dagger, he sprang upon him, not as one man springs upon another, but as a jaguar springs upon the hunter.

They saw the flash of the dagger blades; then, as if uprooted from their pedestal, the two men fell into the sea.

There was a tremendous splashing in the water.

Then one head reappeared, — the blond head of Roland.

He clung with one hand to the points of the rock; then he rested his knee upon it, and finally stood erect, holding in his left hand, by its mass of long hair, the head of his adversary.

He was like Perseus after he had cut off the Gorgon's head.

A tremendous shout rose from the spectators and reached Roland, upon whose lips played a proud smile.

Then, taking his dagger between his teeth, he sprang into the sea and swam to the shore.

The army had halted. The men forgot to think of heat and thirst.

The wounded forgot their wounds.

Even the dying found strength enough to raise themselves upon their elbows.

Roland stopped ten feet away from Bonaparte.

"Here," he said, throwing the bloody trophy at the general's feet, "is the head of your would be assassin."

Bonaparte recoiled, in spite of himself; but as for Roland, he went straight to his clothes and began to put them on as calmly as if he had just come from an ordinary bath, and with a degree of modesty which a woman might have envied him.

CHAPTER XVII.

WHEREIN WE SEE THAT BONAPARTE'S PRESENTIMENTS
DID NOT DECEIVE HIM.

On the 24th the French arrived at Jaffa.

They stayed there the 25th, 26th, 27th, and 28th.

Jaffa was indeed for Bonaparte a city of misfortune.

The reader will remember the four thousand prisoners of Eugène and Croisier who could neither be kept, nor fed, nor sent to Cairo, but had to be, and were, shot.

A graver and still more lamentable necessity awaited Bonaparte on his return.

There was at Jaffa a hospital for patients stricken with the plague.

There is, at the Musée, a magnificent picture by Gros, representing Bonaparte touching the plague-stricken at Jaffa.

The picture is none the less beautiful although it represents an occurrence which did not take place.

Here is what M. Thiers says. We, who are only a paltry romancist, are sorry to find ourselves, on still another point, in opposition to that giant among historians.

It is the author of the "Revolution," and of the "Consulate and Empire," who is speaking.

"When he reached Jaffa, Bonaparte blew up the fortifications. There was a hospital there for our plague patients. To carry them away was impossible; by leaving them where they were, they would be exposed to inevitable death, either from sickness, hunger, or the cruelty of the enemy. Therefore, Bonaparte told Dr. Desgenettes that it would be much more humane to give them opium than to allow them to live; to which the doctor made this much-lauded reply: 'My trade is to cure, not to kill.' The opium was not administered, and this occurrence served to propagate an outrageous *slander*, which has now been disproved."

I humbly beg M. Thiers' pardon, but this reply of Desgenettes, whom I knew well, as I knew Larrey and all the "Egyptians," — I mean the companions of my father in that great expedition, — is as apocryphal as that of Cambronne.

God forbid that I should "slander" (that is the term used by M. Thiers) the man who illuminated the first half of the nineteenth century with the torch of his glory ; and when we come to Pichegru and the Duc d'Enghien, the reader will see whether I simply echo infamous rumors. But truth is indivisible, and it is the duty of him who talks to the people to tell the truth boldly.

We have said that Gros' picture represents something that did not happen, and we will prove it.

Here is Davoust's report, written under the eyes and at the order of the commander-in-chief, in his Official Narrative.

"The army reached Jaffa on the 5th Prairial (May 24th). It remained there the 6th, 7th, and 8th (25th, 26th, and 27th of May). The time was employed in disciplining the villages which had behaved badly. The fortifications of Jaffa were blown up. All the artillery of the place was thrown into the sea. The wounded were sent away both by sea and land. There were only a few ships, and in order to give time for the evacuation by land, we were obliged to defer until the 9th the departure of the army.

"Kléber's division formed the rear-guard, and did not leave Jaffa until the 10th (29th of May)."

You see, not a word about the plague, not a word about the visit to the hospital, and particularly, about touching the plague patients.

Not a word in any official report.

Bonaparte's eyes had been turned towards France ever since they had turned away from the East; and it would have been modesty very much out of place on his part if he had been silent upon such a remarkable fact, which would have done honor, not to his reason, perhaps, but to his daring.

Furthermore, this is how Bourrienne, who was an eye-witness, and a very impressionable actor, relates the occurrence.

"Bonaparte went to the hospital. He found there men with their limbs amputated, wounded men, soldiers afflicted with ophthalmia, who were moaning piteously, and men sick with the plague. The beds of these latter were at the right as we entered the first hall. *I was walking beside the general.* I affirm that I did not see him touch a single one of the plague patients. Why should he? They were in the last stages of the malady; none of them spoke. Bonaparte well knew that he was not specially protected from contagion. Would fortune interfere in his behalf, to shield him? It had certainly not seconded his plans zealously enough during the last two months for him to trust much to it then.

"I ask: Would he expose himself to certain death, and leave his army in the midst of a desert which we had just made into a desert by our own ravages, in a demolished town, without help, or hope of receiving any, — he, so necessary, so indispensable, as everybody must admit, to his army; he, upon whom rested at this moment, beyond any question, the responsibility of the lives of all those who had survived the last disaster, and who had just given proof of their unalterable courage by their devotion, their sufferings, and their endurance of privation; who were doing all that he could humanly ask of them, and who had confidence only in him?"

That is the voice of logic; but here is something convincing.

" Bonaparte walked rapidly through the rooms, lightly striking the yellow part of his boot with the riding-whip which he held in his hand.

" He said these words, as he strode back and forth, —

" 'The fortifications are destroyed. Fortune was against me at Saint-Jean-d'Acre. I must go back to Egypt, to preserve it from the enemies who are coming. In a few hours the Turks will be here. Let all those who are strong enough to get up, come with us; they will be carried on litters and horses.'

" There were, at most, sixty down with the plague. All that has been said of any greater number than that is an exaggeration. Their absolute silence, their complete prostration, and their general weakness announced the near approach of death. To take them away in that state would evidently have been to introduce the plague among the rest of the army.

" If one longs for ceaseless conquests, glory, and brilliant deeds, one must take also his share of ill-fortune. When we think that we have found something to cavil at in the action of a leader who is hurried along by reverses and disastrous circumstances to terrible extremities, it is essential, before passing judgment, to post ourselves thoroughly as to the given condition of affairs, and ask ourselves, with our hands on our hearts, whether we would not have done as he did. Then we must pity the man who is forced to do something which seems cruel, but we must absolve him, since victory — let us be frank about it — cannot be won except with such or similar horrible accompaniments."

Again, here is some one who has every interest in telling the truth.

Listen.

" *He* ordered an examination to be made as to what it would be best to do. The report was that seven or eight men were so dangerously ill that they could not live more than twenty-four hours longer, and that, furthermore, plague-stricken as they were, they would spread the disease among all the soldiers who came in contact with them. Several asked for instant death. *He* thought that it would be an act of charity to advance their death by a few hours."

Do you still doubt? Napoleon shall speak for himself, in the first person : —

" Where is the man who would not have preferred a speedy death to the horror of living exposed to the tortures of these barbarians? If *my son* — and I think I love him as dearly as a child can be loved — *were in a situation like that of those unfortunate wretches, my opinion would be in favor of doing the same to him; and if I were in such a situation myself, I should demand that it be done to me.*"

It seems to me that nothing is clearer than those few lines. How did it happen that M. Thiers did not read them? And if he did read them, why did he deny a fact which is confessed by the one who would have had the most interest in concealing it?

Thus we establish the truth, not for the purpose of accusing Bonaparte, *who could not have acted otherwise* than just as he did, but to prove to the partisans of *pure* history that it is not always *true* history.

The little army, in returning to Cairo, followed the same route that it had taken on leaving it. But the heat grew more terrible each day. When they left Gaza, it registered 35 degrees centigrade, and if the mercury was put upon the sand, it went up to 45 degrees.

A short distance before they reached El-Arich, in the middle of the desert, Bonaparte noticed two men filling up a grave.

He thought he recognized them as the ones to whom he had spoken, a fortnight before.

And when the men were questioned, they said that they were, in fact, the ones who had carried Crosier's litter.

The poor fellow had just died of lockjaw.

" Did you bury his sabre with him ? " asked Bonaparte.

" Yes," they replied, with one voice.

" Are you perfectly sure ? " insisted Bonaparte.

One of the men went down into the grave, thrust away the light sand with his arm, and pulled the hilt of the weapon to the surface.

" Very well," said Bonaparte; " finish your task."

He stayed until the grave was filled up. Then, fearing lest it might be violated, he said, —

" I want a volunteer to stay here as sentinel until the army has passed."

" Here," said a voice, which seemed to come from the sky.

Bonaparte turned, and saw Quartermaster Falou, perched upon his dromedary.

" Ah, is it you ? " he said.

" Yes, Citizen-General."

" And how does it happen that you are on a dromedary when the rest are on foot ? "

" Because two men have died of the plague on my dromedary's back, and no one will ride on it."

" And so it seems you are not afraid of the plague ? "

" I am not afraid of anything, Citizen-General."

" Very well," said Bonaparte, " I will remember that. Go and look for your friend Faraud, and both of you come to me at Cairo."

" We will be there, Citizen-General."

Bonaparte cast a last look towards Crosier's grave.

" Sleep in peace, poor Croisier," he said. " Your modest grave will not often be disturbed."

CHAPTER XVIII.

ABOUKIR.

On the 14th of June, 1799, after a retreat across the burning sands of Syria almost as disastrous as the retreat from Moscow through the snows of the Beresina, Bonaparte entered Cairo amid an immense concourse of people.

The sheik, who was expecting him, presented him with a magnificent horse and the Mameluke Roustan.

Bonaparte had said in his bulletin, dated at Saint-Jean-d'Acre, that he was returning to oppose the landing of a Turkish army which had assembled in the Isle of Rhodes.

Upon this point he had been correctly informed, and on the 11th of July the lookouts at Alexandria signalled that there were seventy-six sail in the offing, of which twelve were ships-of-war flying the Ottoman flag.

General Marmont, who was in command at Alexandria, sent courier after courier to Cairo and Rosetta, ordered the commander at Ramanieh to send him all the troops at his disposal, and sent two hundred men to the fort at Aboukir, to reinforce that point.

The same day the commander at Aboukir, Colonel Godard, wrote to Marmont: —

"The Turkish fleet is moored in the roadstead; I and my men will hold out till the last man falls, rather than yield."

The 12th and 13th of July were employed by the enemy in hastening the arrival of some battalions that were behindhand.

On the evening of the 13th there were in the roadstead one hundred and thirty ships, of which thirteen were vessels of seventy-four guns, nine were frigates, and seventeen were gunboats. The rest were transports.

On the evening of the following day, Godard had kept his word. He and his men were dead, and the redoubt was taken.

There remained thirty-five men shut up in the fort. They were under the command of Colonel Vinache.

They held the fort for two days against the whole Turkish army.

Bonaparte learned all this while he was still at the Pyramids.

He started for Ramanieh, where he arrived on the 19th of July.

The Turks, masters of the redoubt and the fort, had landed all their artillery. Marmont, in Alexandria, who had only eighteen hundred troops of the line and two hundred sailors composing the nautical legion to oppose to the Turks, sent courier after courier to Bonaparte.

Fortunately, instead of marching upon Alexandria, as Marmont feared, or upon Rosetta, as Bonaparte feared, the Turks, with their usual indolence, contented themselves with occupying the peninsula, and with throwing out at the left of the redoubt a great line of intrenchments, bordering on Lake Madieh.

Some five or six thousand feet in front of the redoubt they fortified two little mounds, placing in one of them a thousand men, and in the other two thousand.

They had eighteen thousand men in all.

But these eighteen thousand men seemed to have come to Egypt for the sole purpose of being besieged.

Bonaparte waited for Mustapha Pacha; but seeing that the latter made no movement to march against him, he resolved to take the initiative.

On the 23d of July he ordered the French army, which was now separated from the Turkish army by only two hours' march, to advance.

The advance-guard, composed of Murat's cavalry and three of General Destaing's battalions, with two pieces of artillery, formed the centre.

The division of General Rampon, who had under his orders Generals Fugière and Lanusse, was on the left.

On the right, General Lannes' division advanced along the shore of Lake Madieh.

Placed between Alexandria and the army, with two squadrons of cavalry and a hundred dromedaries, Davoust was ordered to hold off Mourad Bey, or any one else who should come to the help of the Turks, and to keep communication open between Alexandria and the army.

Kléber, who was expected, was to take command of the reserve.

And, finally, Menou, who had gone in the direction of Rosetta, found himself, at sunrise, at the end of the bar of the Nile, near the ferry across Lake Madieh.

The French army came in sight of the intrenchments almost before the Turks were aware of their proximity.

Bonaparte formed the columns of attack. General Destaing, who commanded them, marched straight against the fortified hill at the right, while two hundred of Murat's cavalry, stationed between the two hills, left their position, and riding around on both sides of the right-hand hill, cut off the retreat of the Turks who were attacked by General Destaing.

Meanwhile, Lannes marched against the hill at the left, which was defended by two thousand Turks, and Murat sent two hundred more of his cavalry around this hill.

Destaing and Lannes attacked at almost the same moment, and with equal success. The two hills were carried at the point of the bayonet. The fugitive Turks met the French cavalry, and threw themselves into the sea, at the right and left of the peninsula.

Destaing, Lannes, and Murat then marched against the village, which formed the centre of the peninsula, and attacked it in front.

A column left the camp at Aboukir, and came to the support of the village.

Murat drew his sabre, which he never did until the last moment, gave the word to his cavalry, charged the column, and drove it back to Aboukir.

Meanwhile, Lannes and Destaing captured the village.

The Turks fled on all sides, only to meet Murat's cavalry returning.

Four or five thousand corpses were already strewn around the battle-field.

The French had only one man wounded. He was a mulatto, a compatriot of my father, the commander of a squad of the Hercules Guides.

The French found themselves upon the great road which covered the Turkish front.

Bonaparte had it in his power to box the Turks up in Aboukir, and, while awaiting the arrival of the divisions of Kléber and Regnier, to harass them with bombs and shells; but he preferred to deal a decisive blow, and have done with them.

He ordered the army to march straight upon the second line of defences.

Lannes and Destaing, supported by Lanusse, still bore the brunt of the battle, and won the honors of the day.

The redoubt which defends Aboukir is the work of the English, and is therefore constructed on the most approved scientific plan.

It was defended by nine or ten thousand Turks. A causeway connected it with the sea. The Turks had not had time to dig far enough in the other direction, and therefore it was not connected with the Lake of Madieh.

A space about three hundred feet long remained open, but it was both occupied by the enemy and swept by the gunners.

Bonaparte ordered an attack on the front and right. Murat, in ambush in a grove of palm-trees, was to attack on the left, and cross the space where there was no causeway, under the fire of the gunners, and driving the enemy before him. The Turks, when they saw these dispositions, sent out four detachments of about two thousand men each, who marched to meet our troops.

The battle was sure to be a desperate one, for the Turks realized that they were shut in on the peninsula, with the sea before them, and the wall of French bayonets behind them.

A heavy cannonade directed against the redoubt and the intrenchments on the right was the signal for a fresh attack. General Bonaparte thereupon sent General Fugière forward. He followed the bank, to turn the Turkish right. The Thirty-second, which was stationed at the left of the hamlet which had just been taken, was to hold the enemy in check, and sustain the Eighteenth.

It was then that the Turks left their intrenchments and came to meet us.

Our troops uttered a joyful shout. This was what

they wanted. They rushed upon the enemy with fixed bayonets.

The Turks discharged their guns first, then their two pistols, and finally drew their sabres.

Our soldiers, who were not even checked by the triple discharge, closed upon them with the bayonet.

It was not until then that the Turks realized what quality of men and weapons they had to do with.

With their guns slung over their shoulders, and their sabres hanging by their cords, they began a hand-to-hand fight, trying to snatch from the rifles the terrible bayonets, which pierced their breasts just as they were extending their hands to seize them.

But nothing could stop the Eighteenth. They continued to march forward at the same pace, driving the Turks before them to the foot of the intrenchments, which they attempted to take by storm; but there the soldiers were driven back by a hot fire, which raked them diagonally.

General Fugière, who led the attack, received, in the first place, a bullet in his head. The wound was a slight one, and he kept on, and spoke encouragingly to his men.

But when a ball took away his arm, he was obliged to stop.

Adjutant-General Lelong, who came up with a battalion of the Seventy-fifth, made heroic efforts to induce the soldiers to defy this hurricane of fire. Twice he led them up to it, and twice he was repulsed. The third time he sprang forward, and was just about to leap the intrenchments when he fell dead.

For a long time Roland, who was standing near Bonaparte, had been asking for a command of some sort, which the latter hesitated to give him, until at length he felt that the moment had come to make a supreme effort.

He turned towards him.

"Very well, go!" he said.

"Thirty-second Brigade!" cried Roland.

And the gallant survivors of Saint-Jean-d'Acre ran to him, led by their major, Armagnac.

In the first rank was the *sous-lieutenant,* Faraud, whose wound was healed.

Meanwhile, another attempt had been made by Brigadier-General Morange; but he also was driven back, wounded, leaving thirty men on the glacis and in the ditches.

The Turks believed that they had conquered. Carried away by their custom of cutting off the heads of the dead, for which they received fifty *paras* apiece, they left the redoubt in disorder, and began the bloody work.

Roland pointed them out to his indignant soldiers.

"All our men are not dead," they cried. "There are some wounded among them. Let us save them!"

At the same time Murat saw through the smoke what was going on. He darted forward, under the fire of the artillery, passed through it, cut off the redoubt from the village with his cavalry, and fell upon the men who were engaged in their horrible operation of cutting off heads, on the other side of the redoubt, while Roland attacked it in front, dashed in among the Turks with his accustomed reckless daring, and mowed down the bloody harvesters.

Bonaparte saw that the Turks were taken at a disadvantage by this twofold attack, and he sent Lannes forward with two battalions. Lannes, with his usual impetuosity, attacked the redoubt on the left face and at the gorge.

Pressed thus on all sides, the Turks tried to reach the village of Aboukir; but between the village and the redoubt was Murat with his cavalry, behind them Roland and the Thirty-second Brigade, and at their right Lannes and his two battalions.

Their only refuge was the sea.

They threw themselves into it, wild with terror; for, since they were not in the habit of giving quarter to their prisoners, they preferred the sea, which left them a chance of reaching their ships, to death at the hands of the Christians whom they so despised.

At this point in the battle the French were masters of the two hills where they had begun the assault; of the hamlet, where the remainder of those who had been defending the hills had taken refuge; of the redoubt, which had just cost so many brave men their lives. And now they were before the camp and the Turkish reserve. They fell upon them.

Nothing could now stop our soldiers, who were drunk with the carnage which they had just perpetrated. They dashed in among the tents, and hurled themselves upon the reserve.

Murat and his cavalry fell upon the pacha's guard like a whirlwind, a hurricane, or the simoom.

Ignorant of the result of the battle, Mustapha, when he heard the shouts and cries and uproar, mounted his horse, put himself at the head of his *icoglans*, rushed to meet our men, encountered Murat, fired upon him at close range, and inflicted a slight wound. With the first blow of his sabre, Murat cut off two of his fingers. With the second, he would have cut off his head; but an Arab threw himself in front of the pacha, received the blow, and fell dead. Mustapha gave up his cimeter, and Murat sent him as a prisoner to Bonaparte.

Look at Gros' magnificent picture.

The remnant of the army took refuge within the fort of Aboukir; the rest were killed or drowned.

. Never since two armies first marched against each other has such utter annihilation been seen.   Aside from two hundred janissaries and the hundred men shut up in the fort, nothing remained of the eighteen thousand Turks who had landed.

Kléber arrived at the end of the battle.   He asked about the result of the day, and inquired where Bonaparte was.

Bonaparte was musing, standing upon the most advanced point of Aboukir.   He was looking at the gulf which had swallowed up the French fleet, — his sole hope of returning to France.

Kléber went to him and took him by the arm; and while Bonaparte's eyes remained veiled and thoughtful, Kléber exclaimed, —

" General, you are as great as the world! "

CHAPTER XIX.

DEPARTURE.

DURING the year that this eighth Crusade lasted,— the ninth, if we count Saint Louis' double attempt as two, — Bonaparte did all that it was humanly possible to do.

He took Alexandria, conquered the Mamelukes at Chébreïss and the Pyramids, took Cairo, achieved the conquest of the Delta, and, by means of the marshes of the Delta, completed the conquest of Upper Egypt, took Gaza, Jaffa, and destroyed the Turkish army of Djezzar at Mount Tabor; and, finally, he annihilated a second Turkish army at Aboukir.

The tricolor had floated triumphantly over the Nile and the Jordan.

But he was ignorant of what was happening in France, and that was why, on the evening of the battle of Aboukir, he was gazing dreamily at the sea which had swallowed up his vessels.

He sent for Quartermaster Falou, and questioned him again concerning the fight at Beyrout, the disaster to the flotilla, and the loss of the " Italie; " and his presentiments haunted him more persistently than ever.

In the hope of learning some news, he called Roland.

" My dear Roland," he said, " I have a great desire to open a new career to you."

" What is it ? " asked Roland.

" That of a diplomat."

"Oh, what a dreadful idea that is, General!"

"And yet you must agree to it."

"What! You do not permit me to decline?"

"No."

"Say on, then."

"I am going to send you with a flag of truce to Sidney Smith."

"My instructions?"

"You are to find out what is going on in France, and you will try to distinguish truth from falsehood in what the commodore tells you, which will be no easy matter."

"I will do my best. What will be the ostensible object of my embassy?"

"An exchange of prisoners. The English have twenty-five of our men; we have two hundred and fifty Turks. We will give them the two hundred and fifty Turks, if they will give us our twenty-five Frenchmen."

"When shall I go?"

"To-day."

It was the 26th of July.

Roland went; and that same evening he returned, with a file of newspapers.

Sidney had recognized him as the hero of Saint-Jean-d'Acre, and had not made the slightest objection to telling him what was going on in Europe.

Then, as he had read incredulity in Roland's eyes, he had given him all the French, English, and German papers which he had with him on board the "Tiger."

The news which these papers contained was disastrous.

The Republic, defeated at Sockah and Magnano, had lost Germany at Sockah, and Italy at Magnano.

Masséna, intrenched in Switzerland, had taken an unassailable position on the Albis.

The Apennines had been invaded, and the Var threatened.

The next day, when Bonaparte saw Roland, he said:
" Well ? "

" Well ? " echoed the young man.

" I knew very well that Italy was lost. "

" It will have to be taken again," replied Roland.

" We will try," rejoined Bonaparte. " Call Bourrienne."
Bourrienne was called.

" Ask Berthier where Gantheaume is," said Bonaparte.

" He is at Ramanieh, overlooking the construction of the fleet which is to start for Upper Egypt. "

" Are you sure ? "

" I received a letter from him yesterday. "

" I need a trusty and brave messenger," said Bonaparte to Roland. " Go and find Falou and his dromedary. "

Roland went out.

" Write these words to Alexandria, Bourrienne," continued Bonaparte : —

As soon as this is received, Admiral Gantheaume will report to General Bonaparte.

26th July, 1799.   BOURRIENNE.

Ten minutes later, Roland returned with Falou and his dromedary.

Bonaparte glanced with satisfaction at his messenger.

" Is your animal in as good condition as you are ? " he asked.

" My dromedary and I, General, are in condition to do our twenty-five leagues a day. "

" I ask you to do only twenty. "

" A mere trifle ! "

" You must carry this letter. "

" Where ? "

" To Ramanieh."

" It will reach its address this evening."

" Read the address."

" To Admiral Gantheaume."

" And now, if you should lose it — "

" I shall not lose it."

" We must provide for every possibility.   Listen to its contents."

" It is not very long ? "

" Only one sentence."

" Very well, then.   Let us have the sentence."

" ' As soon as this is received, Admiral Gantheaume will report to General Bonaparte.' "

" That is easy to remember."

" Go, then."

Falou made his dromedary kneel down, climbed upon his hump, and started him off at a trot.

" I am off," he shouted.

And, in fact, he was already some distance away.

The next evening he appeared again.

" The admiral is following me," he said.

The admiral arrived during the night.   Bonaparte had not gone to bed.   Gantheaume found him writing.

" You will prepare," said Bonaparte, " two frigates, the ' Muiron ' and the ' Carrière,' and two smaller vessels, the ' Revanche ' and the ' Fortune,' with provisions enough to last forty or fifty men two months.   Not a word about it to any one.   You are to come with me."

Gantheaume retired, promising not to lose a moment.

Bonaparte sent for Murat.

" Italy is lost," he said.   " The wretches!   They have wasted the fruit of our victories.   We must go. Select five hundred sure men for me."

Then, turning to Roland, he said, —

" You will see that Falou and Faraud are included in this detachment.

Roland bowed assent.

General Kléber, to whom Bonaparte intended to leave the command of the army, was invited to come to Rosetta, " to confer with the commander-in-chief on matters of the utmost importance."

Bonaparte made an appointment with him which he knew very well that he should not keep. He wished, however, to avoid Kléber's reproaches and bitter frankness.

He wrote to him all that he would have said to him, and gave as his reason for not keeping the appointment his fear that the English cruiser might reappear at any moment.

The vessel destined for Bonaparte was once more to carry Cæsar and his fortune. But this time it was not Cæsar sailing eastward, to add Egypt to the conquests of Rome, it was Cæsar revolving in his mind the vast designs which made the conqueror of the Gauls cross the Rubicon.

He was going back, without recoiling at the idea of overturning the Government for which he had fought on the 13th Vendémiaire, and which he had sustained on the 18th Fructidor.

A dream of gigantic proportions had faded away in front of Saint-Jean-d'Acre. A still more vast and soaring vision was taking form in his thoughts as he left Alexandria.

On the 23d of August, — a dark, gloomy night, — a boat pushed off from the Egyptian shore, and put Bonaparte aboard the " Muiron."

THE END.

Lightning Source UK Ltd.
Milton Keynes UK
UKHW020644080221
378420UK00006B/508

9 781377 271033